DEFINING MOMENTS
JACKIE ROBINSON AND THE INTEGRATION OF BASEBALL

DEFINING MOMENTS
JACKIE ROBINSON
AND THE INTEGRATION
OF BASEBALL

Laurie Collier Hillstrom

155 W. Congress, Suite 200
Detroit, MI 48226

Omnigraphics, Inc.

Kevin Hillstrom, *Series Editor*
Cherie D. Abbey, *Managing Editor*

Peter E. Ruffner, *Publisher*
Matthew P. Barbour, *Senior Vice President*

Elizabeth Collins, *Research and Permissions Coordinator*
Kevin M. Hayes, *Operations Manager*

Mary Butler, *Researcher*
Shirley Amore, Joseph Harris, Martha Johns, and Kirk Kauffmann, *Administrative Staff*

Copyright © 2013 Omnigraphics, Inc.
ISBN 978-0-7808-1327-4

Library of Congress Cataloging-in-Publication Data

Hillstrom, Laurie Collier, 1965-
  Jackie Robinson and the integration of baseball / by Laurie Collier Hillstrom.
    pages cm. -- (Defining moments)
  Includes bibliographical references and index.
  Summary: "A comprehensive account of Jackie Robinson's life and career, focusing on the events surrounding the shattering of the "color barrier" in Major League Baseball. Discusses his life after baseball, his influential position in the civil rights movement, and his enduring legacy as a racial pioneer. Includes biographies, primary sources, and more"--Provided by publisher.
  ISBN 978-0-7808-1327-4 (hardcover : alk. paper) 1. Robinson, Jackie, 1919-1972--Juvenile literature. 2. Baseball players—United States--Biography--Juvenile literature. 3. African American baseball players--Biography--Juvenile literature. 4. Racism in sports—United States--History. 5. Discrimination in sports--United States--History. 6. Baseball--United States--History. I. Title.
  GV865.R6H55 2012
  796.357092--dc23
  [B]
                                                                                2012048878

TABLE OF CONTENTS

NARRATIVE OVERVIEW

BIOGRAPHIES

PRIMARY SOURCES

PREFACE

Throughout the course of America's existence, its people, culture, and institutions have been periodically challenged—and in many cases transformed—by profound historical events. Some of these momentous events, such as women's suffrage, the civil rights movement, and U.S. involvement in World War II, invigorated the nation and strengthened American confidence and capabilities. Others, such as the McCarthy era, the Vietnam War, and Watergate, have prompted troubled assessments and heated debates about the country's core beliefs and character.

Some of these defining moments in American history were years or even decades in the making. The Harlem Renaissance and the New Deal, for example, unfurled over the span of several years, while the American labor movement and the Cold War evolved over the course of decades. Other defining moments, such as the Cuban missile crisis and the terrorist attacks of September 11, 2001, transpired over a matter of days or weeks.

But although significant differences exist among these events in terms of their duration and their place in the timeline of American history, all share the same basic characteristic: they transformed the United States' political, cultural, and social landscape for future generations of Americans.

Taking heed of this fundamental reality, American citizens, schools, and other institutions are increasingly emphasizing the importance of understanding our nation's history. Omnigraphics' *Defining Moments* series was created for the express purpose of meeting this growing appetite for authoritative, useful historical resources. This series will be of enduring value to anyone interested in learning more about America's past—and in understanding how those historical events continue to reverberate in the twenty-first century.

Each individual volume of *Defining Moments* provides a valuable resource for readers interested in learning about the most profound events in our nation's history. Each volume is organized into three distinct sections—Narrative Overview, Biographies, and Primary Sources.

- The **Narrative Overview** provides readers with a detailed, factual account of the origins and progression of the "defining moment" being examined. It also explores the event's lasting impact on America's political and cultural landscape.

- The **Biographies** section provides valuable biographical background on leading figures associated with the event in question. Each biography concludes with a list of sources for further information on the profiled individual.

- The **Primary Sources** section collects a wide variety of pertinent primary source materials from the era under discussion, including official documents, papers and resolutions, letters, oral histories, memoirs, editorials, and other important works.

Individually, each of these sections is a rich resource for users. Together, they comprise an authoritative, balanced, and absorbing examination of some of the most significant events in U.S. history.

Other notable features contained within each volume in the series include a glossary of important individuals, places, and terms; a detailed chronology featuring page references to relevant sections of the narrative; an annotated bibliography of sources for further study; an extensive general bibliography that reflects the wide range of historical sources consulted by the author; and a subject index.

New Feature—Research Topics for Student Reports

Each volume in the *Defining Moments* series now includes a list of potential research topics for students. Students working on historical research and writing assignments will find this feature especially useful in assessing their options.

Information on the highlighted research topics can be found throughout the different sections of the book—and especially in the narrative overview, biography, and primary source sections. This wide coverage gives readers the flexibility to study the topic through multiple entry points.

Special Note about
Jackie Robinson and the Integration of Baseball

Some of the quoted material in this volume contains offensive terminology in reference to African Americans. We chose to retain such terminology when it appeared in the original source material in order to provide readers with an accurate picture of the racial atmosphere surrounding Jackie Robinson's achievements.

Acknowledgements

This series was developed in consultation with a distinguished Advisory Board comprised of public librarians, school librarians, and educators. They evaluated the series as it developed, and their comments and suggestions were invaluable throughout the production process. Any errors in this and other volumes in the series are ours alone. Following is a list of board members who contributed to the *Defining Moments* series:

Gail Beaver, M.A., M.A.L.S.
Adjunct Lecturer, University of Michigan
Ann Arbor, MI

Melissa C. Bergin, L.M.S., NBCT
Library Media Specialist
Niskayuna High School
Niskayuna, NY

Rose Davenport, M.S.L.S., Ed.Specialist
Library Media Specialist
Pershing High School Library
Detroit, MI

Karen Imarisio, A.M.L.S.
Assistant Head of Adult Services
Bloomfield Twp. Public Library
Bloomfield Hills, MI

Nancy Larsen, M.L.S., M.S. Ed.
Library Media Specialist
Clarkston High School
Clarkston, MI

Marilyn Mast, M.I.L.S.
Kingswood Campus Librarian
Cranbrook Kingswood Upper School
Bloomfield Hills, MI

Rosemary Orlando, M.L.I.S.
Library Director
St. Clair Shores Public Library
St. Clair Shores, MI

Comments and Suggestions

We welcome your comments on *Defining Moments: Jackie Robinson and the Integration of Baseball* and suggestions for other events in U.S. history that warrant treatment in the *Defining Moments* series. Correspondence should be addressed to:

Editor, *Defining Moments*
Omnigraphics, Inc.
155 West Congress, Suite 200
Detroit, MI 48231

HOW TO USE THIS BOOK

*D*efining Moments: Jackie Robinson and the Integration of Baseball provides users with a detailed and authoritative overview of events surrounding the shattering of Major League Baseball's longstanding "color barrier" on April 15, 1947, as well as background on the principal figures involved in this pivotal episode in U.S. history. The preparation and arrangement of this volume—and all other books in the *Defining Moments* series—reflect an emphasis on providing a thorough and objective account of events that shaped our nation, presented in an easy-to-use reference work.

Defining Moments: Jackie Robinson and the Integration of Baseball is divided into three main sections. The first of these sections, the **Narrative Overview**, provides a comprehensive account of Jackie Robinson's life and career. It chronicles the era of racial segregation in the United States, as well as the rise of Negro League baseball. It covers the development of Brooklyn Dodgers president Branch Rickey's "noble experiment" idea and his selection of Jackie Robinson as the first black player in the major leagues. It also describes the verbal and physical abuse Robinson endured during his rookie season, as well as the admiration and controversy he generated throughout his Hall of Fame career. Finally, this section discusses Jackie Robinson's life after baseball—especially his influential position in the African-American civil rights movement—and explores his enduring legacy as a racial pioneer in the game of baseball and in American society.

The second section, **Biographies**, provides valuable biographical background on Jackie Robinson, as well as other leading figures involved in the integration of Major League Baseball. Among the individuals profiled are sportswriter Wendell Smith, the leading critic of baseball's color line; Branch Rickey, the visionary baseball executive who spearheaded integration; Larry Doby, the first black player in the American League; A. B. "Happy" Chandler, the anti-segregationist commissioner of baseball; and Dodgers shortstop Pee Wee Reese,

Robinson's friend and double-play partner. Each biography concludes with a list of sources for further information on the profiled individual.

The third section, **Primary Sources**, collects essential and illuminating documents related to Jackie Robinson's career and achievements. This diverse collection includes a 1942 *Sporting News* article supporting segregation in baseball; a first-hand account of the historic 1945 meeting between Branch Rickey and Jackie Robinson; an Associated Press writer's recollection of Robinson's major-league debut; personal correspondence between Robinson and President Dwight Eisenhower on the topic of civil rights; and assessments of Robinson's impact by his Dodgers teammate Carl Erskine and former National League president Leonard S. Coleman.

Other valuable features in *Defining Moments: Jackie Robinson and the Integration of Baseball* include the following:

- Attribution and referencing of primary sources and other quoted material to help guide users to other valuable historical research resources.
- Glossary of Important People, Places, and Terms.
- Detailed Chronology of events with a *see reference* feature. Under this arrangement, events listed in the chronology include a reference to page numbers within the Narrative Overview wherein users can find additional information on the event in question.
- Photographs of the leading figures and major events associated with Jackie Robinson's life and the integration of Major League Baseball.
- Sources for Further Study, an annotated list of noteworthy works about Jackie Robinson, baseball history, and the civil rights movement.
- Extensive bibliography of works consulted in the creation of this book, including books, periodicals, and Internet sites.
- A Subject Index.

RESEARCH TOPICS FOR
JACKIE ROBINSON AND THE INTEGRATION OF BASEBALL

When students receive an assignment to produce a research paper on a historical event or topic, the first step in that process—settling on a subject for the paper—can be one of the most vexing. In recognition of this reality, each book in the *Defining Moments* series now highlights research areas/topics that receive extensive coverage within that particular volume.

Potential research topics for students using *Defining Moments: Jackie Robinson and the Integration of Baseball* include the following:

- Discuss some of the political, social, and economic factors that led to the segregation of people by race in the United States.

- Compare the typical experience of white players in Major League Baseball to that of black players in the Negro Leagues during the first half of the twentieth century.

- The Negro Leagues arose out of discrimination, yet black baseball was a source of pride and affirmation for many African Americans. Discuss the impact of segregation on the development of black cultural institutions.

- Explain the key factors that made Jackie Robinson "the right man for the job" of breaking baseball's color barrier, both on and off the field.

- Discuss Brooklyn Dodgers president Branch Rickey's condition that Robinson could not retaliate, no matter how vicious the verbal or physical assault. What would have happened if Robinson had lost his temper and fought back against his tormentors? How did public perceptions of Robinson change when he was finally allowed to speak his mind?

- Pee Wee Reese and other players who witnessed Robinson's early career have said that they never could have endured a similar ordeal. Explain some of the key factors in Robinson's background, temperament, and situation that enabled him to persevere and succeed in the face of tremendous obstacles. Do you think you could have done what Robinson did?

- Assess Jackie Robinson's role as a pioneer in the African-American civil rights movement. How did his experience ending segregation in baseball influence other key events in the fight for racial equality?

- Document the achievements of other African-American athletes who have overcome barriers in sports and society.

- Explore the significance of sports in American society, noting instances in which it has either led the way or lagged behind during periods of social change and upheaval.

- Discuss the legacy of Jackie Robinson and explore the relevance his experiences and example hold for Americans today.

NARRATIVE OVERVIEW

PROLOGUE

One of the earliest landmark events of the African-American civil rights movement took place on April 15, 1947. This event was not a court ruling, or a protest march, or a speech. It was a baseball game between the Brooklyn Dodgers and the Boston Braves. When the Dodgers trotted out of the dugout at Ebbets Field and assumed their defensive positions to start the game, the rookie first baseman wearing number 42—Jackie Robinson—became the first black player in Major League Baseball.

Prior to Robinson's historic debut with the Dodgers, professional baseball had operated under a strict racial segregation policy for more than fifty years. Only white players were allowed in the major leagues, which offered the highest level of competition, the nicest stadiums, the largest crowds, and the greatest prestige. The only option available to black players—regardless of their athletic ability—was the Negro Leagues. Although black baseball featured many talented players, they earned lower salaries than their white counterparts, received less media attention, and played grueling schedules.

Determined to change this unfair situation and extend equal opportunities to black ballplayers—as well as improve his team's performance and increase its fan base—Dodgers president Branch Rickey came up with a daring plan to integrate Major League Baseball. He selected Robinson as the subject of this "noble experiment" and carefully managed his early career. Although Robinson faced resistance from teammates, verbal and physical abuse from opposing players, and even death threats in his quest to break baseball's longstanding color barrier, his courage and perseverance inspired millions of people.

One of these people was Mike Royko, a Pulitzer Prize-winning newspaper columnist who grew up in Chicago and was a lifelong Cubs fan. In the following column, published on the occasion of Robinson's death in 1972, Royko recalls watching the Cubs take on the visiting Dodgers at Wrigley Field in 1947, about a month after Robinson made his first appearance in the majors. Even as a boy, Royko recognized the significance of the event—for the African-American fans in attendance, for the game of baseball, and for society as a whole.

> All that Saturday, the wise men of the neighborhood, who sat in chairs on the sidewalk outside the tavern, had talked about what it would do to baseball. I hung around and listened because baseball was about the most important thing in the world, and if anything was going to ruin it, I was worried. Most of the things they said, I didn't understand, although it all sounded terrible. But could one man bring such ruin?
>
> They said he could and would. And the next day he was going to be in Wrigley Field for the first time, on the same diamond as [Stan] Hack, [Bill] Nicholson, [Phil] Cavarretta, [Johnny] Schmitz, [Andy] Pafko, and all my other idols. I had to see Jackie Robinson, the man who was going to somehow wreck everything.
>
> So the next day, another kid and I started walking to the ballpark early. We always walked to save the streetcar fare. It was five or six miles, but I felt about baseball the way Abe Lincoln felt about education. Usually, we could get there just at noon, find a seat in the grandstand, and watch some batting practice.
>
> But not that Sunday, May 18, 1947. By noon, Wrigley Field was almost filled. The crowd outside spilled off the sidewalk and into the streets. Scalpers were asking top dollar for box seats and getting it.
>
> I had never seen anything like it. Not just the size, although it was a new record, more than 47,000. But this was twenty-five years ago, and in 1947 few blacks were seen in the Loop [Chicago's downtown business district], much less up on the white North Side at a Cub game. That day, they came by the thousands, pouring off the northbound Ls [elevated trains] and out of their cars.

They didn't wear baseball-game clothes. They had on church clothes and funeral clothes: suits, white shirts, ties, gleaming shoes, and straw hats. I've never seen so many straw hats.

As big as it was, the crowd was orderly. Almost unnaturally so. People didn't jostle each other. The whites tried to look as if nothing unusual was happening, while the blacks tried to look casual and dignified. So everybody looked slightly ill at ease. For most, it was probably the first time they had been that close to each other in such great numbers.

We managed to get in, scramble up a ramp, and find a place to stand behind the last row of grandstand seats. Then they shut the gates. No place remained to stand.

Robinson came up in the first inning. I remember the sound. It wasn't the shrill, teenage cry you now hear, or an excited gut roar. They applauded, long, rolling applause. A tall, middle-aged black man stood next to me, a smile of almost painful joy on his face, beating his palms together so hard they must have hurt.

When Robinson stepped into the batter's box, it was as if someone had flicked a switch. The place went silent. He swung at the first pitch and they erupted as if he had knocked it over the wall. But it was only a high foul that dropped into the box seats. I remember thinking it was strange that a foul could make that many people happy. When he struck out, the low moan was genuine.

I've forgotten most of the details of the game, other than that the Dodgers won and Robinson didn't get a hit or do anything special, although he was cheered on every swing and every routine play.

But two things happened I'll never forget. Robinson played first, and early in the game a Cub star hit a grounder and it was a close play. Just before the Cub reached first, he swerved to his left. And as he got to the bag, he seemed to slam his foot down hard at Robinson's foot. It was obvious to everyone that he was trying to run into him or spike him. Robinson took the throw and got clear at the last instant.

I was shocked. That Cub, a hometown boy, was my biggest hero. It was not only an unheroic stunt, but it seemed a rude thing to do in front of people who would cheer for a foul ball. I didn't understand why he had done it. It wasn't at all big league.

I didn't know that while the white fans were relatively polite, the Cubs and most other teams kept up a steady stream of racial abuse from the dugout. I thought that all they did down there was talk about how good Wheaties are.

Late in the game, Robinson was up again, and he hit another foul ball. This time it came into the stands low and fast, in our direction. Somebody in the seats grabbed for it, but it caromed off his hand and kept coming. There was a flurry of arms as the ball kept bouncing, and suddenly it was between me and my pal. We both grabbed. I had a baseball.

The two of us stood there examining it and chortling. A genuine major-league baseball that had actually been gripped and thrown by a Cub pitcher, hit by a Dodger batter. What a possession.

Then I heard the voice say: "Would you consider selling that?" It was the black man who had applauded so fiercely. I mumbled something. I didn't want to sell it. "I'll give you ten dollars for it," he said.

Ten dollars. I couldn't believe it. I didn't know what ten dollars could buy because I'd never had that much money. But I knew that a lot of men in the neighborhood considered sixty dollars a week to be good pay.

I handed it to him, and he paid me with ten $1 bills. When I left the ball park, with that much money in my pocket, I was sure that Jackie Robinson wasn't bad for the game.

Since then, I've regretted a few times that I didn't keep the ball. Or that I hadn't given it to him free. I didn't know, then, how hard he probably had to work for that ten dollars.

But Tuesday I was glad I had sold it to him. And if that man is still around, and has that baseball, I'm sure he thinks it was worth every cent.

Chapter One

THE COLOR LINE
IN BASEBALL

⟨⟨⟨⟨∫⟩⟩⟩⟩

There were all type of restrictions and limitations on what we could do as a race.... There were signs saying Colored Only here, Whites Only there. You could be put in jail or beaten up if you disobeyed. It was like someone always saying, "You've got to know your place." You had to accept what had been set aside for blacks.

—Ed Charles, African-American
minor-league baseball player in the 1950s

Professional baseball, which is widely viewed as America's national pastime, maintained strict racial segregation policies for more than fifty years. Baseball's so-called "color line" prevented great African-American athletes from playing for major-league teams or in their minor-league farm systems. The only option open to these ballplayers was the all-black Negro Leagues. Many black players found this outright discrimination to be extremely frustrating. "A guy could come over here from Italy and play, from Mexico and play, from anywhere in the world and play," noted outfielder Willie Tasby. "I was born here, and I couldn't play. What the hell was going on?"[1] The popularity of Negro League baseball—combined with African-American achievements in other areas of sports, society, and culture—led to heightened resistance to institutionalized racism in the United States and growing demands for integration of the major leagues.

From Slavery to Segregation

The North's victory in the Civil War (1861-65) ended the enslavement of African Americans in the United States. The Thirteenth Amendment to the U.S.

Through the first half of the twentieth century, racial segregation policies in the South required businesses—like this pool hall in Memphis, Tennessee—to maintain separate facilities for blacks and whites.

Constitution, which was adopted in 1865, made slavery illegal throughout the land. Three years later, the Fourteenth Amendment formally extended U.S. citizenship to African Americans. It also required states to provide equal protection under the law to all citizens, without regard to race. The Fifteenth Amendment (1870) affirmed the right of all male citizens to vote. Finally, the Civil Rights Act of 1875 guaranteed all citizens—black or white—"full and equal enjoyment" of public facilities and transportation.

During the postwar period known as Reconstruction (1867-1877), the federal government sent military troops into the South to enforce these laws and protect the civil rights of African Americans. Former slaves took advantage of their newfound freedom to reunite families that had been separated under slavery, establish their own churches and schools, launch new business ventures, and elect black candidates to state and local offices. Many black families dared to hope that they were witnessing the dawn of a new era of racial equality.

Many white Southerners, however, refused to accept these changes. Accustomed to slavery, they continued to hold racist attitudes toward African Americans. In addition, they were determined to maintain the same level of control that they had long held over the region's social and political institutions. They resisted the federal government's efforts to impose equality and resented black citizens' efforts to carve out free and independent lives for themselves. As soon as Reconstruction ended and federal troops withdrew from the former Confederate states, white politicians who had held power before the Civil War regained control of state legislatures across the South.

From the mid-1870s onward, the U.S. Supreme Court handed down a series of decisions that further undermined the effectiveness of federal Reconstruction legislation and eroded the legal standing of African Americans. Emboldened by these rulings, white Southern lawmakers ignored or openly defied the new federal civil rights laws. They passed a flurry of state and local laws designed to restrict the rights of African Americans and force them into a position of second-class citizenship.

Many of these so-called "Jim Crow" laws required private businesses and public institutions to maintain separate facilities for blacks and whites. These racial segregation policies forced black citizens to attend separate schools and churches, use separate bathrooms and water fountains, and sit in different sections on trains and buses. African Americans were also restricted from using public parks, libraries, hospitals, and other facilities that served whites. In 1896 the U.S. Supreme Court sanctioned racial segregation laws in its *Plessy v. Ferguson* ruling, which held that states could require black and white citizens to use different facilities, as long as those facilities were "separate but equal."

In reality, though, the facilities labeled "White" and "Colored" throughout the South were not equal. Instead, those offered to blacks were almost always inferior to those provided for whites. To enforce these discriminatory laws and keep blacks "in their place," whites often resorted to intimidation and violence. Few states in the North passed laws mandating segregation, but racial discrimination still occurred in employment, housing, education, and many other social spheres across the region.

Baseball Draws a Color Line

The American sport of baseball originated shortly before the Civil War. Although the details of its origins are a subject of debate, baseball most likely

John "Bud" Fowler (back row, center) was one of a few black players allowed to play on white professional baseball teams in the 1880s.

grew out of older "stick-and-ball" games, such as cricket and rounders. Various Americans are credited with adapting the rules of these and other European games to create modern baseball around 1845. The first known baseball game using modern rules—including one that made it illegal to throw the ball at an opposing base runner to make an out—took place on June 19, 1846, at Elysian Fields in Hoboken, New Jersey. The New York Baseball Club defeated the New York Knickerbockers in that contest.

The popularity of baseball expanded rapidly during and after the Civil War, from 100 local amateur clubs in 1865 to more than 400 only two years later. As the country was reunited during Reconstruction, baseball quickly spread to distant reaches of the United States and gained its current status as America's national pastime. It became a professional sport in 1869, when the Cincinnati Red Stockings became the first club to offer salaries to its players. In 1876 the professional baseball teams from various cities formed the National Base Ball League (now known as the National League). Twenty-five years later a rival league called the American Base Ball Association (now known as the American League) was established. These groups are considered to be the foundation for modern Major League Baseball.

From its early beginnings, baseball mirrored American society by practicing racial segregation. Most organized leagues maintained unofficial rules that prohibited white teams from having black players on their rosters and barred all-black teams from joining. Although African-American men played the sport, they generally competed as members of separate, "colored" teams and leagues. This division of the sport by race became known as baseball's "color line" or "color barrier" (see "*The Sporting News* Supports Segregation in Baseball," p. 159).

In a few cases, though, black players managed to play on white teams during baseball's early years. Pitcher and utility infielder John "Bud" Fowler became the first black player to break the color barrier in 1878, when he joined a white minor-league professional team in Massachusetts. Although Fowler was widely viewed as a top player, he bounced from team to team throughout his career. "The poor fellow's skin is against him," explained a writer for *Sporting Life*. "With his splendid abilities he would long ago have been on some good club had his color been white instead of black."[2] Star catcher Moses "Fleetwood" Walker became the first African American to play for a major-league franchise in 1884, when his minor-league team, the Toledo Blue Stockings, joined the American Association.

Some black players were greeted with tolerance or even acceptance by white teammates and baseball fans, especially in the North. But many others faced verbal or physical abuse from opposing teams and spectators. Fowler, for instance, found himself the target of competitors' spikes so often that he began taping pieces of wood to his legs as a form of protection. His invention provided the inspiration for modern-day shin guards. "Race prejudice exists in professional baseball ranks to a marked degree," noted a writer for *Sporting News* in 1889, "and the unfortunate son of Africa who makes his living as a member of a team of white professionals has a rocky road to travel."[3]

The situation grew worse for black players in the South after the end of Reconstruction, as they increasingly fell victim to racist attitudes and discriminatory segregation policies. In a world where people were strictly separated by race, many white players and team owners simply refused to associate with African Americans. One infamous incident took place on July 14, 1887, when the Chicago White Stockings refused to take the field for a minor-league game against the Newark Giants because the Giants' roster included black pitcher George Stovey. Around that same time, minor-league team owners reached a "gentleman's agreement" to refuse to offer any contracts to black players in the future. By 1890 there were no black players in organized baseball, and the color barrier remained firmly in place for the next fifty years.

Barnstorming Black Baseball Teams

Despite the fact that they were not welcome in organized white baseball leagues, African-American ballplayers still had the opportunity to play for all-black professional teams in many cities. A group of waiters at the Argyle Hotel in Babylon, New York, formed the first all-black professional baseball club in 1885. They called themselves the Cuban Giants to disguise the fact that the players were African American, figuring that white audiences would be more likely to watch games featuring "Cuban" players. The players even spoke to each other on the field in a made-up language that was supposed to sound like Spanish. The Cuban Giants started out by playing exhibition games against local, amateur white teams to entertain guests at the hotel. They soon began attracting large audiences of both black and white fans. Before long, the talented team began traveling as far as Florida and playing year-round.

"Anything went [in the Negro Leagues]," recalled Hall of Fame catcher Roy Campanella. "Spitballs, shine balls, emery balls; pitchers used any and all of them. They nicked and moistened and treated the ball to make it flutter and spin and break."

The popularity of the Cuban Giants led to the formation of more than 200 all-black independent baseball teams by the turn of the twentieth century. Some of these teams competed against each other in loosely organized leagues, but most early black baseball clubs did what is known as "barnstorming." Each team would travel to various cities and towns and play games against whatever opponents they could find. Most teams would remain on the road for weeks at a time and play up to three games per day (see "A Ballplayer Shares Memories of the Negro Leagues," p. 162). Although the black barnstormers received lower salaries than white professional ballplayers, they made enough to support their families at a time when many African Americans had trouble finding good jobs. Under segregation, however, black players could only stay in colored hotels and eat in colored restaurants. As a result, the teams often ended up eating alongside the road and sleeping on the bleachers at baseball fields.

In the days before television brought professional baseball into American homes, the only way to see a game was to attend one in person. Many small towns would virtually shut down when top black teams arrived so that residents—both black and white—could enjoy the games. These early black teams played an innovative, fast-paced, exciting brand of baseball that was highly entertaining to watch. "I had seen major league baseball, but this is quicker," former player Buck O'Neil recalled. "It's fast, it's quick. You know how the dull moments in baseball can be. In this type of baseball, never a dull moment."[4]

Andrew "Rube" Foster organized the best barnstorming black baseball teams in the Midwest to create the Negro National League in 1920.

To add to the theatrical aspect of the games, certain exceptions to the major-league rules were allowed, or even encouraged. For example, pitchers could coat the ball with saliva or petroleum jelly in order to alter its flight and confuse batters. These trick pitches were known as spitballs and shine balls. Pitchers could also hide sandpaper or emery paper in their belts and use it to create a rough spot on the ball. "Anything went," recalled Hall of Fame catcher Roy Campanella. "Spitballs, shine balls, emery balls; pitchers used any and all of them. They nicked and moistened and treated the ball to make it flutter and spin and break."[5] All of these trick pitches put a premium on quick reflexes, contact hitting, and aggressive base running, which added to the excitement of the game.

The Negro Leagues

The popularity of black baseball continued to grow during the first few decades of the twentieth century. By the time World War I ended in 1918, it had emerged as the premier form of entertainment among African Americans in the nation's cities. Andrew "Rube" Foster, owner of the powerful Chicago Ameri-

The top players from the Negro Leagues competed in the annual East-West All-Star Game during the 1930s and 1940s.

can Giants, decided to organize a league for some of the best black baseball teams in the Midwest. "Rube wanted to put not just a team in organized baseball. No. Rube wanted to put a league into organized baseball," O'Neil explained. "Rube wanted all of the guys that could play to have a chance to play in organized baseball."[6]

Thanks to Foster's efforts, the Negro National League (NNL) was formally established on February 13, 1920, in Kansas City, Missouri. It originally consisted of eight teams: the Chicago American Giants, Chicago Giants, Cuban Stars, Dayton Marcos, Detroit Stars, Indianapolis ABCs, Kansas City Monarchs, and St. Louis Giants. Foster served as its president. Several other regional Negro baseball leagues sprung up around the same time. Thomas T. Wilson, owner of the Nashville Elite Giants, organized the Negro Southern League (NSL) later in 1920. The Eastern Colored League (ECL) formed in 1923, and the first-ever Negro World Series took place the following year between the ECL and NNL champions.

In 1929 the United States entered the severe economic downturn known as the Great Depression. Financial pressures led to the collapse of several black baseball leagues during this time, including the Negro National League in 1931. In fact, the Negro Southern League was the only one to remain in operation during the 1932 season. In 1933, however, Pittsburgh Crawfords owner Gus Greenlee organized a new Negro National League. He also initiated the East-West All-Star Game, an annual showcase of Negro League talent that quickly became the most popular attraction in black baseball. Fans packed Chicago's Comiskey Park each year to see such future Hall of Fame players as Satchel Paige, Josh Gibson, and James "Cool Papa" Bell.

The East-West All-Star Game and other high-profile Negro League contests were important social events within urban black communities in the 1930s and 1940s. In fact, African-American baseball fans often arrived at the ballpark dressed as if they were attending a formal, elegant event. "They were proud, very proud," O'Neil remembered.

> It was the era of dress-up. If you look at the old pictures, you see the men have on ties, hats, everybody wore a hat then. The ladies had on fine dresses. Just the way it happened. And one of the reasons for that was [that] in our faith—Methodist, Baptist, or whatnot—we had eleven o'clock service on Sunday. But when the Kansas City Monarchs were in town or when the East-West game was on, they started church at ten o'clock, so they could get out an hour earlier and come to the ball game. Came straight to the ball game, looking pretty. And we loved it.[7]

By 1940 the new Negro National League and its rival Negro American League, which was launched in 1937, ranked among the largest and most successful black-owned business enterprises in the United States. Many African Americans viewed Negro League baseball as proof that they could achieve great things, even in the face of racial segregation and discrimination (see "Black Achievements during Segregation," p. 16). Young people, in particular, were inspired by the athletic feats they saw on the field and the huge audiences of proud, middle-class African Americans they saw in the stands. Negro League baseball gave them hope that they could overcome social disadvantages and build fulfilling lives for themselves. "It meant everything to me," O'Neil recalled of seeing his first Negro League game. "All the professional baseball players I'd seen, they were white, you know. Now, I was going to see the professionals that were black. And this meant so much to me. It meant getting me out of that celery field [where he worked as a boy]; it meant improving my life."[8]

Black Achievements during Segregation

As Negro League players, sportswriters, and civil rights activists worked to end segregation in Major League Baseball, African Americans were making an impact in various other fields as well. For example, New York City emerged as the center of an exciting black literary, artistic, and cultural movement known as the Harlem Renaissance during the 1920s and 1930s. Writers like Langston Hughes and Zora Neale Hurston, artists like Aaron Douglas and Lois Mailou Jones, and musicians like Louis Armstrong and Josephine Baker gained widespread respect for their talents and helped generate interest in the black experience.

Black athletes also made impressive gains in sports other than baseball. At the 1936 Olympic Games in Berlin, Germany, for instance, African American runner Jesse Owens won four track-and-field gold medals. His achievements, which took place under the watchful eye of German dictator Adolf Hitler, made a forceful statement contradicting Hitler's assertions about white Aryan racial superiority. American boxer Joe Louis, known as the "Brown Bomber," posted another important victory over racism in 1938, when he knocked out German champion Max Schmeling in the first round to claim the world heavyweight title.

African-American soldiers, sailors, and pilots also proved their mettle in combat during World War II. Although the U.S. military remained segregated throughout the war, 125,000 African Americans served overseas in all-black units, and they made vital contributions in many theaters. In addition, nearly 1,000 black men successfully completed an experimental training program in Tuskegee, Alabama, to qualify as U.S. military aviators. These famous Tuskegee Airmen served with distinction and flew 15,500 combat missions. Their achievements further proved the capabilities of African Americans and helped convince President Harry Truman to integrate the U.S. armed forces in 1948.

While the success of the Negro Leagues had a positive impact on many African-American communities, black professional ballplayers continued to confront racism on a regular basis. When Negro League teams played at stadiums that were also used by white teams, for instance, the players were often pro-

Fans dressed in their Sunday best to watch the East-West All-Star Game at Chicago's Comiskey Park.

hibited from using the locker rooms or training equipment. In some cases, black players were forced to change clothes and use restrooms at buildings or private homes located several blocks away from the field. On a few occasions, Negro League games were interrupted or canceled due to intimidation or violence by white racist groups like the Ku Klux Klan. As O'Neil remembered,

> It was terrible, really, in some spots. We got in the ballpark once in Macon, Georgia, and I got the stuff off the bus and went into the dugout and here's the Wizard of the Ku Klux Klan. They're going to march in that field. So you know, when the Ku Klux Klan was marching that means all black people, you closed your windows, you brought the shades down and all. So he says, "You boys

aren't going to play here tonight. We're going to march here tonight." I say, "Yessir." So we get back on the bus and go on. These were some of the things that we had to contend with.[9]

Many Negro League players experienced racism during their travels between cities on team buses. They routinely had trouble finding hotels, restaurants, and gas stations that were willing to serve African Americans, and they sometimes faced ugly taunts or actions. Hall of Fame outfielder Monte Irvin recalled a time when the Newark Eagles bus pulled up outside a café along the road from Montgomery to Birmingham in Alabama. Before the players even got off the bus, the white waitress rushed out to inform them that she would not be serving them anything to eat. After much cajoling, she finally agreed to let the hot and tired ballplayers get a drink of water from a well behind the restaurant. "So we went back to the well and hoisted up a bucket of water," Irvin noted. "There was a gourd nearby. We drank from the gourd, then walked back to the bus to head on down the road. When I looked back, I saw this woman breaking the gourd that we'd drunk out of, smashing it into little pieces."[10]

Demands for Integration Grow

Negro League baseball reached the peak of its popularity during World War II. By this time, millions of African Americans had left the segregated South in hopes of finding greater equality and opportunity in other regions of the country. Many black workers found good-paying jobs in factories that churned out military equipment to support the war effort. This employment trend helped create a small but comfortable black middle-class in many Northern cities. With money to spend and leisure time to fill, these families packed baseball stadiums to see Negro League games.

Sheer talent was another factor in the increasing popularity of Negro League baseball. Some of the greatest athletes ever to grace a baseball field played in the Negro Leagues during their heyday, including such legendary players as Willie Mays, Hank Aaron, Satchel Paige, Josh Gibson, Buck Leonard, and Jackie Robinson. These stars not only proved their skills in high-profile Negro League contests like the East-West All-Star Game, they also showcased their talents in exhibition games against traveling teams composed of white major-league stars. In fact, records indicate that Negro League teams won more than two-thirds of the 167 games they played against white all-star teams during the 1930s.[11] "That's when we played the hardest, to let them know, and to let the

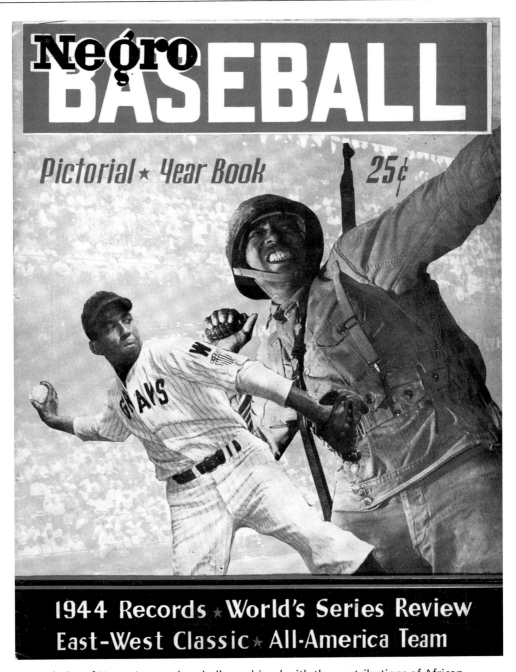

The popularity of Negro League baseball, combined with the contributions of African-American soldiers in World War II, led to calls for an end to racial segregation.

public know that we had the same talent they did and probably a little better lots of times,"[12] declared Negro League star Judy Johnson. Black players' achievements on the field helped break down stereotypes and gave rise to calls for the integration of baseball.

The contributions of segregated African-American military units during World War II also led to increased demands for social justice in the United States. The nation's black-owned newspapers trumpeted the bravery of black soldiers on the battlefield. They also argued that returning veterans who fought for freedom, equality, and democracy overseas also deserved those things at home. "If all Americans were asked to participate in the war, without regard to race or class, then they were entitled to reap the benefits of a democratic society,"[13] as one journalist explained. The so-called "Double V" campaign encouraged African Americans to strive for two victories: over Germany and its allies in World War II and over racial discrimination and segregation in American society. After World War II ended in victory for the United States and its allies in 1945, many people turned their attention toward achieving the second victory.

> *"There's a couple of million dollars worth of baseball talent on the loose ready for the big leagues, yet unsigned,"* wrote Washington Post *columnist Shirley Povich. "Only one thing is keeping them out of the big leagues—the color of their skin."*

As a hallowed American cultural institution, Major League Baseball emerged as a key target for integration. Those in favor of integrating baseball argued that the game did not deserve the title of America's national pastime if its policies prevented black ballplayers from participating at the sport's highest levels. Others supporters of integration made their case from a business perspective. They claimed that the vast pool of talent in the Negro Leagues would raise the level of play, attract new fans to the game, and improve the financial situation of teams and owners. "There's a couple of million dollars worth of baseball talent on the loose ready for the big leagues, yet unsigned," wrote *Washington Post* columnist Shirley Povich. "Only one thing is keeping them out of the big leagues—the color of their skin."[14] Finally, some proponents said that integrating baseball and other institutions was vital if the nation hoped to live up to the principles on which it was founded.

A number of sportswriters worked to generate public support for the integration of professional baseball, including Art Cohn of the *Oakland Tribune*, Sam Lacy of the *Baltimore Afro-American*, Shirley Povich of the *Washington Post*, Wendell Smith of the *Pittsburgh Courier*, and Frank A. Young of the *Chicago Defend-*

er. These journalists directed appeals to fans, players, team owners, and the first commissioner of baseball, Judge Kenesaw Mountain Landis, who held the position from 1920 to 1944.

Wendell Smith (see biography, p. 144), in particular, played an important role in chipping away at baseball's color barrier. He conducted extensive interviews and surveys of players, coaches, managers, and fans to determine the level of support for allowing black players in the major leagues. In a poll conducted in the late 1930s, Smith found that 80 percent of National League players and managers expressed no objection to integration. This result directly challenged claims made by Landis and other officials that white athletes would not tolerate playing with black teammates or against black opponents (see "Sportswriter Wendell Smith Promotes Baseball Integration," p. 155). The work of Smith and other journalists helped to raise awareness of institutionalized racism in baseball and to create an atmosphere where it could be successfully overturned.

Notes

[1] Quoted in Taylor, Matthew. "Move Over, Shoeless Joe: Willie Tasby Was Baltimore's Own Player without Cleats." *Bleacher Report,* August 14, 2009. Retrieved from http://bleacherreport.com/articles/236356-flashback-friday-shoeless-willie-tasby.

[2] Quoted in Tygiel, Jules. *Baseball's Great Experiment: Jackie Robinson and His Legacy.* New York: Vintage Books, 1984, p. 11.

[3] Quoted in Tygiel, p. 15.

[4] O'Neil, Buck. Interview with Ken Burns for *Baseball* [documentary film]. PBS, 1994. Retrieved from http://www.pbs.org/kenburns/baseball/shadowball/oneil.html.

[5] Campanella, Roy. *It's Good to Be Alive.* New York: Signet, 1974, p. 65.

[6] O'Neil.

[7] O'Neil.

[8] O'Neil.

[9] O'Neil.

[10] Quoted in Fussman, Cal. *After Jackie: Pride, Prejudice, and Baseball's Forgotten Heroes: An Oral History.* New York: ESPN Books, 2007, p. 22.

[11] Holway, John. *Voices from the Great Negro Baseball Leagues.* New York: Dodd, Mead, 1975, p. 10.

[12] Quoted in Tygiel, Jules. *Extra Bases: Reflections on Jackie Robinson, Race, and Baseball History.* Lincoln: University of Nebraska Press, 2002, p. 68.

[13] Schall, Andrew. "Wendell Smith: The Pittsburgh Journalist Who Made Jackie Robinson Mainstream." *Pittsburgh Post-Gazette,* March 29, 2012. Retrieved from http://www.post-gazette.com/stories/opinion/perspectives/the-next-page-wendell-smith-the-pittsburgh-journalist-who-made-jackie-robinson-mainstream-300714/#ixzz20EuBK2v8.

[14] Quoted in Peterson, Robert. *Only the Ball Was White.* Englewood Cliffs, NJ: Prentice Hall, 1970, p. 176.

Chapter Two
THE NOBLE EXPERIMENT

—◦◦◦◦∩◦◦◦◦—

There was no doubt about [Brooklyn Dodgers president Branch] Rickey's business objectives, but equally clear to us was his intense commitment to making integration work, which he tended to underplay in public. He and Jack [Robinson] were unequal in power and influence to be sure, but they were always interdependent in this social experiment. Neither could succeed without the other.

—Rachel Robinson

The integration of professional baseball was spearheaded by Branch Rickey, president of the Brooklyn Dodgers. As pressure built to end racial segregation in America after the end of World War II, Rickey came up with a bold plan to recruit a black player from the Negro Leagues to join his major-league roster. The success of his "noble experiment" depended on choosing the right player—one with great athletic talent as well as a strong moral character and flawless public image—and Rickey found his man in Jackie Robinson. After warning Robinson about the difficulties he would inevitably face in attempting to break baseball's color barrier, Rickey signed him to a minor-league contract in 1945.

Rickey Develops a Plan

Born in Ohio in 1881, Wesley Branch Rickey (see biography, p. 130) spent two dismal seasons as a catcher in the major leagues in the early 1900s. After spending a few more seasons as a mediocre coach, he finally found his calling as a front-office executive for the St. Louis Cardinals in the mid-1920s. Rickey proved to be an outstanding judge of baseball talent as well as a brilliant businessman. He is credited with inventing the modern major-league farm system, which allows teams to develop young players by having them work their way up through a series of increasingly competitive minor-league affiliates. He also pioneered the use of baseball statistics as a tool to evaluate players and make decisions, and he introduced protective headgear to baseball by encouraging his players to wear batting helmets. By the time Rickey took over as president of the Brooklyn Dodgers ballclub in 1943, he was already well on his way to earning a reputation as a baseball visionary.

Rickey decided to bring the first black player into major-league baseball for several reasons (see "Branch Rickey Explains His Integration Plan," p. 164). For one thing, the Dodgers organization needed to acquire some young, talented players if the big-league club hoped to win the World Series. Rickey knew that the Negro Leagues offered an untapped source of athletic ability, and he felt that he could gain an advantage over other franchises by moving first. In addition, Rickey believed that adding African-American players to the Dodgers would attract media attention, expand the team's fan base, and increase revenues. Finally, Rickey had personal experience with segregation that made him determined to change the unfair system.

Rickey's most compelling experience of racism occurred in 1906, when he was the baseball coach at Ohio Wesleyan University. His team, which included a black player named Charles Thomas, tried to check into a hotel in Indiana during a road trip. But the hotel manager refused to allow Thomas to stay there with the rest of the team. After arguing with the manager for several minutes, Rickey finally persuaded him to let Thomas sleep on a cot in Rickey's own room. Thomas was deeply humiliated by the situation and took the discrimination very hard. "When I finished registering the rest of the team, I went up to the room, pushed open the door, and went inside. And there was this fine young man, sitting on the edge of his chair, crying," Rickey remembered. "His whole body was wracked with sobs. He was pulling frantically at his hands, pulling at his hands. He looked at me and he said, 'It's my skin. If I could just tear it off, I'd be like everyone else. It's my skin. It's my skin, Mr. Rickey.'"[1]

Rickey started to implement his plan to recruit a Negro Leaguer for the Dodgers by discussing it with the team's banker, George V. MacLaughlin of the Brooklyn Trust Company (see "Branch Rickey's Six-Point Plan for Successful Integration," p. 26). MacLaughlin supported the idea, although he warned Rickey that he would need to find an exceptional player and person to make it work.

Next, Rickey raised the topic at a meeting of the Dodgers' board of directors. The board voted unanimously to approve the plan, but all of the members were sworn to secrecy until Rickey was able to build up support among baseball officials and team owners. As expected, Rickey's proposal encountered serious opposition from Major League Baseball commissioner Kenesaw Mountain Landis. Landis died in November 1944, however, and he was replaced by A. B. "Happy" Chandler (see biography, p. 116) in April 1945. Immediately after taking office, Chandler made a statement to Wendell Smith of the *Pittsburgh Courier* in support of baseball integration. "I'm in support of the Four Freedoms," he declared, "and if a black boy can make it at Okinawa and go to Guadalcanal [sites of World War II battles in the Pacific], he can make it in baseball."[2]

Major League Baseball commissioner Kenesaw Mountain Landis stood in the way of baseball integration for many years.

Even though most team owners did not share the new commissioner's attitude, Rickey moved forward with his plan. He sent Dodgers scouts to Negro League games across the country during the summer of 1945. To hide his true intentions, Rickey claimed that he was looking for players for a new all-black team he planned to launch called the Brooklyn Bombers. In addition to scouting prominent black athletes on the field, Rickey also collected information about the players' personal lives and behavior off the field. He understood that the man he selected to be the first African-American player in major-league baseball would be watched closely by millions of people and come under intense media scrutiny. To ensure that the integration experiment would succeed, Rickey needed to find someone worthy of respect both on and off the baseball diamond. Poor performance or bad behavior would give team owners an excuse to deny other black players the opportunity to play in the majors.

Branch Rickey's Six-Point Plan for Successful Integration

Around 1942, Brooklyn Dodgers president Branch Rickey began thinking about integrating major-league baseball. He knew that he must proceed carefully in order to successfully break the sport's longstanding color barrier. "Americans—both black and white, players and fans—needed time to accommodate themselves to the idea of blacks in baseball," wrote Jules Tygiel. "The slightest false step, Rickey concluded, would delay the entry of nonwhites into the national pastime indefinitely." Accordingly, Rickey came up with a six-point plan that was designed to gradually win the support of team owners, fans, players, and the media. As David Falkner explained in *Great Time Coming,* the plan involved:

1. The backing and sympathy of the Dodgers' directors and stockholders, whose investment and civic standing had to be considered and protected.

2. Picking a Negro who would be the right man on the field.

3. Picking a Negro who would also be the right man off the field.

4. A good reaction from the press and public.

5. Backing and thorough understanding from the Negro race, to avoid misinterpretation and abuse of the project.

6. Acceptance of the player by his teammates.

Although Rickey's "noble experiment" did not proceed exactly according to plan, it did succeed. Jackie Robinson turned out to be the right man, both on and off the field, to achieve Rickey's objectives and open the door for black players to compete in the major leagues. "The Rickey blueprint placed tremendous pressure upon Robinson, his standard-bearer," Tygiel acknowledged. "Robinson's response to this challenge inspired a legend."

Sources

Falkner, David. *Great Time Coming: The Life of Jackie Robinson, from Baseball to Birmingham.* New York: Simon and Schuster, 1995, p. 104.

Tygiel, Bruce. *Baseball's Great Experiment: Jackie Robinson and His Legacy.* New York: Vintage Books, 1984, p. 207.

Choosing Jackie Robinson

Within a few months, Rickey's scouts told him they had found an ideal candidate in Jackie Robinson of the Kansas City Monarchs. Born in Georgia in 1919, Jack Roosevelt Robinson (see biography, p. 134) had originally made a name for himself as the first four-sport varsity athlete at the University of California at Los Angeles (UCLA). As an All-American running back for the school's football team, Robinson led the Bruins to an undefeated season in 1939. He also played basketball and twice led the Pacific Coast Conference in scoring. In track and field, Robinson won the 1940 National Collegiate Athletic Association (NCAA) championship in the long jump with a leap of 24 feet, 10.5 inches. Surprisingly, baseball was his weakest sport during his college career, and he only played one season for the Bruins.

Robinson left UCLA in 1941 to enlist in the military when the United States entered World War II. He attended Officer Candidate School and was commissioned as a second lieutenant in a segregated army unit. After receiving an honorable discharge in November 1944, Robinson signed a contract to play professional baseball for the Kansas City Monarchs of the Negro National League. In 47 games with the Monarchs during the 1945 season, he hit an impressive .387 with 5 home runs and 13 stolen bases. His outstanding performance led to his selection as the starting shortstop for the West team in the Negro Leagues' annual East-West All-Star Game.

Jackie Robinson's military service in World War II was one of the reasons Brooklyn Dodgers president Branch Rickey chose him for his "noble experiment."

Although Robinson's performance on the field was good enough to warrant consideration, Rickey was even more impressed with the player's personal background. Robinson was well-educated, he had experience playing alongside white teammates in college, he had served his country, he was engaged to be married, and he had a deep religious faith. "Integration of the major leagues could, as a result, be debated on its merits, not irrelevant technicalities or character assassinations," wrote journalist Andrew Schall. "Robinson was certainly not the most famous or talented black ballplayer, but he was the least likely to fail for reasons within his own control."[3]

Many fellow Negro League players recognized that Rickey's decision was important and agreed that Robinson was a good choice. "They had to screen the right type of man for it because the whole future could have been killed by picking the wrong man," noted Negro League pitcher Bill Drake. "The boy didn't drink, he didn't smoke, and therefore he made a good leader.... At that time he was the [only] Negro that was logical for that thing."[4] Hank Aaron, who followed Robinson into the major leagues and reigned as baseball's career home run leader from 1974 to 2007, declared that "it's as clear now as it was then that Jackie Robinson was the right man for the right job—intelligent, educated—I think that's what we needed. There were so many temptations put before him. He was a man on trial—not only on the field, but off the field as well—and he had the skills to survive and transcend this ordeal."[5]

A Historic Meeting

Before offering Robinson a contract, though, Rickey wanted to make sure that he was prepared to deal with the inevitable problems that would crop up along the way to integrating major-league baseball. Rickey believed that breaking the sport's longstanding color barrier would require a player who was mentally strong and emotionally secure enough to withstand taunts, threats, and even physical abuse without losing his temper and retaliating. He needed to find out whether Robinson was capable of remaining calm under extreme pressure and provocation.

Rickey sent Dodgers scout Clyde Sukeforth to Chicago to watch one of the Monarchs' games. Afterward, Sukeforth asked Robinson to fly to New York City for a meeting with the Dodgers' president. Their historic, three-hour-long meeting took place on August 28, 1945, in Rickey's office (see "A Dodgers Scout Remembers the Famous Rickey-Robinson Meeting," p. 173). Rickey started off by reading Robinson a passage from *The Life of Christ* by Giovanni Papini, an international best-seller published in 1923. The passage concerned the biblical Sermon on the Mount, in which Jesus told his followers not to respond to violence with violence, advising them instead to "turn the other cheek" toward their attacker. "The results of nonresistance, even if they are not always perfect,

Jackie Robinson and Branch Rickey talked for three hours before signing a contract that made Robinson the first black player in the major leagues.

are certainly superior to resistance or flight," Rickey quoted. "To answer blows with blows, evil deeds with evil deeds, is to meet the attacker on his own ground, to proclaim oneself as low as he. Only he who has conquered himself can conquer his enemies."[6]

> *"It's as clear now as it was then that Jackie Robinson was the right man for the right job," said Hall of Famer Hank Aaron. "He had the skills to survive and transcend this ordeal."*

Rickey went on to explain his view that nonresistance would be key to the success of the "noble experiment." "More than a decade before Martin Luther King Jr. developed techniques of nonviolent protest as a weapon against the violence of southern racism, Rickey urged the same approach on Robinson,"[7] noted civil rights expert Ira Glasser. The Dodgers' executive asked Robinson to promise that no matter what happened during his first few seasons of integrated baseball—whether spectators hurled ugly insults at him, or newspapers printed baseless lies about him, or opposing pitchers intentionally tried to bean him, or opposing base runners slid into him with spikes flying, or racist umpires refused to make any calls in his team's favor—he would resist the urge to fight back. "We can't fight our way through this, Robinson," Rickey stated. "We've got no army. There's virtually no one on our side. No owners, no umpires, and very few newspapermen. And I'm afraid that many fans will be hostile. We'll be in a tough position. We can win only if we can convince the world that I'm doing this because you're a great ballplayer and a fine gentleman."[8]

To see whether Robinson was capable of withstanding racist abuse without retaliating, Rickey decided to test the young ballplayer. Robinson recalled that the test was highly emotional. "To show me what I'd be up against, he acted out a series of one-man dramatic scenes. He was a room clerk in a southern hotel, an insulting waiter at a restaurant, and a sarcastic railroad conductor. Then he took off his coat and played the role of a hot-headed ballplayer and swung his fist at me,"[9] Robinson remembered in a 1955 interview for *Look* magazine. "He knew I would have terrible problems and wanted me to know the extent of them before I agreed to the plan. I was twenty-six years old, and all my life—back to the age of eight when a little neighbor girl called me a nigger—I had believed in payback, retaliation. The most luxurious possession, the richest treasure anybody has, is his personal dignity.... Could I turn the other cheek? I didn't know how I would do it. Yet I knew that I must."[10]

Robinson sat through Rickey's tirade with his fists clenched, but he made it to the end without responding. The exchange convinced the Dodgers' executive that Robinson was indeed the right man for the job. The two men agreed that Robinson would play for the Dodgers' top minor-league affiliate, the Montreal Royals of the International League, during the 1946 season. They waited to announce their agreement until October 23, after the 1945 major-league season had ended. Although Rickey's decision to hire Robinson became front-page news in black-owned newspapers, many national publications downplayed the story or ran it only in the sports section. Nevertheless, Robinson acknowledged the historic nature of the event in his remarks at a press conference. "Of course, I can't begin to tell you how happy I am that I am the first member of my race in organized ball," he told the *New York Times*. "I realize how much it means to me, my race, and to baseball. I can only say I'll do my very best to come through in every manner."[11]

Breaking into Organized Baseball

In February 1946 Robinson married his longtime fiancée, Rachel Isum (see biography, p. 139), who would stand by his side throughout his efforts to break into organized baseball. The couple experienced the effects of racial segregation and discrimination from the very beginning. On their way from California to Florida to attend spring training with the Royals, the Robinsons were bumped off of a flight in New Orleans, Louisiana. "As we were coming in, we were paged, and we were asked to get off the plane. With no real explanation of why we were the only couple taken off, we were told we would be put on another plane later," Rachel Robinson remembered. "We didn't know we had been bumped because in the South, a white couple waiting for seats took priority over a black couple that already had seats. It was my first experience of the South—I had never seen the blacks-whites signs for drinking fountains and ladies rooms."[12]

The problems continued as the Royals traveled around Florida to play exhibition games against other minor-league teams. Although some cities and towns were accommodating toward Robinson, others were not. In Jacksonville, for instance, city officials padlocked the stadium rather than allow Robinson and the Royals to play there. In Daytona Beach, all of the white Royals players and coaches stayed at the oceanfront Mayfair Hotel. It was segregated, however, so Robinson and black sportswriters Billy Rowe and Wendell Smith had to stay in private homes in the surrounding African-American community.

Baseball's First Negro

The Dodgers sign Jackie Robinson — first breach in game's racial barrier

John Roosevelt (Jackie) Robinson, 26-year-old former Army lieutenant and star four-letter athlete at UCLA (University of California in Los Angeles), recently became the first Negro player in the history of organized baseball.

A shortstop, Robinson was signed to an organizational contract by Branch W. Rickey, president of the Brooklyn Dodgers, and ordered to report next February to that club's principal minor-league affiliate, the Montreal Royals of the International League. Before the 1946 season is over Robinson may be in the Dodgers' line-up as their regular shortstop.

In signing Robinson, and several other Negro stars soon after, the Dodgers climaxed a $25,000, three-year scouting search under Rickey's direction throughout the United States and Latin America. They came up with baseball's first honest answer to the vital racial problem it had long evaded and other major-league teams were expected to follow their lead.

The real purpose behind the quest for Robinson and the other Negro stars was shrouded in deep secrecy. Until a month ago, even Brooklyn scouts believed they were seeking material to stock the Brown Dodgers, an All-Negro team Rickey has projected. **(Continued on next page)**

Twenty-six-year-old Jackie Robinson is intelligent, even-tempered, courageous, zealous to help his race.

Robinson's speed, shiftiness delighted Pacific Coast football fans, sparked UCLA to undefeated 1939 season. Here he is in action against Southern California.

On a mediocre team, he led Pacific Coast Conference basketball scorers.

In track, Jackie won national-collegiate broad jump with 25-foot leap.

67

This 1945 article in *Look* magazine announced the historic agreement that shattered baseball's color barrier.

Robinson even encountered racist resistance from the Royals' manager, Clay Hopper, who begged Rickey not to assign the league's first black player to his team. "Please don't do this to me," he complained. "I'm white, and I've lived in Mississippi all my life. If you do this, you're going to force me to move my family and my home out of Mississippi." But the big-league boss had no patience for Hopper's concerns. "You can manage correctly, or you can be unemployed,"[13] Rickey responded.

Robinson soon won over his manager, teammates, and Montreal fans with his spectacular play, which was on full display on the opening day of the 1946 season. In his first regular-season game in a Royals uniform, Robinson hit three singles and a two-run homer, drove in six runs, and stole two bases to lift his team to a 14-1 victory over the Jersey City Giants. "This was the day the dam burst between me and my teammates. Northerners and Southerners alike, they let me know how much they appreciated the way I had come through," Robinson related. "I knew what it was that day to hear the ear-shattering roar of the crowd and know it was for me. I began to really believe one of Mr. Rickey's predictions. Color didn't matter to fans if the black man was the winner."[14]

"I knew what it was that day to hear the ear-shattering roar of the crowd and know it was for me," Jackie Robinson remembered. "I began to really believe one of Mr. Rickey's predictions. Color didn't matter to fans if the black man was the winner."

Robinson's impressive showing continued throughout the 1946 season. He posted a terrific .349 average to claim the International League batting title. He also scored 113 runs and ranked second in the league in stolen bases. His strong performance helped the Royals earn a 100-54 record and win the league championship. At the end of the season, Robinson was honored with the Most Valuable Player award. Even Hopper had to admit that the former Negro Leaguer had proved his value to the team. "You don't have to worry none about that boy," the Royals' manager told Rickey. "He's the greatest competitor I ever saw, and what's more, he's a gentleman."[15]

Early Reactions

Over the course of his rookie season, Robinson emerged as a huge fan favorite in Montreal, and most people he encountered in that multicultural Canadian city treated him and his wife with kindness and respect. Robinson also got an enthusiastic reception from African-American fans, who packed into stadiums across the United States to see him play. In fact, attendance figures for

Robinson had a highly successful 1946 season with the Montreal Royals, the Dodgers' minor-league farm team.

games featuring the Royals topped one million in 1946—a remarkable feat for an International League team.

Robinson's presence on the field was an inspiration for many people, especially African Americans. They rejoiced when they learned that he had finally broken baseball's color barrier, and they expressed hope that his achievements would help end segregation in other facets of American life. "I was thirteen years old when Jackie Robinson signed to play with Montreal," recalled Ed Charles, who went on to play major-league baseball in the 1960s.

> As soon as the media released the news, we got all excited, and it was like, "Hey, we can't hardly wait." I was like a little boy wait-

ing for Christmas and Santa Claus to see what kind of toys he was going to bring us.... I looked at that and said, "Okay, maybe now we're going to begin to start living the American dream like the rest of the citizens, maybe now we're going to make some headway to right what I had seen to be these types of wrongs, the inhuman treatment of our people, the hardships on blacks." And it gave me a little hope that perhaps we were on the right track as far as living the type of American dream, this freedom of opportunity we were supposed to have in this country.[16]

Carrying the hopes and dreams of African Americans gave Robinson a tremendous responsibility and added to the extreme pressure he faced. Many people were counting on him to prove that blacks were equal to whites on the baseball field and beyond. "To tell you the truth, I never thought the day would come when a Negro would be playing in organized baseball, because we [had] always been exploited to the extent that the white man was the best ball player," Negro Leaguer Bill Drake explained. "See, that was my belief, that he was the best ball player because that's all you heard, but I found out that that's not so, he's not the best ball player. He's a good ball player, you got good ball players among the white and you got good ball players among the Negroes. I began to realize late that Negroes are much better ball players than they thought they would be."[17]

Although he appreciated the support he received from the black community, Robinson was under no illusion that his transition to the major leagues would be easy. He had experienced a number of ugly racial incidents at visiting ballparks, and the basketfuls of letters he had received included hate mail and death threats along with notes from fans and admirers. Robinson looked forward to trying to make the Brooklyn Dodgers' roster for the 1947 season, but he also recognized the gravity of his situation. "Jackie began to understand his mission and that the mission went way beyond sports and athletics," Rachel Robinson stated. "He could see that there was more to it than just a social experiment, that it had overtones of being something really big."[18]

Notes

[1] Quoted in Golenbock, Peter. *Bums: An Oral History of the Brooklyn Dodgers.* New York: Putnam, 1984, p. 124.

[2] Quoted in Golenbock, p. 122.

[3] Schall, Andrew. "Wendell Smith: The Pittsburgh Journalist Who Made Jackie Robinson Mainstream." *Pittsburgh Post-Gazette,* March 29, 2012. Retrieved from http://www.post-gazette.com/stories/opinion/

perspectives/the-next-page-wendell-smith-the-pittsburgh-journalist-who-made-jackie-robinson-main stream-300714/#ixzz20EuBK2v8.

[4] Drake, Bill. Interview with Charles Korr and Steven Hause. Negro Baseball League Project, Oral History T-0067, December 8, 1971. State Historical Society of Missouri Research Center, University of Missouri-St. Louis. Retrieved from http://www.umsl.edu/~whmc/guides/t067.htm.

[5] Quoted in Robinson, Jackie. *I Never Had It Made: An Autobiography.* Hopewell, NJ: Echo Press, 1995, p.xvii.

[6] Quoted in Kindred, Dave. "Jackie Robinson: One Man, Alone." *The Sporting News,* April 14, 1997, p. 6.

[7] Glasser, Ira. "Branch Rickey and Jackie Robinson: Precursors to the Civil Rights Movement." *World and I,* March 2003, p. 257.

[8] Robinson, p. 32.

[9] Quoted in Falkner, David. *Great Time Coming: The Life of Jackie Robinson from Baseball to Birmingham.* New York: Simon and Schuster, 1995, p. 107.

[10] Robinson, pp. 33-34.

[11] Quoted in Falkner, p. 116.

[12] Quoted in Golenbock, p. 136.

[13] Quoted in Golenbock, p. 139.

[14] Robinson, p. 47.

[15] Quoted in Golenbock, p. 144.

[16] Quoted in Golenbock, p.135.

[17] Drake.

[18] Quoted in Golenbock, p. 143.

Chapter Three

ROBINSON
JOINS THE SHOW

Let's face it, baseball was at the very core of American life. And all by himself, enduring all that he endured, Jackie Robinson proved what African Americans were capable of accomplishing. Every American, the low and the mighty, had to take note of that.

—Civil rights leader Roger Wilkins

After spending one season in the minor leagues, Jackie Robinson made his major-league debut with the Brooklyn Dodgers in 1947. He overcame resistance from his teammates and hostility from opposing players and fans to have an amazing season. Robinson not only claimed the National League Rookie of the Year Award and led the Dodgers to the World Series, he also earned the admiration of millions of Americans with his quiet courage. "For blacks, Robinson became a symbol of pride and dignity," wrote baseball historian Jules Tygiel. "To whites, he represented a type of black man far removed from prevailing stereotypes, whom they could not help but respect."[1] Robinson's success opened the door for future generations of African-American baseball players to enter the major leagues.

Joins the Dodgers

After the 1946 season ended, Robinson's focus shifted from his baseball career to his personal life. He was thrilled when his wife gave birth to their first child, son Jackie Jr., in November 1946. A few months later, however, Robinson had to leave his family behind to report to a joint Montreal Royals-Brooklyn Dodgers training camp in Cuba. Dodgers president Branch Rickey had decid-

Robinson and his wife, Rachel, welcomed their first child, son Jackie Jr., shortly before he joined the Brooklyn Dodgers.

ed to relocate spring training to the racially diverse Caribbean island nation in order to avoid some of the discrimination that Robinson had encountered the previous year in Florida. He hoped that the move would reduce some of the pressure on Robinson, give him time to get to know his future teammates, and ease his transition into the big leagues.

Unfortunately, playing in Cuba did not help Robinson feel more comfortable. He struggled to find his way around because he did not know Spanish, which is the primary language spoken in Cuba. He also experienced some digestive problems from consuming unfamiliar food and water. Robinson's discomfort also extended to the ball field, as he unexpectedly learned that the Dodgers wanted him to switch from second base to first base—a position he had never played before.

Despite these obstacles, Robinson performed well in spring training. Rickey set up a series of exhibition games between the Royals and the Dodgers. He hoped that Robinson would impress the big-league squad so much that the players would be clamoring for him to join the team. "I want you to be a whirling demon against the Dodgers," the executive told Robinson. "I want you to concentrate, to hit that ball, to get on base by any means necessary. I want you to run wild, to steal the pants off them, to be the most conspicuous player on the field—but conspicuous only because of the kind of baseball you're playing."[2] Robinson took Rickey's advice. In seven exhibition games, he hit a remarkable .625 and stole 7 bases.

Faces Opposition from Teammates

Although the Dodgers were duly impressed by Robinson's talents, many of the players continued to resist the idea of having an African-American teammate. Several of the team's biggest stars hailed from the South, where racial segregation remained firmly in place at that time. Growing up in this environment had created deep-seated prejudices that were difficult to overcome. "I can't say that we really looked down on the blacks," said Dodgers shortstop Pee Wee Reese, who was raised in Kentucky. "We just thought that [segregation] was the way it was supposed to be."[3]

A few of the Dodgers, like Dixie Walker—a veteran outfielder from Alabama—held even stronger racist views. "[They] believed that taking a shower in the same larger shower room with a black ballplayer would infect and contaminate them. They lived by the racial clichés of the time," explained sportswriter Maury Allen. "They thought of blacks as slaves, a generation removed: maids, porters, local laborers, shiftless, dirty, unintelligent. Dixie Walker was a kind, decent, and gentle man [who] saw no question of hatred.... He was a God-fearing man who saw the separation of the races as part of the divine order."[4]

When it appeared likely that Robinson would make the big-league roster for the 1947 season, Walker responded by circulating a petition in the Dodgers' clubhouse. The petition stated that those who signed it would refuse to be on the same team as a black player. Walker and several other southerners affixed their signatures. Most team members who came from northern states refused to sign, however, as did a few key southerners. "I wouldn't sign it," Reese remembered. "I wasn't trying to think of myself as being the Great White Father, really, I just wanted to play the game ... and it didn't matter to me whether he was black or green, he had a right to be there too."[5]

Dodgers outfielder Dixie Walker and several other players signed a petition that said they would refuse to play on the same team as a black man.

When Rickey and Dodgers manager Leo Durocher learned about the petition, they called a late-night meeting of the players responsible. Rickey threatened to trade anyone who had a problem playing for an integrated team. Although a couple of players requested a trade, most of them bowed to Rickey's authority and gave up their protest.

Makes Major League Debut

On April 10, Rickey posted an understated message in the Dodgers' press box that read: "Brooklyn announces the purchase of Jack Roosevelt Robinson from Montreal. Signed, Branch Rickey." With this announcement, Robinson officially became the first African-American player to make a major-league roster in the twentieth century. Still, the mainstream media did not treat it as a big story. Many sportswriters recognized both Robinson's talent and Rickey's determination, so they had fully expected Robinson to be promoted to the Dodgers by the end of spring training. The *New York Times* merely commented that it would have happened earlier if Robinson were white.

The nation's black-owned newspapers welcomed the news with greater fanfare. A headline in the *Boston Chronicle,* for instance, said "Triumph of Whole Race Seen in Jackie's Debut in Major League Ball." At the same time, though, some African-American journalists noted that Robinson's promotion was only one step in the long journey toward racial equality in America. "This of course is just a token victory," wrote Dave Egan in the *Pittsburgh Courier.* "The war against bigotry in baseball will not be won until every team in the major leagues judges every man on his ability to play ball."[6]

Robinson made his first regular-season appearance in a Dodgers uniform on April 15—opening day of the 1947 season. As he prepared to leave the house that morning, he joked with his wife that "in case you have trouble picking me out, I'll be wearing number 42."[7] Over 25,000 people, including about 14,000 African Americans, were in the stands at Ebbets Field to witness his historic shattering of baseball's color barrier. Robinson's performance at the plate did not rise to the occasion, as he went hitless in four at-bats. Nevertheless, the Dodgers defeated the Boston Braves by a score of 5-3 (see "A Sportswriter Recalls Robinson's Major League Debut," p. 176).

Endures Hatred and Hostility

Robinson first experienced racial hostility from an opposing team a week later, during the first game of a home stand against the Philadelphia Phillies. Led by Phillies manager Ben Chapman, who grew up in Tennessee, the opposing dugout launched a vicious verbal assault on Robinson that lasted through most of the game. The Phillies shouted epithets and insults, made obscene gestures, and pretended their bats were machine guns being fired at him.

Some people excused the Phillies' behavior, explaining that verbal exchanges involving taunting, name calling, and even ethnic slurs were common among major-league teams in those days. "You have to realize that baseball is a game in which the guys on the other bench will say almost anything to upset you," said Dodgers pitcher Carl Erskine. "They yell about your mother. They yell about your wife. They call you names. If it gets to you, then it makes you less effective."[8] Yet many people—including families seated in the stands nearby—felt that Chapman's antics went far beyond the level of routine big-league rivalry. "At no time in my life have I heard racial venom and dugout abuse to match the abuse that Ben sprayed on Robinson that night,"[9] declared Dodgers traveling secretary Harold Parrott. Outrage over the incident prompted dozens of fans to send letters of protest to Major League Baseball commissioner A. B. "Happy" Chandler.

At the time, Robinson claimed that the behavior of Chapman and the Phillies did not bother him. He never responded to the endless stream of taunts and gestures coming from the opposing dugout, and he earned widespread praise in newspapers for his restraint. Years later, though, he acknowledged his true feelings about the incident in his autobiography. "I have to admit that this day, of all the unpleasant days in my life, brought me nearer to cracking up than I had ever been," he wrote. "Perhaps I should have become inured to this kind of garbage, but I was in New York City and unprepared to face the kind of barbarism from a northern team that I had come to associate with the Deep South."[10]

Robinson found the abuse so terrible, in fact, that he seriously considered abandoning Rickey's "noble experiment" and retaliating against his tormentors. He admitted that he was sorely tempted to "stride over to that Phillies dugout, grab one of those white sons of bitches, and smash his teeth with my despised black fist."[11] Rachel Robinson could only watch and try to support her husband as he endured such hostility on an almost daily basis. "Every stadium that year was a battleground," she remembered. "For Jack the greatest struggles were internal; the pact he had agreed to with Branch Rickey at his signing—that he would not allow himself to be provoked regardless of the viciousness of the baiting—had to be honored."[12]

> *"This of course is just a token victory," sportswriter Dave Egan wrote of Jackie Robinson's debut. "The war against bigotry in baseball will not be won until every team in the major leagues judges every man on his ability to play ball."*

During that April 22 game against the Phillies, the abuse continued until one of Robinson's teammates came to his defense. Dodgers second baseman Eddie Stanky, who had shown little interest in getting to know the rookie first baseman up to that point, finally reached the limit of his ability to tolerate the Phillies' behavior. He marched over to the opposing dugout and called Chapman a coward for picking on a player who could not fight back. From that time on, the Dodgers seemed more willing to step forward and protect Robinson, as they would any other teammate. "Chapman did more than anybody to unite the Dodgers," said Rickey. "When he poured out that string of unconscionable abuse, he solidified and unified thirty men, not one of whom was willing to sit by and see someone kick around a man who had his hands tied behind his back.... Chapman made Jackie a real member of the Dodgers."[13]

The ugly incident also helped Robinson gain valuable support from the commissioner of baseball. Chandler responded to complaints from fans by warning Chapman that any further racial remarks would result in his suspension. Although the Phillies manager insisted that he had treated Robinson the same way he would have treated any other opponent, the commissioner's message clearly got through. When the Dodgers faced the Phillies again at Shibe Park in Philadelphia, Chapman sent a special request to the visitors' locker room. He asked Robinson to pose for a photograph together to show that they had both put the incident behind them. Robinson earned the respect of many

Robinson (back row, third from left) made his debut with the Brooklyn Dodgers on April 15, 1947.

by agreeing to meet Chapman at home plate before the game. "I can think of no occasion where I had more difficulty in swallowing my pride and doing what seemed best for baseball and the cause of the Negro in baseball than in agreeing to pose for a photograph with a man for whom I had only the very lowest regard,"[14] he admitted. Since neither man relished the idea of a handshake, they posed holding opposite ends of the same bat.

The Phillies incident was only the first of many trials Robinson faced during his rookie season. At one point the media reported that a large group of National League players, led by the St. Louis Cardinals, was planning to go on strike rather than play against Robinson. National League president Ford Frick threatened to suspend any players involved in such a scheme, however, and the rumored strike never happened. Robinson also received many troubling letters in the mail throughout the season, including some in which the writers made death threats against him and his family. The situation became so frightening to Robinson and his wife that the Dodgers assigned a staff member to open their mail and contact the police whenever it contained threatening letters. The authorities followed up on a few of the more credible threats. Before one Dodgers game in Cincinnati, for instance, agents with the Federal Bureau of Investigation (FBI) searched the rooftops of buildings around the stadium looking for a gunman who had vowed to shoot Robinson if he took the field. They never found the man.

In addition to these major scares, Robinson also faced countless minor inconveniences as the only African-American player in the major leagues. Segregation prevented him from staying at the same hotel as his teammates in many southern cities. He was also forced to carry his own luggage through airports and training facilities, while porters handled that duty for the rest of the Dodgers.

Gains Support of Teammates

As the 1947 season wore on, Robinson continued to endure hostility and hatred with courage and dignity. He also proved that he belonged in the major leagues with his daring and spectacular play on the field. After struggling at the plate for the first month of the season, Robinson's hitting improved dramatically in mid-May. On June 14 he started a 21-game hitting streak, and by the end of that month he had raised his batting average to .315 and led the league in stolen bases.

One of Robinson's most important contributions to the game was adding an element of Negro League-style "tricky baseball" to the majors. He turned bunting into an art form, posting a phenomenal .913 success rate (14 hits and 28 sacrifices in 46 attempts). Once on base, his speed and aggressiveness intimidated opposing pitchers and ignited the competitive fire in his team. "Robinson on base—on any base, first, second, third—was the most exciting player I've seen," said legendary Dodgers announcer Red Barber. "When Robinson was on base, every eye in the ballpark was on him."[15]

Robinson's outstanding play served as his personal revenge against fans who taunted him, pitchers who threw at him, and base runners who spiked him in the leg as they crossed first base. "Jack found that the most powerful form of retaliation against prejudice was his excellent play. He 'hurt' the opposition by performing well," Rachel Robinson explained. "We knew that achieving one's

Robinson agreed to pose for a photo with Philadelphia Phillies manager Ben Chapman, who had led a vicious, racially motivated verbal assault against him, in order to advance "the cause of the Negro in baseball."

goals was the most potent method for triumphing over oppressors ... and he did so with great glee."[16]

Robinson's competitive spirit and playing ability helped him gain the support of more and more of his teammates. "Within thirty days, maximum, those of us who were reluctant to sit with Jackie in the dining room car would readily sit down with him," said Dodgers catcher Bobby Bragan, who had signed the petition protesting Robinson's addition to the team. "It soon became apparent to all of us that there wasn't any way we were going to win without Jackie."[17]

One of Robinson's closest allies on the Dodgers was shortstop Pee Wee Reese (see biography, p. 126), who talked and joked with the rookie and invit-

45

> *"I had started the season as a lonely man,"* Jackie Robinson *said of his rookie year. "I ended it feeling like a member of a solid team."*

ed him to play cards and golf with the rest of the players. Reese also demonstrated his support and respect publicly, which helped Robinson feel more confident on the field. During a game in Cincinnati, for example, fans and opposing players began shouting taunts and insults at both Robinson and Reese. They expressed outrage that Reese, as a southerner, was willing to play alongside a black man. The Dodgers captain responded with a subtle but effective display of sportsmanship and camaraderie. "Reese heard the shouting but refused to even glance in the direction of the stands," explained Robinson's daughter Sharon. "Instead, he walked over to my dad on first base. Reese put his hand on my father's shoulder and started talking to him. His words weren't important—in fact, afterward neither man remembered what was said. It was the gesture of comradeship and support that counted."[18]

Dodgers pitcher Rex Barney also found the shortstop's gesture memorable. "Pee Wee went over to him and put his arm around him as if to say, 'This is my boy. This is the guy. We're gonna win with him,'" he recalled. "Well, it drove the Cincinnati players right through the ceiling, and you could have heard the gasp from the crowd when he did it. That's one reason Pee Wee was such an instrumental person contributing to Jackie's success."[19]

With the team captain setting an example, the rest of the Dodgers soon began challenging some of the discriminatory practices that affected Robinson. "I remember Jackie would sit there and wait until everyone else had showered," said outfielder Al Gionfriddo, who joined the team midway through the 1947 season. "One day I hit him on the butt and I said, 'You're part of this team. Why are you waiting to be the last guy in the shower? Just because in some states Negroes can't shower with whites, that doesn't mean it has to apply here in our clubhouse.' And he just looked at me and laughed, and we both got up and took a shower."[20]

Wins the Hearts of Baseball Fans

As the 1947 season continued, people across the country followed Robinson's struggles and triumphs closely. They gathered around their radios to listen to broadcasts of every Dodger game, and they combed through the sports sections of newspapers to get daily updates on Robinson's statistics. The *Pittsburgh Courier* convinced Robinson to write a regular column, "Jackie Robinson

During his rookie season, Robinson gradually gained the support of Dodgers teammates like (from left) Spider Jorgensen, Pee Wee Reese, and Eddie Stanky.

Says," in which he shared his thoughts on various topics and offered insights into his private life and baseball experiences. His portrait appeared on the cover of *Time* magazine, and a public opinion poll found that he was the second-most-popular man in America, after singer and actor Bing Crosby. All of the media attention helped Robinson go from a curiosity to a sensation to a national hero. "Robinson's aggressive play, his innate sense of dignity, and his outward composure under extreme duress captivated the American people,"[21] Tygiel noted.

Although Robinson's fan base was diverse, his popularity was greatest among African Americans. Everywhere the Dodgers played, black fans would fill the stadium to capacity. Some black communities arranged for special trains to

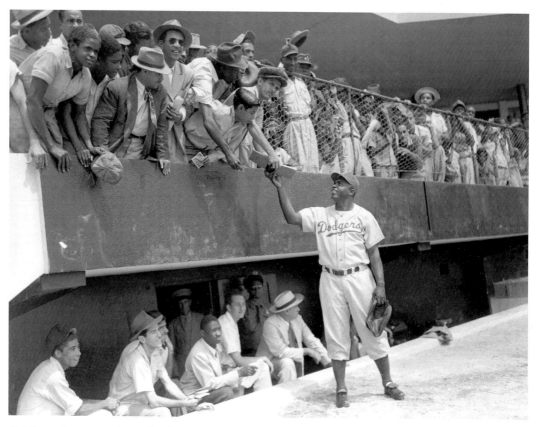

Robinson became a huge fan favorite and helped set attendance records at stadiums across the country.

transport residents to New York or other cities to see Robinson in action. Many black fans arrived at the ballpark dressed in their finest clothes. Some of them did not even know the rules of baseball—they just wanted to witness history in the making. "There's people who come out to see ball games who didn't know who the umpire was. I've heard them holler about that little old man in the blue suit, 'Why don't he get out of the way?' They didn't know he was [the] umpire," recalled former Negro League pitcher Bill Drake. "They used to bring baskets of chicken out there just like going on a picnic. They was just that crazy about Robinson, they was really crazy about Robinson when he was with the Dodgers."[22]

Robinson's extreme popularity was reflected in National League attendance figures. Thanks in part to his presence, the total attendance for 1947 beat the all-time record set the previous year by 750,000 people. Rachel Robinson understood that her husband's achievements carried great meaning for African Americans, and she noted that the support they received from the black community was meaningful for them as well. "Jack and I began to realize how important we were to black America, and how much we symbolized its hunger for opportunity and its determination to make dreams long deferred possible. We would witness the swelling attendance and thunderous support of black fans as the team traveled around the country," she stated. "As a group, black people knew we were involved in something momentous."[23]

Dodgers Capture the NL Pennant

Robinson's outstanding play and the surge in fan support helped lift the Dodgers to the World Series in 1947. Brooklyn posted a 94-60 record on the year to win the National League pennant by five games over the St. Louis Cardinals. Robinson appeared in 151 of the team's 154 games. He batted an impressive .297, led the league in stolen bases with 29, and ranked second in runs scored with 125 runs. He also adjusted well to his new defensive position and became a solid first baseman. At the conclusion of the season, the *Sporting News* presented Robinson with the first-ever National League Rookie of the Year Award. The magazine's editors insisted that they made their choice solely based on his performance on the field. "The sociological experiment that Robinson represented, the trail blazing that he did, the barriers he broke down, did not enter into the decision,"[24] they wrote.

After the Dodgers clinched the pennant, the team recognized Robinson's contributions by declaring "Jackie Robinson Day" at Ebbets Field. They presented him with a Cadillac, a television set, a gold watch, and other gifts. Players, coaches, and team executives all made speeches praising Robinson's accomplishments on and off the field. For Robinson, such recognition marked the successful conclusion of a season-long quest for acceptance by his teammates. "I had started the season as a lonely man," he acknowledged. "I ended it feeling like a member of a solid team. The Dodgers were a championship team because all of us had learned something. I had learned how to exercise self-control—to answer insults, violence, and injustice with silence—and I had learned how to earn the respect of my teammates. They had learned that it's not skin color but talent and ability that counts."[25]

In the 1947 World Series, the Dodgers faced off against a powerful New York Yankees team led by star players Joe DiMaggio, Yogi Berra, and Phil Riz-

Robinson, known for his aggressive base running, is caught in a rundown by the New York Yankees during the 1947 World Series.

zuto. Robinson recalled his first World Series game as one of the best moments of his career. "My greatest thrill in baseball didn't come from any ball I hit, from any base I stole, or from any play I made. It came when I heard the national anthem played just before the start of the 1947 World Series," he declared. "It was a history-making day. It would be the first time that a black man would be allowed to participate in a World Series."[26] The best-of-seven-game series between the two teams is widely considered to be one of the most thrilling in baseball history. After the Dodgers and Yankees split the first six games 3-3, they played a winner-take-all seventh game to decide the championship. Unfortunately for Robinson and his teammates, the Dodgers lost 5-2 (see "Jackie Robinson Looks Back on His Rookie Season," p. 180).

Opens the Door for Other Black Players

Robinson's highly successful rookie season opened the door for other African-American players to enter Major League Baseball (see "First African-American Player for Each Major-League Franchise," p. 52). "In one incredible year, in the face of almost unanimous opposition, Jackie Robinson had proved that the Negro could not only compete in the major leagues but that he could sparkle. Because he was so spectacular, there was a rush by other teams to sign black talent," wrote Peter Golenbock in a history of the Dodgers. "All because of the courage and dignity and skill and intelligence of Jack Roosevelt Robinson."[27]

Twenty-three-year-old World War II veteran Larry Doby (see biography, p. 121) was the second black player in the majors. He broke the American League's color barrier on July 5, 1947, when he played for the Cleveland Indians. Unfortunately, Doby faced some of the same resistance from teammates and hostility from opponents as Robinson did in the National League. "The first day I took the field in Chicago, I stood on the sidelines for five minutes and no one would warm up with me," Doby recalled. Journalist Jerry Izenberg remembered the humiliating treatment Doby endured when the Indians played in the segregated South. "Larry wasn't allowed to use the visitors' clubhouse [in Washington, D.C.]—he had to change in a black boardinghouse. No cab would pick him up, and there he was, walking down the street with his uniform on and his cleats over his shoulder, going to the tradesman's entrance at the ballpark so he could play against the Senators," he wrote. "Unless you've lived it, you don't know. Walk a mile in my shoes."[28]

Like Robinson, though, centerfielder Doby became a breakout star for his new team and gradually gained the acceptance of his teammates. He made the All-Star team in seven consecutive seasons and led the Indians to a World Series championship in 1948. When Doby hit a home run to lift his team to victory in one of the World Series games, the winning pitcher, Steve Gromek, greeted him at home plate with an enthusiastic bear hug. A photographer captured the moment on film, and the image of the teammates' celebration appeared in the sports section of newspapers across the country. It marked the first time that a photo of a black athlete and a white athlete embracing each other had ever been published nationwide. "America really needed that picture," Doby said fifty years later in his Hall of Fame induction speech, "and I'm proud I was able to give it to them."[29]

Several other black players joined major-league teams before the end of the 1947 season. The struggling St. Louis Browns hired two Negro League stars, out-

First African-American Player
for Each Major-League Franchise

Jackie Robinson's success encouraged other major-league teams to add black players to their rosters. The following chart shows the year each team integrated, along with the name of the African-American player who broke the team's color barrier.

TEAM	PLAYER	YEAR
Brooklyn Dodgers	Jackie Robinson	1947
Cleveland Indians	Larry Doby	1947
St. Louis Browns	Hank Thompson; Willard Brown	1947
New York Giants	Monte Irvin; Hank Thompson	1949
Boston Braves	Sam Jethroe	1950
Chicago White Sox	Minnie Minoso	1951
Philadelphia Athletics	Bob Trice	1953
Chicago Cubs	Ernie Banks; Gene Baker	1953
Pittsburgh Pirates	Curt Roberts	1954
St. Louis Cardinals	Tom Alston	1954
Cincinnati Reds	Chuck Harmon; Nino Escalera	1954
Washington Senators	Carlos Paula	1954
New York Yankees	Elston Howard	1955
Philadelphia Phillies	John Kennedy	1957
Detroit Tigers	Ozzie Virgil Sr.	1958
Boston Red Sox	Pumpsie Green	1959

fielder Willard "Home Run" Brown and infielder Hank Thompson, in an effort to win games and increase attendance. When they both appeared in the Browns' lineup on July 20, it marked the first time a major-league franchise had played two African Americans in the same game. The Dodgers added a second black player, pitcher Dan Bankhead, for a brief time in August. Although he hit a home run in his first major-league at-bat, Bankhead also allowed ten hits in a three-inning relief appearance, which resulted in his being reassigned to the minors.

Over the next few seasons, a steady stream of black players poured into organized baseball. By 1952 there were 150 African-American players on major-league rosters or in minor-league farm systems. Once the initial shock of Robinson's debut wore off, "owners and players alike took up cudgels [stick-like weapons] in defense of the move, not from any altruistic motive, but because they recognized ... the competitive value of this new source of man-power,"[30] according to Ford Frick, the former National League president who became the commissioner of baseball in 1951.

Although it would be a dozen years before every major-league team included a black player, the integration of baseball had far-reaching effects on American society. "Through the vehicle of America's pastime, African Americans shattered Jim Crow restrictions while simultaneously challenging long-held stereotypes of racial inadequacy," wrote historian Bruce Adelson. "The mere act of hitting, fielding ... alongside white teammates and opponents, often equal-ing or besting their feats, not only belied the notion of black inferiority but also signaled the eventual demise of Jim Crow."[31]

One unfortunate effect of baseball integration was that it soon led to the demise of the Negro Leagues. Within four years of Robinson's major-league debut, black baseball had lost virtually all of its most talented players. Many of the younger players signed contracts with big-league teams, while most of the older ones retired. At the same time, black baseball fans switched their alle-giance to the newly integrated major-league teams that showcased their heroes. Without stars to attract fans, Negro League team owners suffered financial loss-es and went out of business. The Negro National League disbanded after the 1949 season. Although the Negro American League managed to hold on through the 1950s, it closed its doors in 1962.

Notes

1 Tygiel, Jules. *Baseball's Great Experiment: Jackie Robinson and His Legacy.* New York: Vintage Books, 1984, p. 208.
2 Rowan, Carl T., with Jackie Robinson. *Wait Till Next Year: The Life Story of Jackie Robinson.* New York: Random House, 1960, p. 175.
3 Quoted in Golenbock, Peter. *Bums: An Oral History of the Brooklyn Dodgers.* New York: Putnam, 1984, p. 146.
4 Quoted in Kindred, Dave. "Jackie Robinson: One Man, Alone." *The Sporting News,* April 14, 1997.
5 Quoted in Berkow, Ira. "Standing Beside Jackie Robinson, Reese Helped Change Baseball." *New York Times,* March 31, 1997. Retrieved from http://www.nytimes.com/specials/baseball/bbo-reese-robinson.html.

[6] Quoted in Holtzman, Jerome. *On Baseball: A History of Baseball Scribes.* Champaign, IL: Sports Publishing, 2005, p. 149.

[7] Schall, Andrew. "Wendell Smith: The Pittsburgh Journalist Who Made Jackie Robinson Mainstream." *Pittsburgh Post-Gazette,* March 29, 2012. Retrieved from http://www.post-gazette.com/stories/opinion /perspectives/the-next-page-wendell-smith-the-pittsburgh-journalist-who-made-jackie-robinson-mainstream-300714/#ixzz20EuBK2v8.

[8] Quoted in Fussman, Cal. *After Jackie: Pride, Prejudice, and Baseball's Forgotten Heroes: An Oral History.* New York: ESPN Books, 2007, p. 73.

[9] Parrott, Harold. *The Lords of Baseball.* New York: Praeger, 1976, p. 194.

[10] Robinson, Jackie. *I Never Had It Made: An Autobiography.* Hopewell, NJ: Echo Press, 1995, p. 59.

[11] Robinson, Jackie, p. 64.

[12] Robinson, Rachel. *Jackie Robinson: An Intimate Portrait.* New York: Abrams, 1996, p. 71.

[13] Quoted in Rowan, with Robinson, p. 181.

[14] Rowan, with Robinson, p. 184.

[15] Quoted in Bergman, Irwin B. *Jackie Robinson: Breaking Baseball's Color Barrier.* New York: Chelsea House, 1994, p. 45.

[16] Robinson, Rachel, p. 73.

[17] Quoted in Golenbock, p. 150.

[18] Robinson, Sharon. *Promises to Keep: How Jackie Robinson Changed America.* New York: Scholastic Press, 2004, p. 41.

[19] Quoted in Golenbock, p. 161.

[20] Quoted in Golenbock, p. 161.

[21] Tygiel, p. 195.

[22] Drake, Bill. Interview with Charles Korr and Steven Hause. Negro Baseball League Project, Oral History T-0067, December 8, 1971. State Historical Society of Missouri Research Center, University of Missouri-St. Louis. Retrieved from http://www.umsl.edu/~whmc/guides/t067.htm.

[23] Robinson, Rachel, p. 66.

[24] Quoted in Tygiel, p. 205.

[25] Robinson, Jackie, p. 69.

[26] Quoted in Bergman, p. 47.

[27] Golenbock, p. 166.

[28] Quoted in Fussman, p. 32.

[29] Quoted in Fussman, p. 34.

[30] Frick, Ford C. *Games, Asterisks, and People: Memoirs of a Lucky Fan.* New York: Crown, 1973, p. 99.

[31] Adelson, Bruce. *Brushing Back Jim Crow: The Integration of Minor-League Baseball in the American South.* Charlottesville: The University Press of Virginia, 1999, p. 5.

Chapter Four

STARDOM AND DEATH THREATS

—◀▬▮〰▮▬▶—

When someone breaks through a barrier for the first time, he becomes a great symbol. Jackie was that symbol.... It takes an individual to accomplish something that most people don't think can be accomplished, and then that frees up many people to soar to new heights.

—National Football League (NFL)
Hall of Fame running back Jim Brown

Jackie Robinson's outstanding rookie season was just the start of a ten-year major-league career that featured a Most Valuable Player trophy and a World Series championship. Although Robinson continued to face racial hostility in some quarters, he also became a national celebrity whose fame and influence extended far beyond the baseball diamond. "He was a celebrity in the sports world in a way that no one had been before him," wrote David Falkner in *Great Time Coming*, "recognized as much for what he gave to society as for what he gave to baseball. His moral standing counted for as much as his stat[istic]s."[1] Robinson's success created opportunities for other African-American athletes to showcase their talents in baseball, football, basketball, tennis, and other professional sports.

Becomes "Just Another Guy"

During the months between the 1947 and 1948 seasons, Robinson embarked upon a speaking tour of the South. In each city he visited, he was treated as an honored guest in the homes of prominent black families. Unfortunately, Robinson's enjoyment of the feasts prepared by his hosts resulted in a twenty-

Robinson, shown chatting with Dodgers teammates (from left) Gil Hodges and Gene Hermanski and owner Branch Rickey in 1949, grew more comfortable as his career progressed.

five pound weight gain by the time he reported to spring training in 1948. Manager Leo Durocher, who had returned to the helm of the Dodgers following a one-year suspension, rode Robinson mercilessly for being out of shape. Even though Robinson quickly shed the excess pounds, the antagonistic relationship between the two men continued until Durocher abruptly left the Dodgers in midseason to manage the rival New York Giants. Robinson was relieved when Burt Shotton once again took over the manager job he had held in 1947.

The Dodgers got off to a slow start in 1948 under Durocher. Although the team's play improved under Shotton, the Dodgers never returned to playoff form. Brooklyn posted an 84-70 record and finished a disappointing third in the league standings. Robinson nearly duplicated his offensive numbers from the previous season, batting .296 with 12 home runs, while also increasing his RBI total from 48 to 85. Defensively, Robinson shifted from first base to second base, which was a more natural position for him. He went on to lead the league in fielding average for second basemen at .983. The move also created a potent double-play combination with Pee Wee Reese at shortstop.

Robinson was gratified when the Dodgers added another African-American player to the roster in 1948. Roy Campanella (see biography, p. 111), a future Hall of Famer, joined the team after building a reputation as a gifted catcher and powerful hitter in the Negro Leagues. The other team to move further with integration that season was the Cleveland Indians. In addition to Larry Doby, who had joined the team in 1947, Indians owner Bill Veeck hired the legendary Negro Leagues pitcher Leroy "Satchel" Paige. Although Paige was well past his prime—he was in his forties and had already pitched professionally for more than twenty years—his presence helped the team set attendance records and win the World Series.

As more black players began to appear in the major leagues, Robinson increasingly found himself being treated like any other ballplayer. One of his favorite moments of the 1948 campaign came near the end of the season, when he got kicked out of a game for arguing with the umpire. "He didn't pick on me because I was black. He was treating me exactly as any ballplayer who got on his nerves," he observed. "That made me feel great, even though I couldn't play anymore that day. One of the newspapers said it in the best headline I ever got: 'Jackie Just Another Guy.'"[2]

Wins the MVP

By the start of the 1949 season, Dodgers president Branch Rickey was so pleased with the success of his "noble experiment" that he decided to push baseball integration even further. He scheduled his Brooklyn team to play an exhibition game in Atlanta, Georgia—in the heart of the segregated South. Although black residents were thrilled at the chance to see Robinson and his teammates in action, some white residents were appalled at the idea of black and white players playing together. Local members of the Ku Klux Klan white supremacist group warned that they would resort to violence to prevent the contest from taking place.

Robinson and Campanella received several threatening letters in the weeks leading up to the Atlanta exhibition game. One telegram promised that the two players would be shot if they dared to take the field. The Dodgers' second baseman and catcher responded to the death threats by joking about who could reach

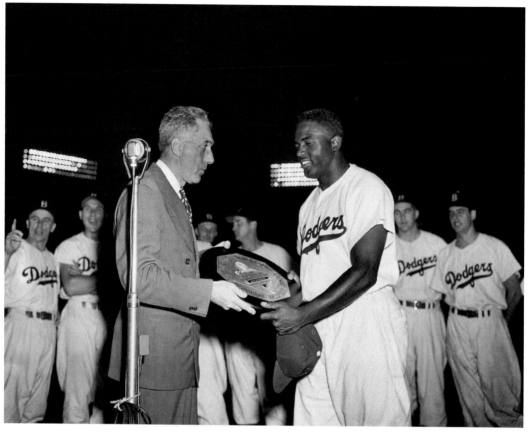

Robinson had his best year in 1949, when he received the Most Valuable Player Award from National League president Ford Frick.

the blacks-only segregated seating section faster if someone started shooting at them. "At the ballpark we couldn't totally dismiss the threats from our minds," Campanella remembered. "They wouldn't let the blacks sit in the grandstand. They made 'em all sit on the banks of the outfield with a cushion.… I told Jackie jokingly, 'You've got it made. You're playing second base. All you have to do is run into center field, and you'll be safe. I have to run all the way from home plate.'"[3] In the end, the game took place without incident. The Dodgers played before 25,000 appreciative fans, about 14,000 of whom were African-American.

In the midst of this tense racial environment, the Dodgers bonded as a team and accepted their black teammates as important contributors to their overall success. "Robinson was no longer a social experiment or a lone-wolf activist but just another teammate, a guy from Brooklyn who happened to be a star," noted Falkner. "His color, like that of any white player, bled into the common hue of a uniform."[4] It helped that Brooklyn added another outstanding black player, pitcher Don Newcombe, who posted a 17-8 record in 1949. At six feet, four inches and 235 pounds, Newcombe was an imposing figure on the mound. His willingness to retaliate made opposing teams think twice before ordering their pitchers to throw at the Dodgers' star hitters (see "Pitcher Don Newcombe Protects His Dodgers Teammates," p. 183). "If you don't protect your men, you're just not gonna get any runs, and they're not gonna have any respect for you. We were going to be sitting ducks," Newcombe explained. "Nobody's gonna protect us? Come on!... You do whatever's necessary to help your players."[5]

> *"Robinson has reached the stage where he says what he believes and says it without reservation, which is a trait unfortunately frowned on in most social circles," Dick Young wrote in the* **Sporting News.**

With the support of his teammates, Robinson put together the greatest statistical year of his career in 1949. He won the National League batting title with an impressive .342 average, led the league with 37 stolen bases, hit a career-high 16 home runs, and tallied 124 RBI. His remarkable performance earned him a spot on the All-Star Team, and at the conclusion of the season he received the prestigious National League Most Valuable Player Award from the Baseball Writers Association of America. Boosted by a team-record 152 home runs, the Dodgers won the pennant with a 97-57 record, but they lost the World Series to the Yankees in five games.

Creates Controversy

Despite his outstanding numbers, the 1949 season was a challenging one for Robinson. After two years of turning the other cheek and ignoring racial hostility, he had convinced Rickey that the time had come for him to fight back. Robinson felt that he had established himself as a player who belonged in the big leagues, so he was ready to show the world his true personality and competitive spirit. The Dodgers president agreed and gave Robinson complete freedom to express his opinions and act upon his anger and frustration. At the beginning of the season, Robinson had made it clear that he would no longer passively accept any sort of abuse from teammates, fans, opponents, or umpires.

Before long, however, Robinson discovered that his new combative attitude did not always go over well with white Americans. When he retaliated on

As he became more outspoken, Robinson was sometimes compared unfavorably to other black players, like 1949 All-Star teammates (from left) Roy Campanella, Larry Doby, and Don Newcombe.

the field or spoke out about an issue, the white press described him as a troublemaker. "Robinson has reached the stage where he says what he believes and says it without reservation, which is a trait unfortunately frowned on in most social circles,"[6] Dick Young wrote in the *Sporting News*. When Robinson defended his right to express himself, some sportswriters claimed that he took everything personally and saw racism where none existed. "It is not terribly difficult for the black man as an individual to enter into the white man's world and be partially accepted," Robinson explained. "As long as I appeared to ignore insult and injury, I was a martyred hero to a lot of people who seemed to have sympathy for the underdog. But the minute I began to answer, to argue, to protest—the minute I began to sound off—I became a swellhead, a wise guy, an uppity nigger. When a white player did that, he had spirit. When a black player did it, he was ungrateful, an upstart, a sorehead."[7]

Once Robinson began to speak his mind, he was often compared unfavorably to Campanella, the laid-back Dodgers catcher. Campanella freely acknowledged that he was interested in playing baseball, not crusading for racial equality, and he often expressed gratitude for the opportunity to play in the major leagues. "Jack and Campy had distinctively different temperaments and approaches to dealing with white people," Rachel Robinson noted. "Jack was reserved and direct at the same time, impatient for signs of progress, and unwilling to accept affronts to his dignity or challenges to the rights of others.... Campy's style and attitude made him more accepted. He was gentler and more accommodating and less apt to challenge."[8] Although the teammates disagreed about many issues, they managed to maintain a cordial, professional relationship. "There's no use in my pretending that we didn't have serious differences of opinion," Robinson said of Campanella, "but I think we always had mutual respect for each other."[9]

Robinson's outspokenness also led to his involvement in a political controversy in 1949. By this time the United States had become engaged in the Cold War, a period of intense military and political rivalry with the Soviet Union and its communist system of government. As the Cold War deepened, both nations sought to promote their political philosophies and expand their spheres of influence around the world. The Cold War created an atmosphere of fear and suspicion within the United States. Many Americans worried that communist spies and sympathizers with ties to the Soviet Union were infiltrating their government and society. Led by U.S. senator Joseph McCarthy of Wisconsin, the U.S. government investigated the activities and questioned the loyalty of thousands of American citizens during this time.

One of these people was Paul Robeson, a prominent African-American singer and stage actor who was active in the fight to end segregation and achieve racial equality in the United States. Robeson had visited the Soviet Union and found it to be free from racial prejudice. He had also worked closely with members of the American Communist Party in the civil rights movement. In an April 1949 speech at a world peace conference in Paris, France, Robeson claimed that if war broke out between the United States and the Soviet Union, it would be "unthinkable" for black Americans to join the fight. Robeson's controversial statement made him a target of the House Un-American Activities Committee (HUAC).

Anxious to discredit Robeson, HUAC sought prominent African Americans to publicly refute his statement. Robinson, as one of the most popular and respected black men in the country, was invited to testify before HUAC in July 1949. Although Robinson did not agree with Robeson's comments, he respected the man and was reluctant to speak out against him. At the same time, though, Robinson felt pressured to testify and worried that refusing to do so might ruin his baseball career. In the end, Robinson agreed to appear before HUAC. In a carefully worded statement, he said that Robeson's views were not representative of fifteen million patriotic African Americans. He denounced communism, but he also criticized racial discrimination in the United States. "There are whites who would love to see us [Negroes] refuse to defend our country because then we could relinquish our right to be Americans," he stated. "It isn't a perfect America and it isn't run right, but it still belongs to us."[10]

Robinson's testimony created a national sensation. The full text of his statement was printed on the front page of the *New York Times* and widely distributed as a pamphlet. Robinson's words were well-received among whites, who praised him for placing loyalty to his country above loyalty to his race. Some blacks, however, resented Robinson for what they viewed as bowing to white authority and betraying a fellow African American. Upset by all the controversy, Robinson was eager to put it behind him and concentrate on baseball.

Stars in a Hollywood Movie

The Dodgers' black stars shone brightly during the 1950 season. Robinson batted .328 with 14 home runs and 81 RBI. Campanella hit 31 home runs, despite missing several weeks of action due to a broken thumb. Newcombe tallied 19 victories, while Brooklyn added another black pitcher, Dan Bankhead, who contributed 9 more wins as a reliever and spot starter. Nevertheless, the Dodgers only managed to post an 89-65 record, and they lost the pennant to the Philadelphia Phillies in the final game of the season.

Robinson's offseason was filled with excitement. First he celebrated the birth of his daughter, Sharon. Then he signed a contract to star in *The Jackie Robinson Story*, a motion picture based upon his life. "Jack's decision to act in a feature film was daring," Rachel Robinson noted. "He had never acted, learned lines, or been involved in any drama—except the one he created on the baseball field."[11] Robinson and his family went to Hollywood, California, for the filming and enjoyed being treated like movie stars. Robinson also enjoyed

Robinson starred alongside Ruby Dee in *The Jackie Robinson Story*, a feature film about his life.

working with veteran actress Ruby Dee, who played Rachel Robinson. Although *The Jackie Robinson Story* was made quickly on a low budget, it enjoyed moderate success in theaters and frequently appeared on television. The financial rewards associated with the film allowed the Robinson family to move from their Brooklyn apartment to a house in the integrated St. Albans neighborhood of Long Island (see "The Insidious Effects of Racial Discrimination," p. 65).

Some less positive developments also occurred prior to the 1951 season. Longtime Dodgers president Branch Rickey was forced to sell his ownership stake in the team, and his rival Walter O'Malley took over. The change meant that Robinson lost the supporter and mentor who had managed his introduction to the major leagues. It also meant that Robinson was stuck playing for a new boss who was openly antagonistic toward him and anyone else associated with Rickey. "For the rest of his career, Robinson knew that whatever he did, whatever he said, O'Malley would be observing him, second guessing," Peter Golenbock wrote in *Bums*. "Much of the fun baseball held for him departed with Branch Rickey."[12] O'Malley also replaced manager Burt Shotton with Chuck Dressen.

Struggles with the Brooklyn Bums

Robinson had another good year in 1951. He batted an impressive .338 and tied the major-league record for double plays by a second baseman with 137. Many observers believe that his performance in the last game of the 1951 season was the greatest of his career. It was a do-or-die situation: a victory over the Phillies would move the Dodgers into a first-place tie with the New York Giants, while a loss would eliminate Brooklyn from pennant contention.

The two teams battled into extra innings. In the bottom of the 12th inning, the Phillies had the bases loaded with two outs. Eddie Waitkus hit a sharp line drive up the middle that looked like a certain game-winner. Instead, Robinson dove toward second base, reached across his body, and made a remarkable diving catch. He landed awkwardly on top of his glove and knocked the wind out of himself, but he still managed to hold on for the out. Two innings later, Robinson came up to bat and hit a game-winning home run off Phillies pitcher Robin Roberts. "Jackie Robinson singlehandedly saved the team from losing," Golenbock related. "Always a clutch performer, in the most important game of the year, Jackie Robinson gave what some experts consider the most clutch performance ever seen."[13] The Dodgers went on to face the Giants in an exciting three-game playoff series, but they failed to win the pennant and had to settle for second place.

Over the next two years, the Dodgers continued to play well during the regular season, only to fall short in the playoffs. Brooklyn won the National League pennant in 1952 with a 96-57 record, but they lost the World Series to the Yankees in seven games. In 1953 the Dodgers were the best team in baseball, posting a record of 105-49. Despite moving to a new defensive position (third base), Robinson batted .329 and knocked in 95 runs. Once again, however, the team could not overtake the powerful Yankees in the World Series. Brooklyn fans grew frustrated with the team's annual plea to "wait 'til next year" and referred to the perennial also-rans as the Bums.

At the end of his seventh season in the majors, Robinson ranked first among active players in career stolen bases (166), second in runs scored (773), and fourth in batting average (.319). Other talented African Americans emerged

The Insidious Effects of Racial Discrimination

In 1952 Jackie Robinson welcomed his third child, son David. The growth of their family encouraged Robinson and his wife to look for a new home outside of New York City. As they toured mostly white suburbs, however, they encountered racial discrimination in the housing market.

In those days, many white people resisted the addition of black families to their neighborhoods—even in the North. Some worried that integration would reduce their property values, while others simply did not care to associate with African Americans. During their search, the Robinsons repeatedly found that houses would suddenly be taken off the market or be listed at a much higher price as soon as they expressed an interest in them. "In the South, the dimensions of the fight [for civil rights] were clear, legislated, and up for challenge," Rachel Robinson explained. "In the North, racism was disguised, denied, and pernicious."

An investigative reporter heard about the Robinsons' struggles and wrote a series of articles that revealed outright housing discrimination in several communities. A group of ministers in Stamford, Connecticut, responded to the articles by forming a committee to address the problem. They helped the Robinson family find and purchase a piece of property in the town to build their dream home, which was completed in 1955.

Outlawing racial discrimination in housing became a major goal of the civil rights movement in the 1960s. The Fair Housing Act, originally included as Title VIII of the Civil Rights Act of 1968, now prohibits discrimination in the sale, rental, or financing of housing on the basis of race, religion, national origin, gender, disability, or family status in the United States.

Source

Robinson, Rachel. *Jackie Robinson: An Intimate Portrait.* New York: Abrams, 1996, p. 133.

as impact players as well. In fact, by 1953 black players had won the National League Rookie of the Year Award five straight times, and six out of the seven seasons since Robinson won it in 1947. Black players had been named Most Valuable Player three times during this stretch, and every World Series except the 1950 contest had featured at least one black player.

In one of the most famous plays in baseball history, Robinson stole home in Game 1 of the 1955 World Series. The Dodgers went on to win the championship over the New York Yankees.

Still, Major League Baseball had a ways to go before it achieved full integration. Only half of the eighteen teams had ever hired a black player by the end of the 1953 season. Although most teams had black players in their minor-league farm systems, it remained difficult for them to make the leap into the big leagues. Some observers noted that team owners held black players to higher standards of ability and character than they did white players. Rather than giving an opportunity to promising young prospects or average performers, they were only willing to promote black athletes whom they considered sure-fire stars.

Captures the World Series Championship

In 1954 the Dodgers changed managers once again, from Chuck Dressen to Walt Alston. Alston took a much more hands-on role in dealing with his veteran players, which created friction between him and Robinson. The Dodgers posted a 92-62 record that season and slipped to second place in the National League behind the New York Giants. Although Robinson batted .311, his defensive skills had declined a bit, and he ended up dividing his time between third base, first base, and left field. "By the end of the 1954 I was getting fed up and I began to make preparations to leave baseball," he recalled. "I loved the game but my experiences had not been typical—I was tired of fighting the press, the front office—and I knew that I was reaching the end of my peak years as an athlete."[14]

Robinson struggled at the plate in 1955 and posted the lowest batting average of his career at .256. The rest of the team showed significant improvement, however, and Brooklyn cruised to the pennant with a 98-55 record. In the World Series, the Dodgers once again faced their hated cross-town rivals, the New York Yankees. The Yankees had taken the World Series title from the Dodgers four times during Robinson's career, and he was determined to do whatever it took to prevent it from happening again.

"Robinson swept across the plate with a hook slide," as biographer David Falkner described the famous steal of home plate in the 1955 World Series, "going away from the Yanks' catcher, Yogi Berra—who went straight up in the air in protest when Robinson was called safe."

In the first game of the series, the aging star made a definitive statement with one of the most memorable and daring plays in baseball history. After advancing to third base against Yankees pitcher Whitey Ford, Robinson stole home. "On Ford's second pitch, taken with a full windup, Robinson broke for the plate and kept on coming," Falkner recalled. "For one implausible instant, the streaking baseball and the runner seemed to converge in perfect balance—the harmony of mayhem. Robinson swept across the plate with a hook slide, going away from the Yanks' catcher, Yogi Berra—who went straight up in the air in protest when Robinson was called safe."[15] The Dodgers went on to win their first World Series championship in seven games.

Retires from Baseball

After finally capturing an elusive World Series title, Robinson felt more certain than ever that his baseball career was winding down. His performance continued to decline in 1956, as he posted the second-lowest batting average of his career (.275) and missed a career-high 37 games. "I was benched a lot," he admitted. "My average was down, and it was obviously time for me to leave the game."[16] The Dodgers won the pennant once again with a 93-61 record, but returned to form and lost yet another World Series to the Yankees.

As Robinson weighed his options at the end of the season, he received a job offer from William Black, president of the Chock Full o' Nuts restaurant chain. Black had started his business career in the 1920s by selling shelled nuts from a stand in New York City's Times Square. He eventually opened a popular chain of lunch counters that served affordable coffee and sandwiches. Chock Full o' Nuts was notable for its minority hiring policies. By the mid-1950s, half of its employees were African-American. Black asked Robinson to become the company's vice president of employee relations and community affairs.

Robinson was strongly considering accepting the position when he received a call from the Dodgers' management informing him that he had been traded to the rival Giants. Robinson was stunned by this turn of events. He felt that he deserved more loyalty from the team owners, and he thought that they should have consulted him before making the deal. The Dodgers' unexpected move sent shock waves through the baseball world. "At the last moment, after all the things he'd done for the Dodgers, after everything he had suffered, they found it necessary to trade a man of his stature, a man who was the Dodgers," declared Hall of Famer Hank Aaron. "Certain people you never trade, and Jackie Robinson should never have been traded."[17]

The Giants offered Robinson a generous salary, but he decided to go ahead with his plan to retire from baseball and join the Chock Full o' Nuts organization. His plan was complicated, though, by a $50,000 deal made by his agent that gave *Look* magazine an exclusive on the story. The deal meant that Robinson could not announce his retirement or even inform the Dodgers of his decision until the news appeared in *Look*. As a result, he stalled the Giants for several weeks and gave vague answers to questions about whether he would join his new team. Finally, in December 1956, Robinson made it official.

As soon as people learned that Robinson's playing days were over, the accolades began flowing. "There never was an easier guy for me to manage," said Chuck Dressen, the Dodgers' manager from 1951 to 1953. "And there was nothing I asked that he didn't do. Hit and run. Bunt. Anything. He was the greatest player I ever managed."[18] "It was a thrill playing on the same team as Jackie Robinson," added pitcher Don Newcombe. "He was such a tremendous competitor.... I owe everything I have, everything I have in my life through baseball, to Jackie Robinson."[19]

Robinson ended his historic ten-year major-league career in 1956, with a career batting average of .311.

Inspires Other Athletes

By the time Robinson ended his decade-long baseball career, there were still three major-league teams that had never hired a black player: the Philadelphia Phillies, Detroit Tigers, and Boston Red Sox. Most other teams featured several black players, however, and some of the best players in the game were African American—including Hank Aaron, Ernie Banks, Roberto Clemente, Willie Mays, and Frank Robinson. "While the game was obviously still infected by old attitudes toward race, black stars were now everywhere,"[20] Falkner noted.

In some ways, the black stars who followed Robinson into the big leagues found their path to be as difficult as his had been. They tended to be younger and less experienced in the ways of the world than Robinson had been when he made his debut. In addition, few players who came later received as much support from their team owners as Robinson had received from Rickey. Finally, the

69

next generation of black players entered the major leagues as the civil rights movement was gaining momentum in the South. Many of these players faced a backlash from angry white Southerners who were determined to resist the changes that were sweeping through American society. "You have to understand what the young black ballplayers after Jackie were walking into. This was racist turmoil far and above anything that had existed since slavery," explained Judy Pace, widow of outfielder Curt Flood, who joined the St. Louis Cardinals in 1957. "That uprising brought an opposing swell of venomous energy. Again, the message was loud and clear: We will put them back in their place. That's what these young black men, who only wanted to play baseball, were confronted with."[21]

Shortly after joining the Cardinals, Flood watched as the team's white clubhouse manager picked up all the other players' dirty uniforms and put them in a laundry hamper. Then, unwilling to touch Flood's uniform, the man used a long pole to pick it up. The man kept Flood's laundry separate from the other players' and sent it to a black-owned cleaning business on the other side of town. Dick Allen, who was the National League Rookie of the Year in 1964 with the Philadelphia Phillies, endured a concerted campaign of racial harassment. "In 1968, pennies began to fly at me from the bleachers at Connie Mack Stadium. Then bolts and batteries. I had to wear a batting helmet on offense *and* defense," he recalled. "If I could have played without all that stuff I had to put up with, what it was all doing to my head ... well, let's just say I'll never know what I could've done."[22]

While black players continued to combat racism in baseball, African-American athletes broke down barriers in other sports as well. Earl Lloyd became the first black player in the National Basketball Association when he took the floor for the Washington Capitols in 1950. "I don't think my situation was anything like Jackie Robinson's—a guy who played in a very hostile environment, where even some of his teammates didn't want him around," Lloyd stated. "In basketball, folks were used to seeing integrated teams at the college level. There was a different mentality."[23] In 1957 professional golfer Charlie Sifford became the first black player to win a PGA Tour event, the Long Beach Open. That same year, tennis star Althea Gibson became the first black player to win the prestigious major tournaments at Wimbledon and the U.S. Open.

Notes

[1] Falkner, David. *Great Time Coming: The Life of Jackie Robinson from Baseball to Birmingham.* New York: Simon and Schuster, 1995, p. 243.

2 Robinson, Jackie. *I Never Had It Made: An Autobiography.* Hopewell, NJ: Echo Press, 1995, p. 76.
3 Quoted in Golenbock, Peter. *Bums: An Oral History of the Brooklyn Dodgers.* New York: Putnam, 1984, p. 224.
4 Falkner, p. 208.
5 Quoted in Golenbock, p. 240.
6 Young, Dick. *Sporting News,* October 12, 1949. Quoted in Tygiel, Bruce. *Baseball's Great Experiment: Jackie Robinson and His Legacy.* New York: Vintage Books, 1984, p. 322.
7 Robinson, Jackie, pp. 76, 80.
8 Robinson, Rachel. *Jackie Robinson: An Intimate Portrait.* New York: Abrams, 1996, p. 86.
9 Robinson, Jackie, p. 262.
10 Robinson, Jackie, p. 84.
11 Robinson, Rachel, p. 113.
12 Golenbock, p. 270.
13 Golenbock, p. 279.
14 Robinson, Jackie, p. 118.
15 Falkner, p. 228.
16 Quoted in Bergman, Irwin B. *Jackie Robinson: Breaking Baseball's Color Barrier.* New York: Chelsea House, 1994, p. 63.
17 Introduction to Robinson, Jackie, p. xvii.
18 Quoted in Bergman, p. 54.
19 Quoted in Bergman, p. 55.
20 Falkner, p. 243.
21 Quoted in Fussman, Cal. *After Jackie: Pride, Prejudice, and Baseball's Forgotten Heroes: An Oral History.* New York: ESPN Books, 2007, p. 83.
22 Quoted in Fussman, p. 184.
23 Quoted in Smallwood, John. "African-American Influence in the NBA." NBA.com, n.d. Retrieved from http://hoopedia.nba.com/index.php?title=African-American_Influence_in_the_NBA.

Chapter Five

ROBINSON AND THE CIVIL RIGHTS MOVEMENT

━━⊶⊷━━

[Baseball] integration made people think, "Why do we still have to be treated as second-class citizens? Why do we have to go through the back door? Why do we have to sit in the lousy seats in the outfield? Why can't we have a grandstand over our head?" All of this happened directly because of integration on the field.

—Bruce Adelson, *Brushing Back Jim Crow*

Jackie Robinson's struggles to integrate professional baseball took place at the same time that the first sparks of the African-American civil rights movement were flaring to life. His courage and perseverance in the face of racial hostility inspired many people who became leaders in the fight to end racial segregation and discrimination. "Jackie Robinson's person and achievement was incontestable proof that such change was possible," David Falkner wrote in *Great Time Coming*. "His fame, and the inspiration he provided, was based on his dramatic and successful single combat against an institution that was a symbol of American culture. How much more could be done when a whole people rose up?"[1] Upon his retirement from baseball, Robinson's involvement in the movement expanded, and he emerged as a powerful advocate of racial equality.

Draws Attention to Segregation

One of Robinson's earliest contributions to the civil rights movement was that he raised public awareness of racial discrimination and its impact on African Americans. Before he stepped onto Ebbets Field in a Dodgers uniform for the first time in 1947, many white Americans never gave much thought to

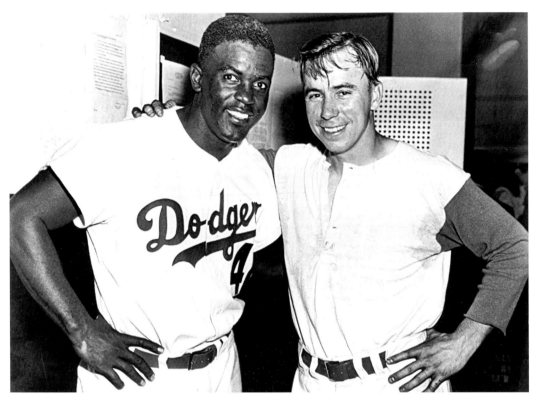

Robinson's friendship with his double-play partner, Dodgers shortstop Pee Wee Reese, helped change people's attitudes about black-white relations.

segregation. People in the North did not recognize the full extent of the problem, and people in the South had grown so accustomed to it that they viewed it as the natural order of things. But Robinson's quest to integrate baseball—and the national attention it received—forced people across the country to confront their prejudices and openly question segregation policies. "He was the figure who made civil rights a popular issue before anyone took to the streets or talked about programs, bills, or social action," Falkner explained. "Robinson was a link, and a crucial one, between despair and a movement. He is a far more important figure than he is given credit for in this country's civil rights movement."[2]

Robinson also set an example of strength and courage that inspired many black civil rights leaders. As he silently endured taunts, physical abuse, and even death threats, Robinson dramatized the plight of blacks under segregation and showed millions of African Americans that it was possible to stand tall and proud in the face of such trials. When Robinson emerged as one of the best and most exciting players of his era, he also proved that blacks had the capacity to match or even surpass the performance of their white counterparts. He thus convinced many people that blacks deserved equal opportunities to succeed.

Every time Robinson took the field alongside his white teammates, he helped demonstrate the possibilities of interracial cooperation. He and shortstop Pee Wee Reese made one of the most potent double-play combinations in baseball. They communicated without words and timed their movements to split-second perfection. Their execution on the field and camaraderie in the dugout helped change the attitudes of innumerable people about black-white relations. "Baseball was THE sport in the 1950s. What happened in a baseball stadium had a huge impact on the society," noted sportswriter Jonathan Mayo. "Seeing black and white players together on the field, and black and white fans sitting together, had a significant and decisive role in the larger integration of society. As Hank Aaron told me, 'A black man crossing home plate and shaking hands with a white teammate in the segregated South in the 1950s had enormous power.'"[3]

> *"Robinson was a link, and a crucial one, between despair and a movement," wrote biographer David Falkner. "He is a far more important figure than he is given credit for in this country's civil rights movement."*

Joins the Civil Rights Movement

Partly due to Robinson's example, challenges to segregation grew more common toward the end of his decade-long career. One of the first major milestones in the civil rights movement occurred in 1954, when the U.S. Supreme Court issued its landmark decision in the case of *Brown v. Board of Education.* The justices unanimously ruled that state laws establishing separate public schools for black and white children violated the Fourteenth Amendment of the U.S. Constitution. This ruling overturned the Court's 1896 decision in *Plessy v. Ferguson,* which had allowed segregation by race as long as the facilities provided to black and white citizens were "separate but equal."

Like many other black activists, Robinson felt gratified by the Court's decision and excited about its implications for ending legalized segregation in other aspects of society. "On May 17, 1954, when the Supreme Court handed down the *Brown v. Board of Education* decision, which outlawed segregation in public schools, and the civil rights movement as we know it surfaced," Rachel

After retiring from baseball, Robinson took on a more active role in the growing civil rights movement. He is pictured with (from left) boxer Floyd Patterson and civil rights leaders Ralph D. Abernathy and Martin Luther King Jr.

Robinson recalled, "Jack and I finally felt connected to something larger than the struggles in baseball, more intensely connected to the destiny of our race."[4]

Another major challenge to segregation came in 1955, when forty-two-year-old black seamstress Rosa Parks was arrested for refusing to give up her seat to a white man on a public bus in Montgomery, Alabama. Her arrest sparked a boycott of Montgomery's public transit system by the city's African-American residents that lasted more than a year. The mass protest was organized by the Montgomery Improvement Organization and its president, a charismatic young black minister named Martin Luther King Jr. It only ended after the U.S. Supreme Court declared segregated seating in public transportation to be unconstitutional in its 1956 decision in *Browder v. Gayle*.

King and other organizers of the Montgomery Bus Boycott employed a strategy that was similar to Branch Rickey's six-point plan for integrating baseball. Like Rickey, they understood that choosing the right person to mount a direct challenge to segregation could help generate public support for the cause. As it turns out, Rosa Parks was not the first person to be arrested for violating the segregated seating policy on a Montgomery bus. "Claudette Colvin was arrested for refusing to give up her seat nine months before Rosa Parks," one writer noted, "but she was an unmarried, pregnant fifteen-year-old."[5] The organizers decided to wait and find a more suitable figure to serve as the symbol of the boycott—someone whose background and reputation would put them above public scrutiny, like Jackie Robinson. "Mrs. Parks was ideal for the role assigned to her by history," according to King. "Her character was impeccable and her dedication deep-rooted," and she was "one of the most respected people in the Negro community."[6]

When Robinson retired from baseball in 1956, the National Association for the Advancement of Colored People (NAACP) honored the occasion by presenting him with its Spingarn Medal. He was the first athlete to receive the prestigious award, which had previously gone to such luminaries as Mary McLeod Bethune, George Washington Carver, and A. Philip Randolph. "At that moment, whatever his popularity among white Americans, Robinson was simply the most admired figure among African Americans in memory,"[7] Falkner stated.

Receiving the Spingarn Medal confirmed Robinson's sense of duty to the emerging civil rights movement. "Robinson recognized that acceptance in organized baseball marked the beginning, not the conclusion, of the struggle for equality," wrote baseball historian Jules Tygiel. "Robinson envisioned the baseball experience as the stepping stone to more significant advances. To Robinson, the aggressive expansion of the beachhead he had established, through the constant assertion of equal rights, represented the obligation of the successful black person. This obligation extended beyond the realm of sport and into the broader society."[8]

Becomes a Social and Political Activist

Upon retiring from baseball, Robinson became involved in a wide variety of new ventures. "Not being on the road [with the Dodgers] meant he had time to

White segregationists rally in Little Rock, Arkansas, to protest the admission of African-American students to Central High School.

give motivational speeches, write newspaper columns, raise money for civil rights organizations, join protest marches, speak to youth groups, play golf, and cut the lawn,"[9] said his daughter, Sharon Robinson. As a pioneering black business executive, Robinson worked at Chock Full o' Nuts for seven years and joined the company's board of directors in 1961. During his employment, he came up with innovative programs to train, promote, and provide incentives to employees of the restaurant chain. Company owner William Black also recognized Robinson's high profile and gave him time off to pursue other interests and opportunities.

Robinson thus accepted an offer from the NAACP to travel around the country making speeches to community groups in order to increase membership in the organization and raise money to support civil rights causes. He also wrote a regular column in the *New York Post* for several years. In addition to sports, Robinson's columns covered civil rights, politics, current events, world affairs, and other issues he considered important. Robinson also hosted his own radio show and provided color commentary for sports broadcasts.

While Robinson settled into his post-baseball career, the civil rights movement continued to expand throughout the South. In 1957 King founded the Southern Christian Leadership Conference (SCLC), an organization that fought for civil rights using the principles of nonviolent resistance. This philosophy encouraged people to peacefully resist unjust laws and promote social change through such strategies as boycotts, strikes, sit-ins, protest marches, and civil disobedience. King credited Robinson as a highly visible example of the power of passive resistance to break down racial barriers. "Jackie Robinson made it possible for me in the first place," he noted. "Without him, I would never have been able to do what I did."[10]

Robinson also influenced the thinking of white leaders during the early years of the civil rights movement. In 1957, for instance, nine African-American students hoping to take advantage of the Supreme Court's school-desegregation ruling enrolled in the previously all-white Central High School in Little Rock, Arkansas. On the first day of school, however, Governor Orval Faubus ordered the Arkansas National Guard to surround Central High and prevent the black children from entering. After the tense standoff gained worldwide media attention and efforts to negotiate a solution failed, President Dwight D. Eisenhower reluctantly sent U.S. Army troops to escort the "Little Rock Nine" into the building. Later, Eisenhower gave a speech suggesting that African Americans should be patient and give white Southerners time to overcome their long-held racial prejudices.

Robinson responded to Eisenhower's remarks in a forceful letter. "Seventeen million Negroes cannot do as you suggest and wait for the hearts of men to change," he wrote. "We want to enjoy now the rights that we feel we are entitled to as Americans."[11] The two men then engaged in a respectful back-and-forth correspondence that ultimately resulted in the president agreeing to meet with King and other prominent civil rights leaders (see "Robinson Pushes Eisenhower to Take Action on Civil Rights," p. 186). Robinson went on to correspond with every president who held office between his retirement from baseball and his death. He encouraged each man to make a strong stand on the issue of civil rights, and in several cases they took his advice.

Expands His Involvement in Politics

Recognizing Robinson's potential appeal to black voters, both Republican candidate Richard M. Nixon and Democratic candidate John F. Kennedy sought

"Jackie Robinson made it possible for me in the first place," declared civil rights leader Martin Luther King Jr. "Without him, I would never have been able to do what I did."

his endorsement in the 1960 presidential race. Robinson met with each candidate personally before making his decision. "He didn't want the lumping of black people with a particular party," his daughter explained. "He wanted to look at each of the candidates, examine the record, and see who could be the most helpful."[12]

To the surprise and dismay of some African-American leaders, Robinson then announced his support for Nixon. In his interview with Kennedy, Robinson had learned that the Democrat was not personally acquainted with many African Americans. Although Kennedy expressed support for the goals of the civil rights movement, Robinson came away from their meeting with the feeling that the son of a wealthy Massachusetts family could not truly understand the race problem in American society.

On the other hand, Robinson was impressed that Nixon had visited Africa and made an effort to understand issues affecting blacks worldwide. He believed that Nixon, if elected, could be a leader who pushed social change from the top—just as Branch Rickey had done in major-league baseball. Robinson's choice was controversial because black leaders typically supported Democratic candidates. Rachel Robinson explained that her husband's support for the Republican reflected "his long-held belief that too-uniform black support of the Democrats had led them to take blacks for granted; leverage would come only when we had influence in both parties."[13] When Nixon lost the election, Robinson did not dwell on the defeat. Throughout Kennedy's time in office, Robinson repeatedly pushed the president to use the power of his office in support of the civil rights movement.

The early 1960s saw a number of important events in the battle to end the segregation of public facilities. On February 1, 1960, four black college students requested service from a segregated lunch counter at a Woolworth's department store in Greensboro, North Carolina. When the establishment refused to serve them, they remained in their seats and refused to leave. More students arrived day after day, and they persevered as angry white segregationists shouted at them, spit on them, and punched them. Their actions launched a wave of similar peaceful protests, known as sit-ins, at segregated restaurants across the South. Civil rights supporters in the North also organized boycotts of national retail chains that maintained segregation policies. When the negative publicity caused business to decline by one-third nationwide, Woolworth's decid-

The Freedom Riders and other civil rights activists worked to end the segregation of public transportation facilities in the South, like this bus station in Durham, North Carolina.

ed to change its policies and allow black and white customers to eat together at its lunch counters. Many other national retailers soon followed suit.

The following year, black and white civil rights activists from the Congress of Racial Equality (CORE) and other groups set out on a series of bus and train trips across the South. They planned to test federal enforcement of the Supreme Court's 1960 ruling in *Boynton v. Virginia*, which declared segregation of interstate transit unconstitutional. The Freedom Riders, as they became known, were attacked and beaten by segregationists in several cities, and one of their buses was set on fire in rural Alabama. Local police either ignored the violence or placed the riders under arrest. The violent reaction to the Freedom Rides garnered international media attention. The Kennedy administration initially responded by asking the protesters to observe a "cooling-off period." When the Freedom Riders refused to comply with this request, President Kennedy finally urged the Interstate Commerce Commission to issue strict new rules to enforce the integration of public transportation systems in the South.

Branch Rickey claimed that all of these civil rights actions could be traced back to his and Robinson's efforts to end segregation in professional baseball. "Integration in baseball started public integration on trains, in Pullmans, in dining cars, in restaurants in the South, long before the issue of public accommodations became daily news,"[14] he stated.

Lends Support to the Cause

The year 1963 was a momentous one in the civil rights movement. It was marked by violent attacks on peaceful protesters by law enforcement officials in cities across the South. That spring, King and the SCLC organized a series of sit-ins, marches, and other protests in Birmingham, Alabama, that were designed to draw attention to the strict segregation policies still in force in the city. They chose Birmingham partly because its police chief, Eugene "Bull" Connor, was a staunch segregationist. They anticipated that Connor would authorize his officers to use violence to repress the protests, which in turn would attract media attention to their cause.

As expected, Connor and the Birmingham police used attack dogs and fire hoses to disrupt peaceful protest marches, which often included women and children. They also arrested hundreds of marchers and held them in overcrowded conditions in the local jail. King himself was arrested on April 12 and spent a week behind bars. During this time, he wrote his influential essay "Letter from Birmingham Jail," in which he defended the use of forceful direct action to create social change. Jackie Robinson was deeply concerned about the events in Birmingham. He organized a jazz concert on his six-acre home site in Stamford, Connecticut, to raise funds to help the jailed protesters and their families. This benefit concert became an annual event that continued for more than three decades and supported various causes and organizations.

The events in Birmingham received widespread media coverage. Many Americans were shocked and appalled by news footage showing children being knocked down by high-pressure water cannons and unarmed marchers being threatened by vicious dogs or clubbed by police officers. President Kennedy responded to the violence in a nationally televised address on June 11, 1963. He promised to promote the passage of federal legislation to ensure the full civil rights of all Americans. "We face," he declared, "a moral crisis as a country and a people. It cannot be met by repressive police action. It cannot be left to increased demonstrations in the streets. It cannot be quieted by token moves or talk. It is a time to act in the Congress, in your State and local legislative body and, above all, in all of our daily lives.... A great change is at hand, and our task, our obligation, is to make that revolution, that change, peaceful and constructive for all."[15]

Kennedy's speech, and his subsequent efforts to secure passage of a major civil rights bill by Congress, effectively changed Robinson's opinion of the president. "The address which Mr. Kennedy made to the American people on the color question is one of the finest declarations ever issued in the cause of human rights," he wrote in his newspaper column. "As consistent readers of this column know, I have been highly critical of this Administration and its handling of the civil rights issue. I must state now that I believe the President has come through with statesmanship, with courage, with wisdom and absolute sincerity."[16]

Robinson attended the 1963 March on Washington with his son David.

In August 1963 Robinson and his family took part in the historic March on Washington, which attracted an estimated 250,000 civil rights supporters to the National Mall in Washington, D.C. "Standing before the Lincoln Memorial shoulder to shoulder with hundreds of thousands of people protesting with strength and dignity was a glorious experience,"[17] Rachel Robinson recalled. The highlight of the event was hearing King deliver his famous "I Have a Dream" speech.

Speaks His Mind

Kennedy was shot and killed by an assassin on November 22, 1963, as he rode in a presidential motorcade through the streets of Dallas, Texas. Robinson and other black leaders initially feared that his successor, Lyndon B. Johnson,

Robinson Supports Free Agency for Baseball Players

In 1970 Robinson testified in court on behalf of Curt Flood, a black baseball player who mounted a legal challenge to the sport's decades-old "reserve clause," which effectively bound a player to a team for life. "Simply put, a player was a team's property," sportswriter Allen Barra explained. "Unless the team chose to trade him or release him, his first big-league team would be his only big-league team for his entire career. A player's only recourse was retirement."

The reserve clause gave team owners complete control over players' careers. It gave players no say in trades or team assignments, regardless of how long they had played for a particular team. Team owners put the clause in place in an effort to eliminate competition between teams for players, which would lead to higher player salaries. Although American antitrust laws prohibited other types of businesses from making such arrangements with their competitors to control worker salaries, Major League Baseball had been granted an exemption from these laws.

Flood initiated his lawsuit when, after twelve seasons with the St. Louis Cardinals, he was traded to the Philadelphia Phillies without his consent. He refused to accept the trade and asked baseball commissioner Bowie Kuhn to declare him a free agent, so that he could sign a new contract with a team of his choosing. "I do not feel I am a piece of property to be bought and sold

would not follow through on Kennedy's promise to seek new civil rights legislation. Despite his Southern roots, however, Johnson committed himself to securing passage of the legislation in Congress as a way of honoring Kennedy's legacy. He signed the Civil Rights Act of 1964 into law on July 2 of that year. A short time later, Robinson wrote a heartfelt letter of appreciation to Johnson. "No President could have affected the progress in our drive for human dignity as you have done," he stated. "The day is rapidly approaching when all Americans will be judged on the contents of character, rather than skin color."[18]

Although the Civil Rights Act of 1964 made important strides toward ending segregation, further legislative action was needed to secure black voting rights. In order to preserve the Jim Crow system of racial segregation and discrimina-

irrespective of my wishes," he declared. "I believe that any system which produces that result violates my basic rights as a citizen and is inconsistent with the laws of the United States." When Kuhn denied his request, Flood decided to sue Major League Baseball. His decision sent shock waves through the world of professional sports, because it had the potential to fundamentally change the relationship between athletes and teams.

The case of *Flood v. Kuhn* went all the way to the U.S. Supreme Court. Fearing reprisals from powerful team owners, no active players appeared on Flood's behalf. The only former players who provided testimony in support of Flood were Robinson and Hank Greenberg. Despite their assistance, however, the Court ruled in favor of the owners in 1972. The justices said that baseball's antitrust exemption could only be removed by an act of Congress, and that the players' union should obtain free agency for players through collective bargaining. Although the dispute effectively ended Flood's baseball career, it also helped future generations of players. The MLB Players' Association successfully negotiated free agency for its members in 1976.

Sources

Barra, Allen. "How Curt Flood Changed Baseball and Killed His Career in the Process." *Atlantic*, July 12, 2011. Retrieved from http://www.theatlantic.com/entertainment/archive/2011/07/how-curt-flood-changed-baseball-and-killed-his-career-in-the-process/241783/.

Flood, Curt, with Richard D. Carter. *The Way It Is*. New York: Trident Press, 1971, p. 236.

tion, many state and local governments in the South used literacy tests, poll taxes, and other requirements to prevent African Americans from registering to vote and exercising their voting rights. People who attempted to circumvent or change these rules faced the threat of losing their homes, their jobs, or even their lives.

During Freedom Summer—a 1964 campaign organized by the Student Nonviolent Coordinating Committee (SNCC) and other civil rights groups to register black voters in Mississippi—three young civil rights workers were ambushed and killed by members of the Ku Klux Klan white supremacist group. Thousands of other activists were beaten by segregationists or arrested by local authorities, while blacks who registered to vote saw their homes, businesses, and churches burned or bombed. The Freedom Summer campaign provided chilling evidence of continued strong resistance to black voting rights in the South and the dangers faced by civil rights workers and black voters.

The quest to secure black voting rights in the South came to a head the following spring, when the SNCC and SCLC organized a protest march from Selma to Montgomery in Alabama. On March 7, 1965, the six hundred peaceful marchers were viciously attacked by state and local law enforcement officers. The police, wearing full riot gear, used billy clubs and tear gas to disperse the protesters. Footage of the incident, which became known as "Bloody Sunday," was broadcast on national television. Millions of Americans were horrified by the violent images, which led to a dramatic increase in support for the civil rights movement. Johnson responded by introducing new legislation in Congress, and he signed the Voting Rights Act of 1965 into law on August 6.

Robinson spent these tumultuous years helping to raise $1.5 million to launch the Freedom National Bank in New York City. This black-owned and operated commercial bank provided start-up loans to encourage and support African-American small-business ventures. It grew out of Robinson's belief that economic power was just as vital as political power in helping African Americans improve their lives and secure equal rights. "I became increasingly persuaded that there were two keys to the advancement of blacks in America—the ballot and the buck," Robinson explained. "If we organized our political and economic strength, we would have a much easier fight on our hands."[19]

After overseeing the successful opening of the bank in 1965, Robinson accepted a position on the staff of New York governor Nelson Rockefeller as special assistant for community affairs in 1966. The following year, he and King had a highly publicized difference of opinion over U.S. military involvement in the Vietnam War. King opposed the war, arguing that it was not necessary to protect U.S. interests and cost the lives of too many American soldiers and Vietnamese civilians. Robinson, on the other hand, supported U.S. military action to stop the spread of communism in Vietnam. He viewed King's antiwar stance as a distraction that pulled people's focus away from the civil rights struggle. Although his decision to speak out against King was unpopular among blacks, Robinson defended his right to express his opinion. "I paid more than my dues for the right to call it like I see it," he declared. "And I could care less if people like me, so long as they respect me"[20] (see "Robinson Supports Free Agency for Baseball Players," p. 84).

Throughout his post-baseball career, Robinson consistently used his fame and influence to support the cause of civil rights. He never shied away from an opportunity to make his voice heard, and his status as an early civil rights pioneer gave him tremendous credibility in the movement. "You simply cannot overstate the importance of Jackie," said historian Ken Burns. "You've got to place him in perspective in the nascent civil rights movement. When Jackie Robinson played that first game in Ebbets Field, Martin Luther King was still in college. There hadn't been a woman refusing to move to the back of the bus. There hadn't been lunch counter demonstrations. The term sit-in hadn't been coined. There were none of the signposts of what we think of as the civil rights movement, which makes Jackie's example one of the first real signs of progress in civil rights since the Civil War."[21]

Notes

[1] Falkner, David. *Great Time Coming: The Life of Jackie Robinson from Baseball to Birmingham.* New York: Simon and Schuster, 1995, p. 259.

[2] Falkner, p. 348.

[3] Mayo, Jonathan. "From the Field to the Stands: Minor Leagues Helped Hasten Integration in South." MLB.com, February 25, 2008. Retrieved from http://www.milb.com/news/article.jsp?ymd=20080223&content_id=350776&vkey=news_milb&fext=.jsp.

[4] Robinson, Rachel. *Jackie Robinson: An Intimate Portrait.* New York: Abrams, 1996, p. 120.

[5] Schall, Andrew. "Wendell Smith: The Pittsburgh Journalist Who Made Jackie Robinson Mainstream." *Pittsburgh Post-Gazette,* March 30, 2012. Retrieved from http://www.post-gazette.com/stories/opinion/perspectives/the-next-page-wendell-smith-the-pittsburgh-journalist-who-made-jackie-robinson-mainstream-300714/#ixzz20ErukrY7.

[6] King, Martin Luther, Jr. *Stride Toward Freedom: The Montgomery Story.* New York: Harper, 1958, p. 44.

[7] Falkner, p. 252.

[8] Tygiel, Jules. *Baseball's Great Experiment: Jackie Robinson and His Legacy.* New York: Vintage Books, 1984, p. 327.

[9] Robinson, Sharon. *Promises to Keep: How Jackie Robinson Changed America.* New York: Scholastic Press, 2004, p. 52.

[10] Quoted in Falkner, p. 237.

[11] Quoted in Long, Michael G., ed. *First Class Citizenship: The Civil Rights Letters of Jackie Robinson.* New York: Times Books, 2007, pp. 56-57.

[12] Quoted in Fussman, Cal. *After Jackie: Pride, Prejudice, and Baseball's Forgotten Heroes: An Oral History.* New York: ESPN Books, 2007, p. 148.

[13] Robinson, Rachel, p. 175.

[14] Quoted in Robinson, Jackie. *Baseball Has Done It.* Brooklyn, NY: Ig Publishing, 2005, p. 55.

[15] Kennedy, John F. "Radio and Television Report to the American People on Civil Rights," June 11, 1963. Retrieved from http://www.jfklibrary.org/Research/Ready-Reference/JFK-Speeches/Radio-and-Television-Report-to-the-American-People-on-Civil-Rights-June-11-1963.aspx.

[16] Quoted in Long, p. 171.

[17] Robinson, Rachel, p. 174.

[18] Quoted in Long, p. 213.

[19] Robinson, Jackie, p. 183.

[20] Quoted in Long, p. 303.

[21] Quoted in Fussman, p. 135.

Chapter Six

THE LEGACY OF JACKIE ROBINSON

⋘⟨⟩⟫⋙

A life is not important except in the impact it has on others.

—Jackie Robinson

Jackie Robinson's pioneering role in baseball integration and leadership position in the civil rights movement helped spark enduring changes in American society. From the time he made his major-league debut until the end of his life, Robinson "would elate and empower blacks, help trigger the seismic changes of the civil-rights era, and force all Americans—even those with no interest in sports—to confront their nation's most confounding problem: race,"[1] wrote journalist Frank Fitzpatrick. Remembering Robinson's legacy still prompts discussions about racial issues affecting American society today.

Major League Baseball (MLB) has honored Robinson in a variety of ways over the years. The number he wore on his Dodgers uniform, 42, is the only one in history to be retired by every big-league ballclub. The number is brought back on one special day at the beginning of each season, though, when every modern-day player wears it as a way of reminding themselves and their fans of the contributions Robinson made. Although racial controversies still flare up on occasion in the world of sports—and minorities remain underrepresented in team ownership and management—the unprecedented diversity of today's college and professional team rosters stands as a testament to Robinson's fight for equality.

Inducted into the Hall of Fame

One of the highlights of Robinson's post-baseball life came in 1962, when he became the first African-American player to be inducted into the MLB Hall

At his Major League Baseball Hall of Fame induction ceremony in 1962, Robinson was accompanied by his wife, his mother, and former Dodgers owner Branch Rickey.

of Fame in Cooperstown, New York. To be eligible for the Hall of Fame, a player must: have played in the major leagues for at least ten years; have been retired from professional baseball for at least five years; and receive at least 75 percent of votes cast by members of the Baseball Writers Association of America.

Since Robinson had frequently clashed with sportswriters during his career, some people questioned whether he would receive enough votes to make it into the Hall of Fame in his first year of eligibility. But a sportswriter with whom Robinson had a particularly abrasive relationship, Dick Young of the *New York Daily News*, wrote a highly persuasive article in favor of Robinson's election. "Jackie Robinson made baseball history and that's what the Hall of Fame is, baseball history,"[2] he argued.

For his part, Robinson insisted that Hall of Fame voters should only consider his accomplishments as a player—such as his lifetime batting average of

.311 and career fielding percentage of .922—rather than his historic role in breaking baseball's color barrier. In the end, Robinson received 124 out of a possible 160 votes, or 77.5 percent. Despite the closeness of the result, he was gratified to be elected to the Hall of Fame. "It is the ultimate in recognition, the highest honor in baseball," he noted. "All the greats of the past have been elected to the Hall of Fame, that is, all the white greats."[3] At the induction ceremony, Robinson was joined on stage by his wife, his mother, and the man who had launched his major-league career, Branch Rickey.

Years of Sorrow and Failing Health

The late 1960s and early 1970s were years of hardship and heartbreak in Robinson's personal life. He was saddened by the death of Rickey in 1965, and he lost his beloved mother, Mallie Robinson, in 1968. That was also the year when his oldest son, Jackie Robinson Jr., was arrested for possessing illegal drugs and carrying a concealed weapon.

Jackie Jr. and his siblings had often struggled under the pressure of growing up with a famous father. "Their search for identity was complicated by Jack's fame as a baseball star and racial pioneer," Rachel Robinson explained. "That challenge had a special impact on Jackie, who, as our first-born son and the bearer of Jack's name, had shared with us from infancy the bright glare of the public spotlight."[4] Jackie Jr. had learning disabilities that made school difficult for him. Although he was a good athlete, he resented it when people compared him to his father. By the time he reached high school, Jackie Jr. often stayed out late and got into trouble. One time, he ran away from home and tried to hitchhike to California.

In an effort to straighten out his life, Jackie Jr. joined the U.S. Army. He was deployed to Vietnam in 1965, where he endured nightmarish combat situations and was wounded in an explosion that killed two of his friends. By the time he returned home, Jackie Jr. was addicted to drugs. His 1968 arrest resulted in a court-ordered stay in a rehabilitation facility. Jackie Jr. eventually recovered and got a job as a counselor helping other people overcome drug addiction. Just as his life appeared to be on a productive path at last, however, Jackie Jr. was killed in a car accident in 1971.

As he struggled to cope with the tragic loss of his oldest son, Robinson also faced serious health problems of his own. Around the time he retired from baseball, Robinson had been diagnosed with diabetes—a chronic condition in which

Robinson's friends and family gathered to honor his memory at the 1977 MLB All-Star Game. Pictured are (clockwise from left) Willie Mays, baseball commissioner Bowie Kuhn, Branch Rickey III, David Robinson, Rachel Robinson, Sharon Robinson, Roy Campanella, and Pee Wee Reese.

the body loses its ability to manufacture the hormone insulin, which it needs in order to process sugar and turn it into energy. While there is still no cure for diabetes, modern medicine enables people with diabetes to monitor their blood-sugar levels closely and inject insulin as needed to maintain healthy levels. Back in the 1960s, though, medical treatment for diabetes was not as effective. Although Robinson took insulin injections, he could not control his blood-sugar levels well enough to avoid major health complications. He developed problems with his eyesight, poor circulation in his feet and legs, and heart disease related to diabetes.

Robinson made one of his last public appearances in the spring of 1972, when he attended a ceremony at Dodgers Stadium in Los Angeles (where the Brooklyn Dodgers had relocated in 1958) honoring the 25th anniversary of his major-league debut. The Dodgers acknowledged Robinson's important role in the history of the franchise by retiring his jersey number, 42.

Robinson's final public appearance came in October of that year, during the second game of the World Series in Cincinnati. A record crowd in the stadium and a television audience estimated at 60 million people watched as Robinson—silver-haired, walking with a limp, and nearly blind—threw out the ceremonial first pitch. It became clear that his spirit remained intact when he used the occasion to call for the inclusion of African Americans in baseball management and administration. "I'm extremely proud and pleased to be here this afternoon," said Robinson, "but must admit, I'm going to be tremendously more pleased and more proud when I look at that third base coaching line and see a black face managing in baseball."[5]

"By watching Jackie Robinson and the players who followed him, we learned ... that skin color had nothing to do with talent, ability, hard work, strength of character, or any other trait that mattered," wrote historian Ira Glasser.

Only two weeks later, on October 24, 1972, Robinson died of a heart attack at his home in Stamford, Connecticut. He was fifty-three years old. More than 2,500 mourners attended his funeral at Riverside Church in New York City, where the Reverend Jesse Jackson gave the eulogy. "Jackie, as a figure in history, was a rock in the water, hitting concentric circles and ripples of new possibility," the civil rights leader and political figure stated. "When Jackie took the field, something within us reminded us of our birthright to be free. And somebody without reminded us that it could be attained. There was strength and pride and power when the big rock hit the water, and concentric circles came forth and ripples of new possibility spread throughout this nation."[6] Six former athletes served as pallbearers, including Robinson's Dodger teammates Joe Black, Ralph Branca, Junior Gilliam, Don Newcombe, and Pee Wee Reese, as well as basketball star Bill Russell of the Boston Celtics. Robinson was buried in Cypress Hills Cemetery in Brooklyn.

Impact on Baseball and Society

From the time of his passing onward, people have continually assessed Robinson's impact on baseball and the wider world. "The events unleashed by the historic alliance between Robinson and Rickey significantly altered American society," wrote biographer Jules Tygiel. "Federal legislation, court actions, and moral pressures precipitated most of these advances. But throughout the nation, black athletes represented both the harbingers and the agents of change."[7]

Among Robinson's major contributions was raising public awareness of racial discrimination and its effects. "As much as Robinson meant directly to his own people—as an example and inspiration and pioneer—he meant even more to the white society," added *Sporting News* writer Leonard Koppett. "He did more than any other single human being could do to focus their attention on the inequities of a system in which lily-white baseball was only one small symptom. The consequences of the waves his appearance made spread far beyond baseball, far beyond sports, far beyond politics, even to the very substance of a culture."[8]

Robinson's strength and perseverance in the face of racial hostility, and the camaraderie he established with his Dodger teammates, forced many people to rethink their long-held views about African Americans (see "Teammate Carl Erskine Reflects on Robinson's Legacy," p. 191). "It opened eyes," said biographer Jonathan Eig. "Factory workers suddenly saw that they could work alongside a black man. White kids began to root for Robinson without even considering his race. And fans at ballparks who experienced those kind of racist taunts for maybe a first time were forced to examine their own views."[9]

Robinson's remarkable athletic ability, which helped him earn a coveted spot in the Hall of Fame, proved to many fans that blacks were equal to whites. "By watching Jackie Robinson and the players who followed him, we learned when we were very young and in a way deeply meaningful to us, that skin color had nothing to do with talent, ability, hard work, strength of character, or any other trait that mattered," wrote historian Ira Glasser. "Skin color, it seemed to us then, was like eye color or hair color. It told you nothing about a man's character or his ability to hit a baseball. From there it was not a hard jump to understanding that skin color also told you nothing about a person's ability to play the violin, do mathematics, or help build a tall building in New York."[10]

Robinson also had a tremendous impact on black athletes who came after him. He not only broke down barriers to participation, he also set an example of honor, dignity, and self-respect for future generations to follow. "What Jackie brought to baseball and America was a unifying ethos," said Roy Campanella II, son of the great Dodgers catcher. "If I were to give you a visual metaphor, it would be of Jackie as a vessel that traveled on very troubled waters and cut a

Hall of Famer Lou Brock explores the Jackie Robinson exhibit at the Negro Leagues Baseball Museum in 2012.

wake deep and wide enough so that others coming behind him would encounter less turbulence. ... The ethos was that the African-Americans who followed Jackie owed their community and the nation their best effort. Jackie established a tradition for a couple of waves of ballplayers. They became disciples. Only each spread the message in his own way."[11]

Honoring Robinson's Legacy

Many people and organizations have established programs to honor and promote Robinson's legacy over the years. In 1973 his widow, Rachel, founded a nonprofit organization called the Jackie Robinson Foundation (JRF) to provide tuition assistance, summer jobs, mentoring services, and other resources to help underprivileged youth attend college and achieve their dreams. "We strengthen young people by providing education and leadership development opportunities with the expectation that the path selected by each student will include giving back to their communities," Sharon Robinson explained. "More than thirty years after his death, the JRF scholars remain a living tribute to my father.... And so, the ranks of dedicated young leaders and followers committed to building a vibrant, productive, and richly diverse world are growing."[12] The JRF has sent hundreds of individuals to college over the years, and its programs boast a 90 percent graduation rate (see "A Major League Baseball Executive Describes Robinson's Impact," p. 188).

In the ensuing years, communities across the United States named parks, schools, streets, and buildings after Robinson. His alma mater, the University of California at Los Angeles, renamed its baseball stadium in his honor, for instance, and Major League Baseball named its Rookie of the Year award after him. In 1984 Robinson posthumously received the Presidential Medal of Freedom, which is the nation's highest civilian honor. President Ronald Reagan presented the award to Rachel Robinson in a special White House ceremony. Two decades later Robinson was awarded the Congressional Gold Medal. The U.S. government has also issued postage stamps and commemorative coins bearing Robinson's image.

In 1997, on the fiftieth anniversary of Robinson breaking baseball's color barrier, his number 42 was permanently retired by every major-league team. Five years later Robinson's grandson, Jesse, helped reenact his historic first appearance in the majors at the All-Star Game in Milwaukee, Wisconsin. Wearing a replica 42 Dodgers jersey, he trotted out of the dugout and took his grandfather's original position at first base, to the roaring approval of 43,000 fans. In 2005 Major League Baseball established April 15 as Jackie Robinson Day, which would be marked with special events and celebrations in stadiums across the nation each year (see "MLB Stars Reflect on Jackie Robinson," p. 99).

Professional baseball expanded its annual tributes to Robinson in 2007, when all major-league players, managers, and coaches started to wear a number 42 jersey on April 15 of each year. Every team also autographed one of the special jerseys to be auctioned on the MLB.com website, with all proceeds benefitting the Jackie Robinson Foundation. Many players appreciated the chance to be a part of history for one day each year. "Just to have the opportunity to tell my kids one day that I wore Jackie Robinson's number for at least one day every season," Minnesota Twins center fielder Denard Span said, "it's a great thing for me."[13]

Jackie Robinson Day festivities have also featured video tributes to his life and legacy, public appearances and speeches by his wife and daughter, honors

New York Yankees Alex Rodriguez, Derek Jeter, and Robinson Cano (who was named after Jackie Robinson) wear number 42 on April 15, 2010—the sixty-third anniversary of Robinson breaking baseball's color barrier.

for other black pioneers, such as the Tuskegee Airmen of World War II, and ceremonial first pitches thrown by former Negro League baseball stars like Don Newcombe and Monte Irwin. MLB star Curtis Granderson, an enthusiastic promoter of the idea of having all big-league players wear 42 for a day, explained the importance of the occasion for today's kids. "I think it's a great thing for baseball. I think it's a great thing for life in general, continuing to promote his legacy," he said. "I don't think it's been forgotten, by the number of kids that are coming up to me saying, 'Hey, my first book report was on Jackie Robinson.' These are 6, 7, 8, 9-year-olds that are doing it."[14]

Another way in which MLB has encouraged young people to learn about and honor Robinson's legacy is the Breaking Barriers initiative. This "baseball-themed character education program ... offers a curriculum based on values demonstrated by barrier breaker Jackie Robinson—determination, commitment, persistence, integrity, justice, courage, teamwork, citizenship, and excellence."[15] Since it was established in 1996, the program has served more than 19 million youth in the United States and Canada. It culminates in an annual essay contest that challenges students in fourth through eighth grades to write about how they have used values exemplified by Robinson to overcome obstacles or barriers in their own lives.

The Negro Leagues Baseball Museum (NLBM) in Kansas City, Missouri, features a special exhibit honoring Robinson. It also presents an annual Jackie Robinson Legacy Award to a current or former MLB player, coach, or executive for "career excellence in the face of adversity." Founded in 1990, the NLBM tells the story of black baseball from the late 1800s to the 1950s through exhibits, multimedia displays, historic photographs, and artifacts. During the 2012 All-Star Game weekend in Kansas City, dozens of MLB stars visited the museum, paid tribute to legendary players of the past, and participated in fundraising activities. "This was a league anchored in the ugliness of segregation," NLBM president Bob Kendrick said. "But out of it came this tremendous story of triumph and conquest. It became the driving force of integration. For the African-American and Hispanic players, this is their Mecca."[16]

Interest in Robinson's life and career seems certain to increase further in April 2013, when a new feature film called *42* is scheduled for release. Written and directed by Brian Helgeland, the movie stars Chadwick Boseman as Robinson and Harrison Ford as Branch Rickey. Its soundtrack features the rap anthem "Brooklyn Go Hard" by Jay-Z.

Racial Controversies in Sports

Sixty-five years after Robinson broke the color barrier, race remains a significant issue in American society. Although the problems black athletes encounter today are different than those they faced in earlier eras, racial controversies have continued to crop up over the years in baseball and other professional sports. Bigotry in baseball returned to the news shortly after Robinson's death, when Hank Aaron closed in on the legendary Babe Ruth's record of 714 career home runs. Aaron's quest to break Ruth's record carried many reminders of Robinson's quest to break into the majors. "Aaron's assault on Ruth's record, his calm, unassuming dignity under pressure, and his good-natured acceptance of the media circus which followed in his wake, captured the public imagination, much as Jackie Robinson had a quarter of a century ear-

MLB Stars Reflect on Jackie Robinson

Many Major League Baseball stars use the occasion of Jackie Robinson Day to reflect on Robinson's legacy and what it has meant in their own lives and careers. Several current and former players share their thoughts below:

Retired three-time All-Star David Justice: "Jackie Robinson's name should be thrown in there with Frederick Douglass, Harriet Tubman.... It's the sort of thing that should be taught in school. Because of Jackie Robinson, we [African Americans] are playing today."

Toronto Blue Jays outfielder Rajai Davis: "Jackie paved the way with his sweat, his blood, his tears, all the adversity he had to face in a trying time in U.S. history, and it's amazing that he was able to gather the strength to deal with all the hatred that the world showed, even Major League Baseball.... I can only imagine how difficult it was, but yet he kept persevering."

Retired seven-time National League MVP Barry Bonds: "The man was heroic. I've been inspired by his courage and strength.... Jackie was an educated African-American who had the background to be able to handle the pressures and adversities for the rest of us to not only achieve as athletes but as human beings.... It took someone with his caliber to pave the way for the rest of us."

Retired eight-time National League batting champion Tony Gwynn: "The one thing that impresses me most about Jackie was his character, because it takes quite a man to be able to go through all of the stuff [he did].... There's no way in hell that anybody playing the game today—no matter what they say, no matter what they think—could have gone through what he went through."

Sources

Gonzalez, Alden. "MLB Family Honors Jackie Robinson." MLB.com, April 15, 2011. Retrieved from http://mlb.mlb.com/news/article.jsp?ymd=20110415&content_id=178 36932&vkey=news_mlb&c_id=mlb.

Leavy, Walter. "Baseball's Biggest Superstars Salute a Legend." *Ebony,* July 1997, p. 52.

Hank Aaron blasts career home run number 715, breaking Babe Ruth's record.

lier,"[17] remarked Tygiel. Unfortunately, Aaron's quest also resembled Robinson's in that it was accompanied by an outpouring of hate mail and death threats.

When Aaron made his debut with the Milwaukee Braves in 1954, he was the last player to join the majors from the Negro Leagues. Over the next twenty years, during which the Braves moved to Atlanta, Aaron consistently ranked among league leaders in home runs. The likelihood that he would eclipse Ruth's record—which had stood since 1935 and had long been considered unbreakable by baseball experts—became clear in 1973, when the thirty-nine-year-old star hit 40 home runs to end the season with a career mark of 713. Over the course of that season, Aaron received an average of 3,000 letters per day. Many of the letters were hate-filled diatribes telling him that a black man was not worthy of breaking Ruth's record and threatening him with violence if he tried. Aaron also received fan mail and public support, however. Ruth's widow insisted that her husband would have applauded Aaron's efforts, for instance, and cartoonist Charles M. Schulz covered the controversy in his popular "Peanuts" comic strip.

Aaron tied Ruth's record in his first at-bat of the 1974 season. He went on to break the record on April 8 in front of 53,775 people—the largest crowd in Braves history. Aaron ended his Hall of Fame career in 1976 with 755 total home runs. His record stood for more than thirty years until it was finally broken in 2007 by Barry Bonds. After retiring as a player, Aaron became one of the first African Americans in MLB upper-level management when he accepted a position as the Braves' vice president of player development.

Racist attitudes and racial stereotypes remain a problem in professional sports. Over the years, many team owners, coaches, fans, and sportswriters have tended to attribute the achievements of white athletes to hard work, intelligence, and character. The achievements of black athletes, on the other hand, are more often attributed to biological advantages and natural physical abilities. CBS Sports football commentator Jimmy "The Greek" Snyder ignited a firestorm of controversy in 1988—and was quickly fired by the TV network—when he claimed that selective breeding during the era of slavery was responsible for the physical strength and speed of black athletes.

In 2012, though, African-American Olympic sprinter Michael Johnson returned to the controversial "slave theory" to explain black athletic success. "All my life I believed I became an athlete through my own determination, but it's impossible to think that being descended from slaves hasn't left an impact through the generations," he said. "Difficult as it was to hear, slavery has benefited descendants like me—I believe there's a superior athletic gene in us."[18] Experts in the field of genetics discounted the theory, pointing to numerous studies showing that skin color has no effect on a person's innate athletic ability.

Stereotypes Limit Opportunities

In addition to stereotypes relating race to athletic ability, there are also persistent stereotypes relating race to intelligence in sports. In the National Football League (NFL), for example, about 70 percent of players are African American. For many years, however, the league had virtually no black quarterbacks. As the on-field leader of the offense, the quarterback is the most important, prestigious, and mentally demanding position in football. Although there was no official rule prohibiting black athletes from playing quarterback, prevailing racial attitudes seemed to create informal "positional segregation." "Deep-seated American racial stereotypes, which assumed that blacks were naturally more gifted athletes while whites possessed superior mental capabilities, led coaches at every level of the game—from Pop Warner to the pros—to favor one race over the other for particular positions on the team," one writer explained. "Racial stereotypes thus became self-fulfilling prophecies, as black domination of the speed positions [such as running back and wide receiver] and white control of the QB spot seemed to confirm assumptions that each race had certain natural advantages over the other."[19]

Although black quarterbacks became increasingly common in the NFL during the 1990s and 2000s, they often seemed to be subjected to a higher level of fan expectations, media scrutiny, and pressure to perform than their white counterparts. In 2003, for instance, conservative talk show host Rush Limbaugh served as a commentator on ESPN's *Sunday NFL Countdown* program. Limbaugh created controversy by suggesting that Donovan McNabb, the black quarterback of the Philadelphia Eagles, was overrated by the media because of his race. "I think what we've had here is a little social concern in the NFL. The media has been very desirous that a black quarterback do well—black coaches and black quarterbacks doing well," Limbaugh said. "There is a little hope invested in McNabb, and he got a lot of credit for the performance of this team that he didn't deserve." McNabb responded by expressing disappointment in Limbaugh's attitude. "It's sad that you've got to go to skin color," he stated. "I thought we were through with that whole deal."[20] Limbaugh ended up resigning from ESPN as a result of the controversy.

Racial stereotypes have also contributed to the underrepresentation of African Americans in team ownership, administration, management, and coaching positions in professional sports. As of 2011, there was only one black majority owner (Michael Jordan of the NBA's Charlotte Bobcats) among the 122 franchises in the four biggest professional sports (baseball, basketball, football, and hockey). "Make no mistake," noted a writer for the *Philadelphia Tribune*. "There is still a lingering issue of potential black owners having to be 'approved' for participation by those already at the table in these very private 'clubs.'"[21]

African Americans have also held relatively few head coaching jobs in the NFL, given the high percentage of black football players. Fritz Pollard was the only minority coach in professional football history until 1989, when Art Shell was named head coach of the Los Angeles Raiders. Over the next fourteen years, only five other black head coaches took the reins of NFL franchises, and most of them remained in those positions for only a short time. In 2003 the NFL attempted to address this situation by establishing the Rooney Rule, which

In the 2013 movie *42*, actor Chadwick Boseman portrays Jackie Robinson during his rookie season with the Brooklyn Dodgers.

required teams to interview at least one minority candidate before filling any high-level coaching or front-office vacancy. The rule was named after Dan Rooney, owner of the Pittsburgh Steelers and chairman of the NFL's diversity committee. It helped increase the number of African-American head coaches in the NFL from three in 2003 to a record eight in 2011. Rooney himself hired one of those coaches, Mike Tomlin, who in 2009 became the youngest head coach (at thirty-six) ever to win a Super Bowl.

The NBA has been more progressive than other professional sports leagues in hiring black head coaches. In 2012, for example, fourteen of the NBA's thirty teams were helmed by African Americans. Although this percentage is much higher than any other sport, it remains relatively small considering that nearly 80 percent of NBA players are black. The NBA and the NFL have also come under criticism for charging high ticket prices that prevent many black fans from attending games. "Franchise owners and league officials in the multibillion-dollar sports business would like to present their sports as twenty-first century models of racial harmony and color-blind opportunity," said Orin Starn, a professor of cultural anthropology. "But, in reality, the dynamics of race and money are clear enough in professional basketball arenas and football coliseums nationwide, where the majority of the athletes are black and yet, because of expensive ticket prices, there are few African Americans in the stands."[22]

Another frequent complaint involves the limited range of professional sports that feature black athletes. Whereas black players dominate pro basketball and football, there are many popular and lucrative sports that feature very few, if any, African-American participants. There are no black drivers in NASCAR racing, for instance, and as of 2011 Tiger Woods and Joseph Bramlett were the only African Americans among the more than 250 active golfers on the men's and women's professional tours. Professional tennis is only slightly more inclusive, with a handful of black players active on both the men's and the women's sides. The most successful current African-American players are sisters Venus and Serena Williams, who had combined to win twenty-two Grand Slam singles titles and four Olympic gold medals as of 2012.

> "Baseball is at the point where the social barriers have been knocked down," said Chicago White Sox chairman Jerry Reinsdorf. "I don't think there's a general manager in baseball who makes a decision on a player other than, 'Is this the best guy I can have on my team?'"

A number of theories have been advanced to explain the lack of black athletes competing in auto racing, hockey, and "club sports" like golf and tennis. One theory is that young black athletes have few role models to emulate in these sports. Another is that the expense involved in pursuing these sports can be prohibitive for families with low or moderate incomes—a disproportionate number of whom are racial minorities. Blacks, for example, have the highest rate of poverty of any racial group in America. In 2010, according to a Pew Research Center analysis of U.S. government data, 27.4 percent of blacks and 26.6 percent of Hispanics were poor, compared to 9.9 percent of non-Hispanic whites and 12.1 percent of Asians. African Americans also have the lowest rates of income and household wealth (defined as assets minus debts) of any group. The median household wealth for black families was about $5,700 in 2010, while the figure for white families was about $113,000—or twenty times higher.[23]

Finally, golf in particular had segregation policies and elitist membership requirements that long prevented African Americans from participating. Clifford Roberts, one of the founders of the Augusta National Golf Club in Georgia—which did not accept its first black member until 1990—once declared that "As long as I am alive, all the golfers will be white and all the caddies will be black."[24] Many people hope that the high-profile successes of black athletes in sports in which they have historically been underrepresented—such as Tiger Woods in golf, the Williams sisters in tennis, and 2012 Olympic gold medalist Gabby Douglas in gymnastics—will lead to greater African-American participation in these sports.

Declining Numbers of Black Baseball Players

If recent trends continue, baseball may become another sport that sees relatively little participation by black athletes. In the years after Robinson made his historic MLB debut, African-American players like Willie Mays and Hank Aaron ranked among the sport's biggest stars. The percentage of black players in the majors grew from 17 percent in 1959—the year that the Boston Red Sox, under segregationist owner Tom Yawkey (see biography, p. 149), became the last team to integrate its roster—to reach an all-time high of 27 percent in 1975. Ever since that time, however, the percentage of black players in MLB has declined steadily—to 19 percent in 1995, 13 percent in 2000, and under 9 percent in 2012. Baseball's minor leagues and college programs have seen lower rates of participation by black players, as well.

Few people attribute the decline to racism, however. In fact, the global recruitment of players has made the racial and ethnic composition of MLB more diverse than ever before. The percentage of Hispanic players on major-league rosters, for instance, more than doubled from 13 percent in 1990 to 28 percent in 2012. Latin American nations have produced some of today's biggest stars, including Miguel Cabrera of the Detroit Tigers, Albert Pujols of the Los Angeles Angels of Anaheim, Alex Rodriguez of the New York Yankees, and Alfonso Soriano of the Chicago Cubs. "We've come a long way," said Chicago White Sox

Venezuela-born Miguel Cabrera, winner of the elusive Triple Crown (leading the league in batting average, home runs, and RBIs) in 2012, is one of many Latino players making an impact on Major League Baseball.

chairman Jerry Reinsdorf. "Baseball is at the point where the social barriers have been knocked down. I don't think there's a general manager in baseball who makes a decision on a player other than, 'Is this the best guy I can have on my team?' We've come definitely beyond where society in general is. Sports really is equal opportunity."[25] MLB has also received high marks for minority hiring in coaching and administration, with black or Latino managers at the helm of five teams and 31 percent of overall coaching and administrative staffs comprised of people of color, as of 2011.

Some observers attribute the declining number of black baseball players to increased competition from other professional sports. Both the NBA and the NFL have dozens of high-profile African-American stars who are idolized by young fans across the country. In addition, top athletes may be attracted to basketball or football because they offer a shorter path to fame and fortune than baseball does. Rather than toiling away in the minor leagues for several years, NBA and NFL players can jump to the pros straight out of college—or sometimes even high school. "That's what's so disturbing about this business of the dwindling number of African-Americans in the major leagues," said Frank Robinson, a Hall of Fame player who became the first black manager in the major leagues in 1975. "It's happening right in front of us. We see it. If we don't address it, pretty soon, there's not going to be any of us here to remember when there stopped being blacks in baseball."[26]

Other analysts attribute the decrease in black players in MLB to social and economic problems affecting African-American families and communities. "When the family started to break down in the inner cities, that attacked the No. 1 place where kids start playing baseball: Little League," explained Darrell Miller, director of the MLB Urban Youth Academy. "If you're a single mother working two jobs, you're looking for a turn-key sports program that the parks offer in football and basketball. You drop your kid off, then come back and pick him up."[27]

Jackie Robinson's legacy still inspires millions of Americans, both black and white. But the battle for full racial equality in America continues. "If [Robinson] were alive today, he would be reminding us—and not gently—that racial inequalities still limit the opportunities and stifle the dreams of too many black children, who have not been able to escape from the layers of racial exclusion laid down over so many decades. The laws we passed, as transforming as they were, have not proved to be enough," Glasser stated. "He would be talking to us, as he did in his last public appearance shortly before he died, about the unfinished struggle, both in and out of baseball. For many who remain in that struggle, Robinson remains among us, pushing us to go further, stutter-stepping off third base, eyes flashing, heading home."[28]

Notes

[1] Fitzpatrick, Frank. "Jackie Robinson: The Man and the Event." *Philadelphia Inquirer*, April 7, 2007.

[2] Quoted in Tygiel, Jules. *Baseball's Great Experiment: Jackie Robinson and His Legacy.* New York: Vintage Books, 1984, p. 143.

[3] Quoted in Tygiel, p. 141.

[4] Quoted in Robinson, Rachel. *Jackie Robinson: An Intimate Portrait.* New York: Abrams, 1996, p. 192.

[5] Quoted in Robinson, Sharon. *Promises to Keep: How Jackie Robinson Changed America.* New York: Scholastic, 2004, p. 57.

[6] Quoted in Robinson, Rachel, p. 217.

[7] Tygiel, p. 343.

8 Quoted in Gould IV, William B. "In Memoriam, Leonard Koppett." Sports Radio Service, July 13, 2003. Retrieved from http://www.sportsradioservice.com/misc/misc-071303.html.

9 Quoted in Fitzpatrick.

10 Glasser, Ira. "Branch Rickey and Jackie Robinson: Precursors of the Civil Rights Movement." *World and I,* March 2003, p. 257. Retrieved from http://www.worldandi.com/newhome/public/2003/march/mtpub.asp.

11 Quoted in Fussman, Cal. *After Jackie: Pride, Prejudice, and Baseball's Forgotten Heroes: An Oral History.* New York: ESPN Books, 2007, p. 257.

12 Robinson, Sharon, p. 61.

13 Gonzalez, Alden. "MLB Family Honors Jackie Robinson." MLB.com, April 15, 2011. Retrieved from http://mlb.mlb.com/news/article.jsp?ymd=20110415&content_id=17836932&vkey=news_mlb&c_id=mlb.

14 Quoted in "MLB Celebrates Jackie Robinson Day." ESPN.com, April 16, 2012. Retrieved from http://espn.go.com/mlb/story/_/id/7817037/mlb-honors-jackie-robinson-ballpark-tributes.

15 "Breaking Barriers: In Sport, In Life." MLBCommunity.org, 2012. Retrieved from http://web.mlbcommunity.org/programs/breaking_barriers.jsp?content=inside.

16 Quoted in Nightengale, Bob. "Negro Leagues Museum Gets All-Star Showcase." *USA Today,* July 6, 2012. Retrieved from http://www.usatoday.com/sports/baseball/story/2012-07-05/negro-leagues-museum-gets-all-star-showcase/56052852/1.

17 Tygiel, p. 342.

18 Quoted in Turner.

19 Shmoop Editorial Team. "Race in NFL History." *Shmoop University,* November 11, 2008. Retrieved from http://www.shmoop.com/nfl-history/race.html.

20 "Limbaugh Resigns from NFL Show." ESPN.com, October 2, 2003. Retrieved from http://espn.go.com/gen/news/2003/1001/1628537.html.

21 Crawley, A. Bruce. "122 Teams, One Black Major Owner." *Philadelphia Tribune,* October 23, 2011. Retrieved from http://www.phillytrib.com/commentaryarticles/item/1164-122-teams-one-black-major-owner.html.

22 "Race Remains 'Flashpoint of Controversy' in American Sports." Phys.org, May 3, 2007. Retrieved from http://phys.org/news97426086.html#jCp.

23 Kochhar, Rakesh, Richard Fry, and Paul Taylor. "Wealth Gaps Rise to Record Highs Between Whites, Blacks, Hispanics." *Pew Social and Demographic Trends,* July 26, 2011. Retrieved from http://www.pewsocialtrends.org/2011/07/26/wealth-gaps-rise-to-record-highs-between-whites-blacks-hispanics/.

24 Quoted in Crouse, Karen. "Treasure of Golf's Sad Past, Black Caddies Vanish in Era of Riches." *New York Times,* April 3, 2012, p. A1. Retrieved from http://www.nytimes.com/2012/04/03/sports/golf/from-a-symbol-of-segregation-to-a-victim-of-golfs-success.html?_r=2&pagewanted=all.

25 Quoted in Gonzalez.

26 Quoted in Fussman, p. 232.

27 Quoted in Fussman, p. 230.

28 Glasser.

BIOGRAPHIES

Roy Campanella (1921-1993)
First Black Catcher in Major League Baseball

Roy Campanella, often referred to by the nickname Campy, was born on November 19, 1921, in Philadelphia, Pennsylvania. His father, John Campanella, was the son of Sicilian immigrants. His mother, Ida Mercer Campanella, was African American. Roy was the youngest of their five children. Growing up in the racially integrated Nicetown neighborhood of Philadelphia, Roy was often teased by both black and white children for being a "half-breed," or a person of mixed race. But his mother always told him that he should never be ashamed about his background, and she emphasized that he was just as good as anyone else.

In 1929 the U.S. economy entered a severe downturn that became known as the Great Depression. Roy and his older siblings had to work in their father's small grocery business to help support the family. Roy helped deliver groceries after school and on weekends, and he grew strong lugging boxes of produce and sacks of potatoes. He also shined shoes and sold newspapers to earn money. In his spare time, Roy played sports with neighborhood friends. His favorite sport was baseball, and he became a star in local sandlot games. He also frequently walked the two miles to Shibe Park to see Major League Baseball's Philadelphia Athletics play. Unable to afford a ticket, Roy and his friends would watch through the outfield fence or from the roof of a nearby building.

By the time he reached Simon Gratz High School, Campanella was an outstanding athlete who competed in football, basketball, track and field, amateur boxing, and baseball. When he first tried out for the school baseball team, the coach divided the hopeful players by position—infielders, outfielders, pitchers, and catchers. When Campanella noticed that no one else wanted to play catcher, he adopted it as his position, figuring it would be the surest way to make the team. As it turned out, his short, stocky body, strong throwing arm, and quick, catlike reflexes made him ideally suited to become a catcher.

111

Joins the Negro Leagues

Campanella was such a good defensive catcher—as well as a powerful hitter—that it soon became clear that he had the potential to play professional baseball. In those days, however, Major League Baseball (MLB) operated under a longstanding segregation policy that barred African Americans from playing. Instead, talented African-American players were forced to play in the all-black Negro Leagues. Accustomed to watching all-white MLB teams, Campanella never even dreamed of playing in the majors. "If I wondered at all about why there weren't any colored players, I just thought there weren't any good enough,"[1] he acknowledged.

In 1938, when he was sixteen, Campanella quit school in order to play professional baseball for the Baltimore Elite Giants in the Negro National League. He soon proved his durability by catching four consecutive games in one day. "You didn't get hurt when you played in the Negro leagues," he explained. "You played no matter what happened to you because if you didn't play, you didn't get paid."[2] Despite the demanding schedule, Campanella quickly emerged as a star. He was named Most Valuable Player of the Negro Leagues' annual East-West All-Star Game in 1941, while he was still a teenager.

In 1942 Campanella signed a contract to play for the Monterrey Sultans of the Mexican League. He learned to speak Spanish in order to communicate with the team's pitchers. After returning to the Giants in 1944, he impressed scouts for the major-league Brooklyn Dodgers during an exhibition game at Ebbets Field. Unbeknownst to Campanella, Dodgers president Branch Rickey was then searching for a talented black player to join his team and shatter MLB's color barrier.

Becomes a Teammate of Jackie Robinson

In fact, Campanella was one of the players Rickey considered before he selected Jackie Robinson to integrate the majors. Some of Rickey's scouts argued that Campanella was a stronger player, and he certainly had more pro baseball experience than Robinson, who had only played one season in the Negro Leagues by 1945. Rickey worried that white MLB pitchers might be reluctant to listen to a black catcher, however, and he also liked the fact that Robinson was a military veteran with a college education. Campanella's mixed racial background was another factor working against him. Biographer Arnold Rampersad suggested that the darker-skinned Robinson "was probably far more Rickey's idea of what the first Negro player should look like—and what he thought black Americans would want the first to look like—than Campanella."[3]

Although Rickey chose Robinson to become the first black player in the major leagues, Campanella followed close behind. In 1946 the Dodgers' boss signed him—along with Negro Leagues pitcher Don Newcombe—to a minor-league contract with the Class B Nashua Dodgers of the New England League. As the most experienced player on the young team, Campanella once took over as manager when Walt Alston was ejected from a game. He thus became the first African American to manage a team of white professional ballplayers. In 1947, while Robinson was making his historic debut in MLB, Campanella played for the Class A Montreal Royals and was named Most Valuable Player of the International League. On April 20, 1948, when he made his big-league debut with the Dodgers, Campanella became the first black catcher in MLB.

Campanella and Robinson were teammates for the next nine seasons. Sportswriters inevitably drew comparisons between the Dodgers' black stars and the ways in which they approached their role as racial pioneers. Campanella was generally described as laid-back, unassuming, jovial, and full of enthusiasm for the game of baseball. He was popular among his teammates and often joked around with reporters. Robinson, on the other hand, "always struck us as being deadly serious and conscious at all times," recalled Dink Carroll of the *Montreal Gazette*. "If he had any light moments, they came when we weren't around."[4]

Whereas Robinson had a fiery temper and often spoke out against racial discrimination, Campanella had a more placid temperament and avoided clashes over civil rights. He usually pretended not to notice racial hostility from opposing players and fans, for instance, and he declined to join in fellow black players' protests against segregated hotels and restaurants. Robinson found his teammate's attitude frustrating, and it created a distance between them. Red Smith of the *New York Herald Tribune* summed up the difference between the two Dodgers: "Jackie Robinson was the trail blazer, the standard bearer, the man who broke the color line, assumed the burden for his people and made good. Roy Campanella is the one who made friends."[5]

Career Cut Short by Injury

Over the course of his career, Campanella came to be viewed as one of the greatest catchers ever to play the game. In 1949 he was among the first black players to be selected to the MLB All-Star Team, along with Robinson, Newcombe, and Larry Doby. He returned to the All-Star Game every year through 1956, and he was named Most Valuable Player of the National League three times, in 1951, 1953, and 1955. Campanella's greatest season came in 1953, when he batted an impressive .312 and established three single-season records for a catcher: for most putouts (807), most home runs (41), and most runs batted in (142). His career statistics include a .276 batting average, 1,161 hits, 242 home runs, and 856 RBIs. He also threw out 227 of the 445 base runners who attempted to steal against him, for a career percentage of 51.01—third on the all-time list.

Campanella's statistics might have been even more notable had his career not been cut short—first by segregation, which prevented him from entering the major leagues until age twenty-six, and later by a serious injury. In early 1958, as the Dodgers prepared to relocate from Brooklyn to Los Angeles, Campanella was involved in a terrible automobile accident. He was driving back to his home on Long Island late at night when his car skidded on a patch of ice, collided with a telephone pole, and flipped upside down. Campanella broke two vertebrae in his neck and was paralyzed from the shoulders down. Months of physical therapy returned most of the use of his arms and hands, but he required a wheelchair for mobility for the rest of his life. In the aftermath of the accident, Campanella struggled to come to terms with his disability. He also went through a divorce and was forced to sell his house in order to pay his medical bills.

Campanella found the strength to carry on, however, and he gained new insights from his experience. "I know that breaking your neck is a tough way to learn a lesson," he stated, "but lying in bed paralyzed, I learned two things: tolerance and patience. Toward myself and everybody else. That's love, isn't it?"[6] In 1959 the Dodgers organized a special exhibition game against the New York Yankees to honor and benefit Campanella. A record crowd of over 93,000 fans showed their support and admiration by attending the game at the Los Angeles Coliseum, which raised $75,000 to help pay the catcher's medical bills. Later that year, Campanella published *It's Good to Be Alive,* a book that describes his recovery from injury and the restoration of his spirit. The story was made into a TV movie directed by Michael Landon in 1974.

After his playing career ended, Campanella remained involved with the Dodgers organization. He served as a scout, coached catchers in spring training, and worked in community relations. In 1969 he became the second African-American player (after Robinson) to be inducted into the National Baseball Hall of Fame. "This completes my baseball career," he said. "All my disappointments are behind me. There is nothing more I could ask for in baseball."[7] In 1972 the Dodgers retired his uniform number, 39, and in 2006 the franchise established an award in his name for the player who best exemplified his spirit and leadership.

Campanella died of a heart attack on June 26, 1993, in Woodland Hills, California. He was survived by his third wife, Roxie Doles, and his five children from his previous marriages to Bernice Ray and Ruthe Willis. By the end of his life, Campanella had emerged as a spokesman for people with disabilities. "People look at me and get the feeling that if a guy in a wheelchair can have such a good time, they can't be too bad off after all,"[8] he noted. Campanella inspired many people with his courage and determination. "I'm having a wonderful second life," he once said. "I want to tell everybody about it. I want them to remember that when trouble comes, it ain't always bad. Take it with a smile, do the best you can, and the good Lord will help you out."[9]

Sources

Campanella, Roy. *It's Good to Be Alive.* New York: Dell, 1959.

Lanctot, Neil. *Campy: The Two Lives of Roy Campanella.* New York: Simon and Schuster, 2011.

"The Official Site of Roy Campanella." Retrieved from http://www.roycampanella.com/.

Swaine, Rick. "Roy Campanella." Society for American Baseball Research (SABR), 2012. Retrieved from http://sabr.org/bioproj/person/a52ccbb5.

Notes

[1] Quoted in Lanctot, Neil. *Campy: The Two Lives of Roy Campanella.* New York: Simon and Schuster, 2011, p. 11.

[2] Thomas, Robert McG. Jr. "Roy Campanella, 71, Dies; Was Dodger Hall of Famer." *New York Times,* June 28, 1993. Retrieved from http://www.nytimes.com/1993/06/28/obituaries/roy-campanella-71-dies-was-dodger-hall-of-famer.html.

[3] Rampersad, Arnold. *Jackie Robinson: A Biography.* New York: Random House, 1997, p. 292.

[4] Quoted in Lanctot, p. 144.

[5] Quoted in "Sport: The Man behind the Plate." *Time,* February 10, 1958. Retrieved from http://www.time.com/time/magazine/article/0,9171,868262,00.html#ixzz2AATSXdZS.

[6] Quoted in Anderson, Dave. "Baseball: Sport of the Times; In Roy Campanella, the Heart of a Hero." *New York Times,* June 28 1993. Retrieved from http://www.nytimes.com/1993/06/28/sports/baseball-sports-of-the-times-in-roy-campanella-the-heart-of-a-hero.html.

[7] Quoted in Anderson.

[8] Quoted in Anderson.

[9] Quoted in Anderson.

A. B. "Happy" Chandler (1898-1991)
Politician and Second Commissioner of Major League Baseball

Albert Benjamin Chandler was born in the farming community of Corydon, Kentucky, on July 14, 1898. His mother, Callie (Saunders) Chandler, abandoned the family when he was four years old. His father, Joseph Sephus Chandler, ended up raising Albert and his younger brother, Robert, with help from relatives. Growing up without a mother made young Albert very independent. By the age of eight he was helping to support the family by doing odd jobs for neighbors and delivering newspapers.

After graduating from Corydon High School, Chandler entered Transylvania College in Lexington, Kentucky. "I had arrived at Transylvania College—a small-town Kentucky school of 280 but a great hall of learning to me—in 1917 with a $5 bill, a red sweater, a smile, and a fierce love for sport that won me varsity letters in football, basketball, and baseball,"[1] he recalled in *Sports Illustrated*. During his college years, Chandler earned the nickname "Happy" because of his outgoing, jovial nature.

Following a brief stint in the U.S. Army during World War I, Chandler completed his bachelor's degree in 1921. He tried out for several minor-league baseball teams in hopes of becoming a professional athlete, but none offered him a contract. Chandler then decided to study law at Harvard University. He soon found that he was unable to afford Harvard's tuition, though, so he returned home after one year and completed his law degree at the University of Kentucky in Lexington in 1924. Chandler launched his career as a lawyer in Versailles, Kentucky, the following year. He also married Mildred Watkins, a teacher. They would eventually have four children: Marcella, Mildred, Albert Jr., and Joseph Daniel.

Governor of Kentucky

Long interested in politics, Chandler was elected to the Kentucky State Senate as a Democrat in 1930. The following year—thanks to the support of powerful party "bosses" on the nominating committee—he became lieutenant governor of Kentucky. Almost immediately after taking office, though, Chandler and Governor Ruby Laffoon disagreed over a proposed law creating a state sales tax. Laffoon eventually managed to pass the tax by one vote, and from that time on he actively opposed Chandler's bid to succeed him as governor.

As the next election approached in 1935, however, Laffoon traveled to Washington, D.C., for a meeting with President Franklin D. Roosevelt. Taking advantage of a state law that made him acting governor in Laffoon's absence, Chandler quickly ushered a bill through the state legislature that required gubernatorial candidates to be selected by voters through a primary election, rather than by party bosses through a nominating convention. The change helped Chandler, at age thirty-seven, overcome Laffoon's opposition to his candidacy and win election as the nation's youngest governor.

The young Kentucky governor led a repeal of the unpopular sales tax and oversaw a money-saving reorganization of the state government. He supported programs that improved the state's roads and schools, increased citizens' access to electricity, and created pension programs for teachers and mine workers. In 1938 Chandler launched an unsuccessful campaign to represent Kentucky in the U.S. Senate. The following year, however, he arranged to be appointed to the position upon the death of Senator Marvel Mills Logan, and he held onto the seat in the 1942 elections. As a fiscal conservative, he fought against some of Roosevelt's New Deal reforms, which were intended to use federal spending to create jobs and provide assistance to Americans who were struggling during the Great Depression.

Commissioner of Baseball

By 1944 Chandler had set his political sights on the White House. His presidential hopes were dashed, however, when he failed to gain enough support within the Democratic Party to be nominated as Roosevelt's vice presidential running mate. In November of that year, longtime Major League Baseball commissioner Kenesaw Mountain Landis died, and the owners of the sixteen teams launched a search for a replacement. Chandler won the job in recognition of his outstanding college baseball career and his many political connections. He officially became the second commissioner of baseball on April 24, 1945.

In many ways, Chandler was the opposite of his stern, stately predecessor, who had built a reputation as a tough, law-and-order federal judge in Chicago. "Picture him and imagine me, a man named 'Happy,' succeeding him," he remarked. "Happy does not frown. He smiles. He does not try to look mean. He laughs."[2] In the beginning of his tenure, sports journalists had trouble taking Chandler seriously and often criticized him for seeming like a country bumpkin. He did not help his cause by singing a song to entertain the crowd at an introductory press conference.

Before long, however, Chandler began to make full use of the power of his office. Much to the chagrin of the owners, he often supported the interests of players, umpires, and fans over the financial interests of teams. "I told the owners when I took the job in 1945, 'You don't own this game. You merely own a franchise in it. The game belongs to the American people, and as long as they think it is theirs they'll be loyal and support it. If ever they get to feeling it's nothing but a bloody business and run just for profit by you fellows, the stands will go empty,'"[3] he explained.

Controversial Tenure

Chandler made several controversial decisions during his tenure as baseball commissioner. One of the first was his decision to support Branch Rickey, the maverick president of the Brooklyn Dodgers, when he hired Jackie Robinson to integrate Major League Baseball. Landis had always stood by the other team owners who steadfastly rejected the idea of allowing African-American players to join the big leagues. But as soon as Chandler got the job, he allowed Rickey to proceed with his plan. "Many of the owners didn't want the change," he recalled. "I wasn't asked for a decision, so I never gave one. The dissenters had to think they were on firm ground because Judge Landis had been in office twenty-four years and never lifted a finger for black players. He always said, 'The owners have the right to hire whom they please.' Obviously Branch Rickey ... thought so, too."[4]

Chandler's support enabled Robinson to break baseball's longstanding color barrier in 1947. Although that event is now considered a defining moment in the history of the game and an early triumph in the civil rights movement, Chandler's decision was extremely controversial at the time. It angered not only the other team owners, but also many white baseball players, fans, and corporate sponsors. During the first few seasons of Rickey's "noble experiment," the commissioner intervened on several occasions to protect Robinson from racially motivated abuse and boycotts. For instance, Chandler warned Philadelphia Phillies manager Ben Chapman to stop taunting Robinson or face disciplinary action, and he threatened to suspend any St. Louis Cardinals players who refused to take the field against the integrated Dodgers. "Although Robinson may not know it, we watched over him as we would a baby. We had fellows at many of his games to see that he wasn't mistreated," Chandler noted. "Robinson didn't always help much because he had a little bit of a chip on his shoulder and many people resented him. ... We stayed on it all the time, and Robinson won his spurs."[5]

Chandler also created the first pension fund to support players whose careers ended due to injury or old age. He negotiated a lucrative deal with the Gillette Safety Razor Company and the Mutual Broadcasting System for exclusive radio and television rights to the World Series and the All-Star Game, then applied the proceeds to the player pension fund. Chandler made several other decisions that went against the wishes of most team owners. He strictly enforced rules limiting the number of times teams could assign players to the minor leagues, for instance, and he prohibited teams from negotiating with young prospects before they graduated from high school. Although the owners expected him to "wink" at behavior that flaunted the rules, Chandler was determined to preserve the integrity of the game. "There are sixteen teams in this game," he declared. "If I wink at one, I'll have to wink at fifteen others. That's not a wink, that's a twitch."[6] The team owners did not appreciate Chandler's efforts to serve interests besides their own, so they voted against renewing his contract in 1951.

Returns to Public Service

After his six-year term as baseball commissioner ended, Chandler returned home to Kentucky. In 1955 he waged a successful campaign to return to the governor's office. Highlights of his second term included establishing a medical school at the University of Kentucky, which was later named after him, and calling out the National Guard on two occasions to enforce racial integration in the state's public schools. Chandler left office in 1959, and he later made three unsuccessful bids for reelection. He was elected to the Kentucky Sports Hall of Fame in 1957, and his contributions as baseball commissioner were recognized with his 1982 induction into the National Baseball Hall of Fame.

Chandler died of a heart attack at his home in Versailles, Kentucky, on June 15, 1991, at the age of ninety-two. "I have, counting all, followed the course I charted for myself almost to the letter," he once said. "Looking back, I wouldn't change a jot for anything.... I have been going, and winning, all my life."[7]

Among Chandler's surviving family members is his grandson Ben Chandler, who represented the state of Kentucky in the U.S. Congress from 2004 to 2013.

Sources

Chandler, Happy, with Vance H. Trimble. *Heroes, Plain Folks, and Skunks: The Life and Times of Happy Chandler: An Autobiography.* Chicago: Bonus Books, 1989.

"Happy Chandler." National Baseball Hall of Fame, n.d. Retrieved from http://baseballhall.org/hof/chandler-happy.

"History of the Game, Doubleday to Present Day: Albert Benjamin 'Happy' Chandler." MLB.com, 2012. Retrieved from http://mlb.mlb.com/mlb/history/mlb_history_people.jsp?story=com_bio_2.

Notes

[1] Chandler, A. B., with John Underwood. "How I Jumped from Clean Politics into Dirty Baseball." *Sports Illustrated,* April 26, 1971. Retrieved from http://sportsillustrated.cnn.com/vault/article/magazine/MAG 1084797/1/index.htm.

[2] Chandler, with Underwood. "How I Jumped from Clean Politics into Dirty Baseball."

[3] Chandler, with Underwood. "How I Jumped from Clean Politics into Dirty Baseball."

[4] Chandler, with Underwood. "How I Jumped from Clean Politics into Dirty Baseball."

[5] Chandler, with Underwood. "How I Jumped from Clean Politics into Dirty Baseball."

[6] Chandler, A. B., with John Underwood. "Gunned Down by the Heavies." *Sports Illustrated,* May 3, 1971. Retrieved from http://sportsillustrated.cnn.com/vault/article/magazine/MAG1084821/1/index.htm.

[7] Chandler, with Underwood. "Gunned Down by the Heavies."

Larry Doby (1923-2003)
Professional Baseball Player Who Integrated the American League

Lawrence Eugene Doby was born on December 13, 1923, in Camden, South Carolina. His parents were David Doby, who worked as a horse groomer and played semi-professional baseball, and Etta Doby, who worked as a housekeeper. Young Larry grew up playing baseball in the street, using broom handles for bats and tin cans for bases. He also helped support the family by picking cotton in nearby fields for one dollar per day. Larry's father drowned when he was eleven years old. The tragedy forced his mother to move north in search of work. Larry lived with relatives for several years before eventually joining his mother in Paterson, New Jersey.

Doby attended Paterson Eastside High School, where he was an all-state athlete in baseball, basketball, and football and also earned a varsity letter in track. He encountered very little racial discrimination during these years. "I grew up in a mixed neighborhood in Paterson. I ate in my classmates' homes, and they ate in mine," he remembered. "I was the only black on the football team, and when we were invited to play segregated high school bowl games in Florida, the team voted to stay home rather than play without me."[1]

Doby's athletic talents helped him earn a basketball scholarship to attend Long Island University. At that point, his future plans included becoming a high-school teacher and coach and marrying his girlfriend, Helyn, with whom he would eventually have five children. In 1942, however, his powerful hitting and stellar defense impressed a baseball umpire, who contacted the owner of the Newark Eagles about the high-school star. "They gave me a tryout, and I made the team," Doby recalled. "That's how I got involved in Negro League Baseball."[2]

Doby played in the Negro Leagues for parts of the 1942 and 1943 seasons. He was then drafted into the U.S. Navy during World War II and served in the Pacific Theater. When Jackie Robinson signed a minor-league contract with the Montreal Royals (the Brooklyn Dodgers' top farm team), Doby heard the news

121

on Armed Forces Radio. It was the earliest indication that Major League Base-ball's longstanding color barrier might fall, allowing African Americans to showcase their skills alongside the best white professional ballplayers. "I never looked that far ahead, because growing up in a segregated society, you couldn't have thought that was the way life was gonna be," Doby explained. "There was no bright spot as far as looking at baseball until Mr. Robinson got the oppor-tunity to play in Montreal in '46."[3]

First Black Player in the American League

Doby returned to the Eagles that year. He batted .360 and helped lift the team to victory in the Negro Leagues World Series. In 1947, shortly after Robinson made his historic major-league debut with the Dodgers, Cleveland Indians owner Bill Veeck approached Doby about joining his team. Veeck had expressed interest in signing Negro League players for years, but then-Major League Baseball commissioner Kenesaw Mountain Landis had consistently rejected the idea. Once Robinson broke the color barrier, however, Veeck decided to move forward with his integration plan.

Unlike Robinson, Doby did not have an opportunity to ease his way into white baseball by playing in the minor leagues. Instead, he joined the Indians straight out of the Negro Leagues, where he had been hitting .458. When he made his first appearance with the team on July 5, 1947, in Chicago's Comiskey Park—only two days after signing a contract—Doby became the first black play-er in the American League. The twenty-three-year-old rookie did not receive a particularly warm welcome when he was introduced to his new teammates. "I walked down that line, stuck out my hand, and very few hands came back in return. Most of the ones that did were cold-fish handshakes, along with a look that said, 'You don't belong here,'" he recalled. "I put on my uniform, and I went out on the field to warm up, but nobody wanted to warm up with me. I had never been so alone in my life. I stood there alone in front of the dugout for five minutes. Then Joe Gordon, the second baseman who would become my friend, came up to me and asked, 'Hey, rookie, you gonna just stand there or do you want to throw a little?' I will never forget that man."[4]

Doby experienced the same sort of racial hostility and discrimination as Robinson had when he entered the major leagues only eleven weeks earlier. Doby was forced to stay in separate hotels and change in separate locker rooms from his white teammates, for instance, and he also endured verbal taunts and physical abuse from opposing players. "The things I was called did hurt me. They hurt a lot. The things people did to me, spitting tobacco juice on me, sliding into me, throwing baseballs at my head,"[5] he acknowledged. "Jackie got all the publicity for putting up with it. But it was the same thing I had to deal with. He was first, but the crap I took was just as bad. Nobody said, 'We're gonna be nice to the second black.'"[6]

A Picture Worth a Thousand Words

Although Doby struggled in his rookie season, he emerged as a key contributor to the Indians' success in 1948. Despite changing his defensive position from second base to center field, Doby batted .301 with 14 home runs and 66 runs batted in (RBI) to help Cleveland reach the World Series. In Game 4 Doby became the first black player ever to hit a home run in the World Series—a shot that gave Indians pitcher Steve Gromek a 2-1 complete-game victory. Gromek reacted by wrapping his teammate in a joyful bear hug. When a photograph of their spontaneous celebration appeared in newspapers nationwide, it played a role in improving race relations. "It was such a scuffle for me, after being involved in all that segregation, going through all I had to go through, until that picture," Doby related. "The picture finally showed a moment of a man showing his feelings for me. But the picture is not just about me. It shows what feelings should be, regardless of differences between people. And it shows what feelings should be in all of life, not just in sports. I think enlightenment can come from such a picture."[7] The Indians went on to defeat the Boston Braves in six games to claim the World Series championship.

In 1949 Doby was selected to the All-Star Team for the first of seven times in his career. He thus joined Robinson, Roy Campanella, and Don Newcombe as the first black players to appear in the All-Star Game. In 1950 Doby posted career highs in batting average (.326) and hits (164) and collected more than 100 RBIs for the first of five seasons. He went on to lead the American League in home runs twice (in 1952 and 1954) and set a major-league record of 164 consecutive games without a fielding error that stood for seventeen years. After leading the Indians back to the World Series in 1954 (where they were swept by the New York Giants), Doby was traded to the Chicago White Sox the following year. He returned to the Indians in 1958, then was traded to the Detroit Tigers in 1959. Doby retired from baseball on July 26, 1959, after breaking his ankle while sliding into second base.

In thirteen major-league seasons, Doby batted .283 with 253 home runs and 970 RBIs. "Perhaps his greatest achievement lay outside the statistics that are such a central part of the culture of baseball," wrote Robert E. Botsch. "Larry Doby, without the months of preparation that helped Jackie Robinson endure his ordeal, endured two ordeals of his own. The first involved his entry into a hostile world where many wanted him to fail, and the second was being ignored by history because he was not the first to enter that world. Doby endured both without complaint, never saying anything about Jackie Robinson that could be construed as even hinting at jealousy. He endured with quiet pride and great dignity."[8]

Honored for His Achievements

Once his playing career ended, Doby became a successful major-league scout, batting coach, and executive. In 1978 he was appointed manager of the Chicago White Sox, making him the second African American (after Frank Robinson) to lead a major-league ballclub. Doby's managerial career only lasted one season. Afterward, he served as the director of community relations for the NBA's New Jersey Nets and became involved in a number of inner-city youth programs.

In 1994 the Indians recognized Doby's legacy by retiring his jersey number, 14. In 1997 he was honored at the All-Star Game in Cleveland. He served as the American League captain and threw out the ceremonial first pitch, and a portion of the proceeds from the game was used to build the Larry Doby All-Star Playground in the city. In 1998 Doby was inducted into the National Baseball Hall of Fame in Cooperstown, New York. In his induction speech, he expressed pride in the role he played in integrating baseball. Doby said his experience proved "that we can live together, we can work together, we can play together, and we can be successful together. And I'm very happy and proud that I've been a part of this [game of] baseball and I'm still a part of it.... Everything I've got, everything my family's got, we've got it from baseball."[9]

Doby died on June 18, 2003, at his home in Montclair, New Jersey, following a long battle with cancer. He was seventy-nine. Upon his passing, many observers asserted that Doby deserved as much credit as Jackie Robinson for his pioneering role in the integration of baseball. "Many forget that Doby was the first black player in the American League in a time when the leagues did not play each other. So, like Robinson, he was a lone black face in a league of his own," wrote Justice B. Hill of MLB.com. "Without taking anything away from Robinson's significant achievement, it is fair to say that plenty of trail-blazing remained to be done when Doby joined the Indians on July 5, 1947. These two black pioneers should have been tied together with the same thread. As history told the Jackie Robinson story, it also should have been telling the Larry Doby story."[10]

Sources

Botsch, Robert E. "Larry Doby." University of South Carolina Aiken, July 31, 2008. Retrieved from http://www.usca.edu/aasc/doby.htm.

Crowe, Chris. *Just as Good: How Larry Doby Changed America's Game.* Somerville, MA: Candlewick Press, 2012.

"Larry Doby." National Baseball Hall of Fame, n.d. Retrieved from http://baseballhall.org/hof/doby-larry.

Moore, Joseph. *Pride against Prejudice: The Biography of Larry Doby.* New York: Praeger, 1988.

Notes

[1] Quoted in Hill, Justice B. "Doby, AL's First Black Player, Dies." MLB.com, June 19, 2003. Retrieved from http://mlb.mlb.com/news/article.jsp?ymd=20030619&content_id=381932&vkey=news_mlb&fext=.jsp&c_id=null.

[2] Quoted in Hill. "Doby, AL's First Black Player, Dies."

[3] Quoted in Hill. "Doby, AL's First Black Player, Dies."

[4] Quoted in Izenberg, Jerry. "Larry Doby Should Be Honored by Newark." NJ.com, July 7, 2012. Retrieved from http://www.nj.com/sports/ledger/izenbergcol/index.ssf/2012/07/izenberg_larry_doby_should_be.html.

[5] Quoted in Crowe, Chris. *Just as Good: How Larry Doby Changed America's Game.* Somerville, MA: Candlewick Press, 2012, p. 28.

[6] Quoted in "Larry Doby Doesn't Mind Being 'Second Black' Again." *Jet,* July 20, 1978, p. 52.

[7] Quoted in Moore, Joseph. *Pride against Prejudice: The Biography of Larry Doby.* New York: Praeger, 1988, p. 4.

[8] Botsch, Robert E. "Larry Doby." University of South Carolina Aiken, July 31, 2008. Retrieved from http://www.usca.edu/aasc/doby.htm.

[9] "Lawrence Eugene Doby: Induction Speech." National Baseball Hall of Fame, 1998. Retrieved from http://baseballhall.org/node/11492.

[10] Hill, Justice B. "Doby Stood Tall in the Face of Adversity." MLB.com, June 19, 2003. Retrieved from http://cleveland.indians.mlb.com/news/article.jsp?ymd=20030619&content_id=383394&vkey=news_cle&fext=.jsp&c_id=cle.

Pee Wee Reese (1918-1999)
Brooklyn Dodgers Captain Who Befriended
Jackie Robinson

Harold Henry Reese, known by the nickname "Pee Wee" from his days as a young marble-shooting champion, was born on July 23, 1918, in Ekron, Kentucky. His father, Carl Reese, worked as a detective for a railroad company. When Pee Wee was about ten years old, his father pointed out a tree in nearby Brandenburg, Kentucky, that had a long, thick, horizontal branch. He told his son that mobs of white people sometimes murdered black people by hanging them from that branch. This terrifying act, known as lynching, served as a highly visible warning to any blacks who did not "know their place" in Kentucky's segregated society.

Segregation meant that Pee Wee had little contact with African Americans in his youth. Nevertheless, he always remembered the lynching tree and his feelings of sadness about the cruel and inhumane treatment of black people. "When I was growing up, we never played ball with blacks because they weren't allowed in the parks. And the schools were segregated, so we didn't go to school with them. And there'd be some mischief between blacks and whites, but, as I remember, it was just mischief," he explained. "It wasn't hatred, at least not from me."[1]

Reese attended DuPont Manual High School in Louisville. He was slow to develop physically, so he only played organized baseball during his senior year. After graduating, he got a job laying cable for a telephone company and continued playing amateur baseball in a church league. One season, Reese's team made it to the league championship, which was held at the home field of a local minor-league franchise, the Louisville Colonels. Reese's strong performance in that game attracted the attention of Colonels management, and they signed him to a contract for $200.

Joins the Brooklyn Dodgers

Reese steadily improved his skills in the minor leagues. He turned into a sure-handed shortstop with a knack for making big plays and getting clutch hits.

In 1940 the Boston Red Sox signed him to a major-league contract. But the team's player-manager, Joe Cronin, was not willing to give up his position as shortstop, so he arranged for Reese to be traded to the Brooklyn Dodgers. Reese turned into a solid big-league performer almost immediately, and in 1942 he made the first of ten career appearances in the All-Star Game.

In addition to his contributions on the field, Reese also brought leadership and competitive fire to the Dodgers' dugout and locker room. He earned the respect of his teammates, and they often looked to him for advice and support. "He was the heart and soul of the 'Boys of Summer,'" noted longtime Dodgers broadcaster Vin Scully. "If a player needed to be consoled, Pee Wee would console him. If a player needed to be kicked in the fanny, Pee Wee would do that, too. If a player really needed a friend, Pee Wee was there for him."[2]

In 1943 Reese enlisted in the U.S. military, and he served in the Pacific Theater during World War II. On his way back to the United States in 1945, he learned that Dodgers president Branch Rickey had just hired Negro League star Jackie Robinson to break Major League Baseball's longstanding color barrier. The idea of playing on the same team as a black man did not bother Reese. "I was on a ship coming back to the States from Guam, in the middle of the ocean, and was playing cards. Someone hollered to me: 'Hey, Pee Wee, did you hear? The Dodgers signed a nigger.' It didn't mean that much to me and I kept playing cards," he recalled. "Then the guy said, 'And he plays shortstop!' My God, just my luck, Robinson has to play my position! But I had confidence in my abilities, and I thought, well, if he can beat me out, more power to him. That's exactly how I felt."[3] (As it turned out, Robinson never competed for Reese's shortstop position and became his double-play partner at second base instead.)

Stands Up for Robinson

Reese returned to the Dodgers for the 1946 season and was elected captain by his teammates. The following year, Robinson joined the team for spring training. Reese was the first player to approach the rookie and introduce himself. "It was the first time I'd ever shaken the hand of a black man," Reese said. "But I was the captain of the team. It was my job, I believed, to greet the new players."[4] Not all of Robinson's new teammates were so welcoming. Outfielder Dixie Walker tried to convince his fellow Dodgers to sign a petition saying that they would not play on the same team as a black man. Reese refused to sign it, though, and many other players followed his lead, which basically put an end to the protest.

Once the 1947 season got underway, Robinson frequently endured streams of vicious verbal harassment from opposing players and fans. At one ballpark, the abuse grew so intolerable that Reese walked over to Robinson, draped an arm around his shoulder, and stood talking to him for several minutes. This gesture of solidarity both comforted Robinson and quieted the crowd. "Something in my gut reacted to the moment," Reese related. "Something about—what?—the unfairness of it? The injustice of it? I don't know."[5] The moment was immortalized nearly six decades later when a statue depicting the two players was erected at Keyspan Park in Brooklyn.

Reese and Robinson played together on the Dodgers for ten years. For much of that time, with Reese at shortstop and Robinson at second base, they made one of the most potent double-play combinations in baseball history. The two men also established a personal friendship that included many rounds of golf and late-night card games. Witnessing Robinson's struggles firsthand gave Reese a deep appreciation for his teammate's role in history. "Thinking about the things that happened, I don't know any other ballplayer who could have done what he did," he noted. "To be able to hit with everybody yelling at him. He had to block all that out, block out everything but this ball that is coming in at a hundred miles an hour. To do what he did has got to be the most tremendous thing I've ever seen in sports."[6]

Reese remained modest about his own role in Robinson's success. He insisted that he never went out of his way to help Robinson, but merely treated him the same way as he treated other players. "I get a lot of credit and I appreciate it," he said, "but after a while, I thought of him as I would Duke Snider or Gil Hodges or anyone else. We never thought of this as a big deal. We were just playing ball and having fun."[7]

Hall of Fame Career

Reese remained with the Dodgers throughout his sixteen-year career, until he retired from baseball in 1959 (the year the franchise relocated to Los Angeles). He led the team to seven National League pennants and one World Series championship (in 1955). His career statistics include a .269 batting average, 126 home runs, and 885 RBIs. He led the National League in walks in 1947 (with 104), in runs scored in 1949 (with 132), and in stolen bases in 1952 (with 30). Although his statistics are respectable, Reese was probably best known for the intangible qualities he brought to the Dodgers. Somehow, he always managed to beat out bunts, extend hits for extra bases, make diving catches, and turn key double plays.

After his playing days ended, Reese launched a successful career as a sports broadcaster for CBS (with partner Dizzy Dean), NBC (with partner Curt Gowdy), and the Cincinnati Reds. He also worked as a sales representative for Hillerich and Bradsby, the company that produced Louisville Slugger baseball bats. In 1984 he was inducted into the National Baseball Hall of Fame, and the Dodgers retired his uniform number, 1.

Reese died on August 14, 1999, at his home in Louisville. He had fought prostate cancer and lung cancer in the last few years of his life. He was survived by his wife of fifty-seven years, Dorothy (Walton) Reese, and their two children, Mark and Barbara. Upon Reese's passing, many baseball greats honored him for his public acceptance and support of Robinson, which played an important role in breaking down resistance to baseball integration. "Pee Wee helped make my boyhood dream come true to play in the Majors, the World Series," declared former Dodgers pitcher Joe Black. "When Pee Wee reached out to Jackie, all of us in the Negro Leagues smiled and said it was the first time that a white guy had accepted us. When I finally got up to Brooklyn, I went to Pee Wee and said, 'Black people love you. When you touched Jackie, you touched all of us.' With Pee Wee, it was number one on his uniform and number one in our hearts."[8]

Sources

Berkow, Ira. "Standing Beside Jackie Robinson, Reese Helped Change Baseball." *New York Times,* March 31, 1997. Retrieved from http://www.nytimes.com/specials/baseball/bbo-reese-robinson.html.

Golenbock, Peter. *Teammates.* New York: Gulliver Books, 1990.

"Official Site of Pee Wee Reese." Retrieved from http://www.peeweereese.com/.

Schoor, Gene. *The Pee Wee Reese Story.* New York: J. Messner, 1956.

Notes

1 Quoted in Berkow, Ira. "Standing Beside Jackie Robinson, Reese Helped Change Baseball." *New York Times,* March 31, 1997. Retrieved from http://www.nytimes.com/specials/baseball/bbo-reese-robin son.html.

2 Quoted in "Hall of Fame Shortstop Pee Wee Reese Dead at 81." *Los Angeles Times,* August 14, 1999. Retrieved from http://www.baseball-almanac.com/deaths/pee_wee_reese_obituary.shtml.

3 Quoted in Berkow.

4 Quoted in Berkow.

5 Quoted in Berkow.

6 Quoted in "The Official Site of Pee Wee Reese." Retrieved from http://www.peeweereese.com/quotes .htm.

7 Quoted in "Pee Wee Reese Quotes." *Baseball Almanac,* 2012. Retrieved from http://www.baseball almanac.com/quotes/pee_wee_reese_quotes.shtml.

8 Quoted in "Pee Wee Reese Obituary." *Baseball Almanac,* August 14, 1999. Retrieved from http://www.baseball-almanac.com/deaths/pee_wee_reese_obituary.shtml.

Branch Rickey (1881-1965)
Brooklyn Dodgers Executive Who Led Baseball Integration

Wesley Branch Rickey was born on December 20, 1881, in Lucasville, Ohio. He went by his middle name from childhood to avoid being confused with a cousin who was also named Wesley. Branch was the second of three sons born to Jacob Franklin Rickey and Emily Brown Rickey. He was raised in a deeply religious farming family, and he maintained those values throughout his life. He was famous for telling down-home country stories, for instance, and he never drank alcohol, used curse words, or worked on Sundays.

Rickey received an elementary school education and also studied mathematics, Latin, and other subjects on his own. He served as a country schoolteacher for a few years before continuing his education at Ohio Wesleyan University. Rickey worked his way through college by playing catcher for several professional baseball teams. He initially signed a contract with the Cincinnati Reds in 1903, but the team released him because he refused to practice or play games on Sundays. He then bounced between the St. Louis Browns and the New York Highlanders.

For a man who eventually became known for his vast baseball knowledge, Rickey had an undistinguished playing career. His lifetime batting average was only .239, and as a catcher he once allowed an opposing team to steal thirteen bases in a single game—a major-league record that has stood since 1907. In between stints as a player, though, Rickey earned his bachelor's degree from Ohio Wesleyan in 1905. He entered graduate school at the University of Michigan in 1908 and served as head coach of Michigan's baseball team while earning his law degree.

Innovative Baseball Executive

After completing his education, Rickey returned to professional baseball as a scout, club secretary, and field manager. He launched his career as a major-league manager in 1913, the first of his three seasons at the helm of the St. Louis Browns. During World War I Rickey was posted in France as an officer in a chemical warfare unit of the U.S. military. Upon his return from overseas in 1919, he accepted a lucrative deal to become manager of the St. Louis Cardinals.

Rickey's tenure as a big-league manager proved to be a disappointment. His teams posted records below .500 in seven of his ten seasons and never finished above third place in their respective leagues. In 1925, however, Rickey found his calling as a front-office executive. After being fired as the Cardinals' manager, he became vice president and general manager of the team. Over the next seventeen years, he took a struggling team that was $175,000 in debt and built a dynasty that captured six National League pennants and four World Series championships. Rickey's ability to recognize talent, develop young players, and negotiate smart business deals made him one of the most effective baseball operations executives of all time.

Rickey also proved to have a knack for innovation. During his long career, he came up with a number of ideas that revolutionized various aspects of the game. "Rickey had a reputation for intelligent design," wrote historian Ira Glasser. "He devised new and effective ways to instruct players and sharpen their skills; invented training devices, like base-sliding pits and batting tees, that are commonplace today but were unheard of then; and pioneered the use of complex statistical measures to evaluate performance."[1] Rickey is credited with helping to grow the fan base for baseball—and thus the salaries of players and earnings of team owners—by increasing its appeal to children. He was also instrumental in popularizing the use of batting helmets to protect players' heads.

One of Rickey's most significant innovations was creating the "farm system," a network of minor-league teams that are owned by or affiliated with a major-league franchise. He used the farm teams to teach, develop, and evaluate young talent that could eventually be "harvested" by the parent club. Baseball commissioner Kenesaw Mountain Landis opposed Rickey's idea and tried to limit each major-league team to one minor-league affiliate. Eventually, though, Rickey's scheme created such a wealth of talented young players that other teams fought for the right to establish their own farm systems.

Breaks Baseball's Color Barrier

In 1943 Rickey left the Cardinals and became president and part-owner of the Brooklyn Dodgers. Upon moving to a northern city, he immediately began making plans to hire a black player to shatter baseball's longstanding "color barrier," an informal rule that had kept the game strictly segregated since the 1880s.

Rickey believed that integrating the major leagues would make good business sense. He knew that the all-black Negro Leagues were full of great players, and he also recognized that African-American fans would flock to major-league ballparks to see them in action.

But Rickey also believed that segregation was unjust. He had developed this view during his years as a college baseball coach, when the lone black player on his team was prohibited from staying in a hotel with his teammates. Following this experience, Rickey "vowed that I would always do whatever I could to see that other Americans did not have to face the bitter humiliation that was heaped upon [him]."[2]

Rickey came up with a detailed plan to achieve baseball integration. First and foremost, he knew that he needed to find the right man for the job, both on and off the field, if his "noble experiment" were to succeed. "I must be sure that the man was good on the field," he explained. "[But I also] wanted a man of exceptional intelligence, a man who was able to grasp and control the responsibilities of himself to his race and could carry that load. That was the greatest danger point of all."[3]

After scouting international leagues and the Negro Leagues, Rickey finally set his sights on Jackie Robinson of the Kansas City Monarchs. A college-educated World War II veteran with a stable family life, Robinson possessed both the character and the athletic ability that Rickey sought. During a three-hour meeting in Brooklyn, Rickey tested Robinson's temperament by role-playing situations of discrimination and abuse that he likely would face as the first black player in the major leagues. Robinson passed the test, and Rickey signed him to a contract. After spending one season with the minor-league Montreal Royals, Robinson made his historic major-league debut on April 15, 1947.

Forced Out as Dodgers Owner

Robinson went on to play ten spectacular seasons for the Dodgers, overcoming all obstacles to earn Rookie of the Year and Most Valuable Player honors before retiring in 1956. Rickey monitored Robinson's career closely until 1950, when his Dodgers' co-owners forced him out as president of the ballclub. He then sold his share of the team for more than one million dollars and took over as executive vice president and chairman of the Pittsburgh Pirates. Rickey oversaw a rebuilding program in Pittsburgh that resulted in a World Series title in 1960, the year after he retired.

During the early 1960s Rickey turned his attention to launching a new professional baseball league, the Continental League. When the existing American League and National League expanded to include new teams, however, it effectively killed his plan. In poor health for the last few years of his life, Rickey collapsed on stage while giving a speech to mark his induction into the Missouri Sports Hall of Fame. He died three weeks later, on December 9, 1965, in Columbia, Missouri. He was survived by his wife, Jane Moulton Rickey, and their five daughters. Robinson described his mentor's passing as "a great loss not only to baseball but to America."[4]

In 1967 Rickey's contributions as a visionary executive were honored by his election to the National Baseball Hall of Fame. Sportswriter Red Smith of the *St. Louis Post-Dispatch* once summed up Rickey's many roles as "player, manager, executive, lawyer, preacher, horse-trader, spellbinder, innovator, husband and father and grandfather, farmer, logician, obscurantist [someone who is intentionally vague or withholds information], reformer, financier, sociologist, crusader, sharper, father confessor, checker shark, friend and fighter."[5]

Sources

Breslin, Jimmy. *Branch Rickey.* New York: Viking Penguin, 2011.

Lowenfish, Lee. *Branch Rickey: Baseball's Ferocious Gentleman.* Lincoln: University of Nebraska Press, 2007.

"On This Day: Branch Rickey, 83, Dies in Missouri." *New York Times,* December 10, 1965. Retrieved from http://www.nytimes.com/learning/general/onthisday/bday/1220.html.

Polner, Murray. *Branch Rickey: A Biography.* Jefferson, NC: McFarland, 2007.

Notes

[1] Glasser, Ira. "Branch Rickey and Jackie Robinson: Precursors of the Civil Rights Movement." *World and I,* March 2003, p. 257. Retrieved from http://www.worldandi.com/newhome/public/2003/march/mtpub.asp.

[2] Quoted in Glasser.

[3] Rickey, Branch. Speech delivered at the "One Hundred Percent Wrong Club" Banquet, Atlanta, Georgia, January 20, 1956. Library of Congress, American Memory Collection. Retrieved from http://memory.loc.gov/ammem/collections/robinson/branch.html.

[4] Quoted in "On This Day: Branch Rickey, 83, Dies in Missouri." *New York Times,* December 10, 1965. Retrieved from http://www.nytimes.com/learning/general/onthisday/bday/1220.html.

[5] Quoted in "Baseball, the Color Line, and Jackie Robinson." Library of Congress, American Memory Collection, n.d. Retrieved from http://memory.loc.gov/ammem/collections/robinson/jr1940.html.

Jackie Robinson (1919-1972)
Player Who Broke Major League Baseball's Color Barrier

Jack Roosevelt Robinson was born on January 31, 1919, in Cairo, Georgia. His father, Jerry Robinson, was a sharecropper who farmed a plot of land on a large plantation owned by a wealthy white family. His mother, Mallie McGriff Robinson, was the daughter of freed slaves who had worked on a nearby plantation. Jackie was the youngest of their five children. He had three brothers, Edgar, Frank, and Mack, and one sister, Willa Mae. Jerry Robinson abandoned the family when Jackie was six months old, leaving Mallie to raise the children as a single parent. "I could only think of him with bitterness," Jackie wrote of his father years later. "He had no right to desert my mother and five children."[1]

In the area of southern Georgia where Robinson was born, discriminatory "Jim Crow" laws kept people strictly segregated by race. Blacks were expected to "know their place" in society, which meant they served as farm labor and domestic help, deferred to white people, and never complained about unfairness or mistreatment. White supremacists used intimidation and violence to keep this system in place. Mallie Robinson decided that she was unwilling to raise her children in the Jim Crow South. Six months after her husband left, she packed up their belongings and joined a small group of relatives in a cross-country migration to Pasadena, California.

Jackie grew up in a mostly white, working-class neighborhood of Pasadena. Although some neighbors initially resisted the idea of having a black family on the block, Mallie eventually won them over with patience and determination. "My mother never lost her composure," Jackie remembered. "She didn't allow us to go out of our way to antagonize the whites, and she still made it perfectly clear to us and to them that she was not at all afraid of them and that she had no intention of allowing them to mistreat us."[2]

Shows Athletic Ability and Racial Pride

Throughout his youth, Robinson competed in soccer, tennis, football, basketball, baseball, and track and field. He appreciated how sports enabled him to relate to white teammates and opponents on equal terms, and how it placed an emphasis on ability and performance rather than skin color. Following in the footsteps of his brother Mack—a world-class sprinter who won a silver medal (behind American superstar Jesse Owens) in the 200 meters at the 1936 Olympics in Berlin, Germany—Robinson earned varsity letters in football, baseball, basketball, and track at John Muir Technical High School.

After graduating from high school in 1937, Robinson continued to pile up athletic achievements at Pasadena Junior College before transferring to the University of California, Los Angeles (UCLA) in 1939. Robinson became the first athlete in UCLA history to earn varsity letters in four sports (football, basketball, baseball, and track) in a single year. He earned All-American honors as a running back on the Bruins' undefeated football team, led the Pacific Coast Conference in scoring as a guard on the basketball team, and won the 1940 collegiate national championship in long jump. Robinson's performance in his single season of baseball was the least impressive, as he posted a weak .095 batting average while playing shortstop for the Bruins.

In 1941 Robinson ran into financial difficulties and had to leave UCLA without earning a degree. He went to Hawaii to play semi-professional football and work in construction. He returned to California shortly before the December 1941 Japanese attack on Pearl Harbor convinced the United States to enter World War II. Robinson then enlisted in the U.S. Army and was assigned to a segregated unit at Fort Riley, Kansas, where he successfully protested against a policy that prohibited black soldiers from becoming officers. He completed officer training and was commissioned as a lieutenant in 1943.

While stationed at Fort Hood, Texas, Robinson was involved in a racially charged incident that threatened to end his military career. When a bus driver on the base ordered Robinson to move to the back of the bus to make room for white soldiers, he refused to leave his seat. Robinson then faced a court martial for willful disobedience and conduct unbecoming an officer. Thanks to intervention by civil rights organizations and black-owned newspapers, though, Robinson was exonerated on all charges. He left the service in 1944 with an honorable discharge.

Shatters Baseball's Color Barrier

In 1945 Robinson played professional baseball for the Kansas City Monarchs of the Negro National League. He had a great season, batting .387 and earning a spot as starting shortstop for the annual East-West All-Star Game. Like much of the rest of American society, organized baseball was segregated by race at that time. A longstanding "color barrier" prohibited black ballplayers from playing for Major League Baseball teams or their minor-league affiliates. Branch Rickey, president and part-owner of the Brooklyn Dodgers, was determined to change this unfair system. After scouting the Negro Leagues and various international leagues, he identified Robinson as the ideal subject for a "noble experiment" in baseball integration.

A short time later, the two men discussed Rickey's scheme in a three-hour meeting. Rickey made Robinson promise not to retaliate, no matter how much racial hostility he might encounter as the first black player in the majors. Robinson realized that fighting back would inflame the passions of African-American spectators and confirm the dire predictions of critics, while passive resistance would increase public support for integration. "It was one thing for me out there on the playing field to be able to keep my cool in the face of insults," he acknowledged. "But it was another for all those black people sitting in the stands to keep from overreacting when they sensed a racial slur or an unjust decision. They could have blown the whole bit to hell by acting belligerently and touching off a race riot. That would have been all the bigots needed to set back the cause of black men in sports another hundred years."[3]

After spending one season with the Montreal Royals, the Dodgers' top minor-league affiliate, Robinson made his historic major-league debut on April 15, 1947. Robinson faced resistance from some of his teammates and endured vicious verbal and physical abuse from opposing players and fans. He withstood this ordeal with courage and determination, however, and never wavered in the commitment he made to Rickey not to retaliate. "I had to fight hard against loneliness, abuse, and the knowledge that any mistake I made would be magnified because I was the only black man out there," Robinson remembered. "I had to fight hard to become 'just another guy.' I had to deny my true fighting spirit so that the 'noble experiment' could succeed.… But I never cared about acceptance as much as I cared about respect."[4]

After shattering baseball's color barrier in 1947, Robinson batted .297, led the league in stolen bases, and received Rookie of the Year honors. He went on to have a spectacular ten-year career with the Dodgers, highlighted by six National League pennants, six All-Star Game appearances, and Most Valuable Player honors in 1949. Robinson also led the Dodgers to the World Series championship in 1955. His daring decision to steal home in Game 1 set the tone for the entire series, in which the Dodgers finally defeated their hated rivals, the New York Yankees, in seven games.

Robinson's electrifying performance on the field brought him the respect of fans and teammates, while his strength in overcoming obstacles helped make him a symbol of hope for millions of Americans. His trailblazing career and on-field exploits—.311 batting average, 1,518 hits, 137 home runs, 947 runs scored, 734 RBIs, 197 stolen bases, and .983 fielding percentage—enabled him to win election to the National Baseball Hall of Fame in his first year of eligibility in 1962. He was the first African-American player ever to be inducted. "Robinson could hit and bunt and steal and run," Roger Kahn wrote in *The Boys of Summer*. "He had intimidation skills, and he burned with a dark fire. He wanted passionately to win. He bore the burden of a pioneer and the weight made him stronger. If one can be certain of anything in baseball, it is that we shall not look upon his like again."[5]

Becomes a Notable Civil Rights Activist

Following his retirement from baseball at the end of the 1956 season, Robinson became a business executive with the Chock Full o' Nuts restaurant chain. He also wrote a newspaper column, hosted a radio show, and provided commentary for sports telecasts. In 1965 he launched the Freedom National Bank in New York City, which provided loans to help black entrepreneurs start up small business ventures. He also established a construction company to build affordable housing for working families.

Robinson expanded his involvement in the civil rights movement after his baseball career ended. He gave speeches and raised money to support the National Association for the Advancement of Colored People (NAACP), for instance, and organized an annual jazz concert to benefit various causes. Robinson attended the 1963 March on Washington, where the Reverend Martin Luther King Jr. presented his famous "I Have a Dream" speech, and kept up a lively correspondence with presidents and other public figures on the topic of civil rights. His status as an early pioneer in the fight for racial equality gave him tremendous credibility and influence within the movement.

Throughout his post-baseball years, Robinson suffered from health problems related to diabetes. He died of a heart attack at his home in Stamford, Connecticut, on October 24, 1972, at the age of fifty-three. He was survived by his wife, Rachel Isum Robinson, and two children, daughter Sharon and son David. His eldest son, Jackie Jr., had been killed in an automobile accident a year earlier.

Robinson made an enduring impact on the game of baseball and on American society. He opened the door for other black athletes to make their mark in professional sports, inspired millions of African Americans to break down barriers to participation in other aspects of life, and forced white Americans to confront their prejudices and change their attitudes about race. "[Integrating Major League Baseball] was earth-shattering," explained former president Bill Clinton. "It was a milestone for sports, but also a milestone in the fifty-year effort that really began at the end of World War II to change America's attitudes on the question of race. It was not long after that President Truman signed an order to desegregate the military.... A whole series of things happened and they were triggered by Jackie Robinson."[6]

Robinson's legacy has been honored in many ways over the years. His widow established the Jackie Robinson Foundation in 1973 to provide scholarships and other assistance to help underprivileged youth to attend college. In 1984 Robinson posthumously received the Presidential Medal of Freedom, which is the nation's highest civilian honor. In 1997 his uniform number 42 was permanently retired by every team in Major League Baseball, and in 2005 MLB designated April 15 of every year as Jackie Robinson Day, to be marked with special events and celebrations at stadiums across the country.

Sources

"Jackie Robinson: The Official Website." Retrieved from http://www.jackierobinson.com/about/bio.html.
Rampersad, Arnold. *Jackie Robinson: A Biography.* New York: Random House, 1997.
Robinson, Jackie. *I Never Had It Made: An Autobiography.* Hopewell, NJ: Echo Press, 1995.
Tygiel, Jules. *Baseball's Great Experiment: Jackie Robinson and His Legacy.* New York: Vintage Books, 1984.

Notes

[1] Quoted in Rampersad, Arnold. *Jackie Robinson: A Biography.* New York: Random House, 1997.

[2] Quoted in Rampersad.

[3] Robinson, Jackie. *I Never Had It Made: An Autobiography.* Hopewell, NJ: Echo Press, 1995.

[4] Quoted in Newman, Mark. "MLB Celebrates Robinson's Enduring Impact." MLB.com, April 14, 2011. Retrieved from http://mlb.mlb.com/news/article.jsp?ymd=20110414&content_id=17767716&c_id=mlb.

[5] Kahn, Roger. *The Boys of Summer.* New York: Harper and Row, 1972, p. xix.

[6] Quoted in Bodley, Hal. "No Measuring Robinson's Impact." MLB.com, April 15, 2010. Retrieved from http://mlb.mlb.com/news/article.jsp?ymd=20100415&content_id=9331356&vkey=news_mlb&fext=.jsp&c_id=mlb.

Rachel Robinson (1922-)
Wife of Jackie Robinson and President of the Jackie Robinson Foundation

Rachel Robinson was born as Rachel Annetta Isum on July 19, 1922, in Los Angeles, California. She was one of three children born to Charles Raymond Isum and Zellee Isum. She grew up as part of a close-knit extended family that had already lived in Los Angeles for a generation. As a girl Rachel enjoyed walking to museums, violin lessons, and family gatherings. "Within a two-mile radius, I had everything I needed to support my growth," she recalled. "The church was central to our social activities. It wasn't something where you needed to have money or any social resources."[1]

After graduating from Manual Arts High School in 1940, Rachel entered the University of California at Los Angeles (UCLA) to study nursing. During her freshman year she could not help but notice a handsome African-American senior, Jack Roosevelt Robinson, who had recently become the first athlete to earn a varsity letter in four sports in the same year at UCLA. "He was big, he was broad-shouldered, he was very attractive physically, and he had pigeon toes you couldn't miss," she remembered. "He was also proud of his color, which was something many of us didn't have at that age. . . . There was a kind of dignity about him and a sense of purpose that attracted me."[2]

The two began dating and soon got engaged. While Rachel completed her nursing degree and worked as a riveter in an aircraft factory, Jackie served in the U.S. military during World War II. Once the war ended, Jackie signed a contract to play professional baseball in the Negro Leagues for the Kansas City Monarchs. His performance on the field, as well as his reputation as an upstanding citizen off the field, attracted the attention of Brooklyn Dodgers president Branch Rickey, who was looking for an ideal person to become the first black player in Major League Baseball. Following a three-hour meeting in the fall of 1945, Rickey signed Robinson to a contract with the Dodgers' top minor-league affiliate, the Montreal Royals. A few months later, in February 1946, Jackie and Rachel Robinson were married. They would eventually have three children: Jackie Jr., Sharon, and David.

Supports the "Noble Experiment"

After spending one season with the Royals, Jackie made his historic debut with the Dodgers on April 15, 1947, shattering Major League Baseball's long-standing color barrier. Rachel stood by her husband's side throughout this often difficult ordeal. She supported him as he faced racially motivated abuse from opposing players and fans, and she endured discrimination in cities and stadiums across the country during the era of segregation. "She was not simply the dutiful little wife. She was Jack's co-pioneer," wrote journalist and civil rights activist Roger Wilkins. "She had to live through the death threats, endure the vile screams of the fans, and watch her husband get knocked down by pitch after pitch. And because he was under the strictest discipline not to fight, spike, curse, or spit back, she was the one who had to absorb everything he brought home. She was beautiful and wise and replenished his strength and courage."[3]

Throughout Jackie's ten-year career with the Dodgers, Rachel attended as many games as possible. Although she found it difficult to hold her tongue in the face of vicious name calling and race baiting, she felt it was important to bear witness to her husband's experiences so that she could provide much-needed understanding and support. "My most profound instinct as Jack's wife was to protect him—an impossible task," she noted. "I would, however, be a consistent presence to witness and validate the realities, love him without reservation, share his thoughts and miseries, discover with him the humor in the ridiculous behavior against us, and, most of all, help maintain our fighting spirit. I knew our only chance to survive was to be ourselves."[4] Rachel always tried to comfort her husband during the drive back from the stadium, so that their home would remain a sanctuary from the tensions of baseball integration.

Thanks to Jackie's courage and Rachel's support, Rickey's "noble experiment" turned out to be a tremendous success. Robinson went on to become the first African-American player inducted into the National Baseball Hall of Fame, and his achievements helped open the door for a new generation of black athletes in baseball and other professional sports. "I think the lesson for us is: if you have an overriding goal, a big goal that you're trying to achieve, there are times when you must transcend the obstacles that are being put in your way. Rise above them," Rachel stated. "Jack wanted to integrate athletics."[5] Jackie insisted that he could not have done it without Rachel by his side, "strong, loving, gentle, and brave, never afraid to either criticize or comfort me."[6]

Launches Her Own Career

While her husband maintained the busy travel schedule of a professional baseball player, Rachel relished her role as a homemaker. "Being home allowed me to enjoy my children and support their development," she explained. "I was one of those suburban mothers so often caricatured as a den mother, scout leader, the works: participating in neighborhood drives and causes; racing here and there with a car full of children to events, lessons, games; and present when they came home for talks, snacks, and homework." But when Jackie retired from baseball and became a business executive, and their youngest child went to school full time, she began pursuing her own career goals. "I needed to develop as a separate person with interests, skills, personal challenges, and victories all my own," she stated. "I was indeed buoyed by the changing role of women. I knew that what I wanted for myself wasn't aberrant and that women had the right to pursue their dreams."[7]

In 1959 Rachel earned a master's degree in psychiatric nursing from New York University. Over the next five years she worked as a psychiatric nurse, therapist, and medical researcher at the Albert Einstein College of Medicine. In 1965 she became an assistant professor at the Yale School of Nursing and director of nursing at the Connecticut Mental Health Center. Rachel also managed to find time to contribute to the civil rights movement during these years. When police in Birmingham, Alabama, threw the Reverend Martin Luther King Jr. and other peaceful protesters in jail in 1963, for example, she helped organize an outdoor jazz concert to raise bail money. The concert—held on the Robinsons' property in Stamford, Connecticut—became an annual event that benefitted many causes over the years.

Honors Her Husband's Legacy

The early 1970s proved to be a tough time emotionally for Rachel and her family. Her oldest son died in an automobile accident in 1971, and Jackie Robinson died from complications of diabetes in 1972. Rachel immediately began looking for ways to honor her husband's memory and legacy. One of her first acts was to establish the Jackie Robinson Development Corporation to build housing for low- and moderate-income families. She served as president of the company for ten years and oversaw the construction of more than 1,300 housing units.

In 1973 Rachel created the Jackie Robinson Foundation (JRF), a nonprofit organization aimed at helping deserving young people go to college. "It had to be more than just naming a building or a street for him," she explained. "It had to be something active, alive, and something in the area of education."[8] As of 2013, JRF had provided more than $22 million in scholarships to help more than 1,400 minority students graduate from colleges and universities across the country.

Rachel participated in many ceremonies honoring Jackie Robinson and the integration of baseball. She used each of these opportunities to spread her husband's message of racial justice and equality to new generations of Americans. "This [fiftieth] anniversary [of Jackie Robinson's debut]," she said at Dodger Stadium in 1997, "has given us an opportunity as a nation to celebrate together the triumphs of the past and the social progress that has occurred. It has also given us an opportunity to reassess the challenges of the present. It is my passionate hope that we can take this reawakened feeling of unity and use it as a driving force so that each of us can recommit to equality of opportunity for all Americans."[9]

Rachel also protected her husband's image by carefully controlling the manner in which his name, number, and likeness were used. She has turned down countless requests over the years, for instance, to produce a Jackie Robinson bobblehead doll. "If there's one thing that man always had, it was dignity," she stated. "I could not see Jack's head bouncing around."[10]

Receives Awards for Her Own Contributions

Rachel received a number of prestigious honors for her own involvement in breaking baseball's color barrier and promoting civil rights for all Americans. In 2007 MLB commissioner Bud Selig presented her with the Commissioner's Historic Achievement Award. "We give this great honor very rarely to people who have had a major impact on the sport," he explained. "She'll be the first person to receive it for what she has done off the field. But she's made an enormous impact. Jackie had her to talk to in 1947 and '48 during those extraordinary years. Their participation in the civil rights movement. Her work with the Robinson Foundation. She not only made baseball better, she made society better."[11] In 2009 Rachel received the UCLA Medal, the highest honor presented by her alma mater.

As she entered her ninth decade, Rachel Robinson offered the following advice for young people seeking to honor the legacy of Jackie Robinson in their own lives and make a difference in their own communities:

> I think at any age, one can look around in your own setting and
> in your own family and find ways to contribute to social change.

When you see attitudes that hurt others, or limit their opportunities, you can say to yourself: what is my part in this? Can I be a catalyst for change in my school, on my block, in my church, wherever I am? The question is: do I have a responsibility for others? I would say yes because I passionately believe that we are linked as human beings. Our destinies are intertwined. And what is happening to me ultimately is having an impact on you. So, if someone is homeless, uneducated, without medical care, without support, I have to feel some responsibility for them, and do whatever I can think to do. We all need to stand up and be counted.[12]

Sources

Chass, Murray. "And Cheers to You, Mrs. Robinson." *New York Times,* April 16, 1997. Retrieved from http://www.nytimes.com/1997/04/16/sports/and-cheers-to-you-mrs-robinson-eleganly.html?src=pm.

"Rachel Robinson, Founder." Jackie Robinson Foundation, n.d. Retrieved from http://www.jackierobinson.org/about/RachelRobinson.php.

Robinson, Rachel. *Jackie Robinson: An Intimate Portrait.* New York: Abrams, 1996.

Robinson, Sharon. *Promises to Keep: How Jackie Robinson Changed America.* New York: Scholastic, 2004.

Notes

1 Quoted in Libman, Gary. "Rachel Robinson's Homecoming." *Los Angeles Times,* September 2, 1987. Retrieved from http://articles.latimes.com/1987-09-02/news/vw-3579_1_house-today.

2 Quoted in Libman.

3 Quoted in "Ohio Wesleyan Honors Rachel Robinson with Branch Rickey Award." Ohio Wesleyan University, News and Media, January 12, 2011. Retrieved from http://news.owu.edu/2011/20110112-rickey Award.html.

4 Robinson, Rachel. *Jackie Robinson: An Intimate Portrait.* New York: Abrams, 1996, p. 52.

5 Quoted in "Interview with Rachel Robinson." Scholastic.com, February 11, 1998. Retrieved from http://www.scholastic.com/teachers/article/interview-rachel-robinson.

6 Robinson, Jackie. *I Never Had It Made.* Hopewell, NJ: Echo Press, 1995, p. xxiv.

7 Robinson, Rachel, pp. 144, 147.

8 Quoted in Lee, Cynthia. "Rachel Robinson to Receive UCLA's Highest Honor." *UCLA Today,* May 5, 2009. Retrieved from http://www.today.ucla.edu/portal/ut/rachel-robinson-to-receive-ucla-90830.aspx.

9 Quoted in Chass, Murray. "And Cheers to You, Mrs. Robinson." *New York Times,* April 16, 1997. Retrieved from http://www.nytimes.com/1997/04/16/sports/and-cheers-to-you-mrs-robinson-elegantly.html?src=pm.

10 Quoted in Kennedy, Kostya. "Keeper of the Flame." *Sports Illustrated,* April 16, 2012. Retrieved from http://sportsillustrated.cnn.com/vault/article/magazine/MAG1197112/3/index.htm.

11 Quoted in Bloom, Barry. "Commissioner Honors Rachel Robinson." MLB.com, April 15, 2007. Retrieved from http://mlb.mlb.com/news/article.jsp?ymd=20070415&content_id=1900049&vkey=news_mlb&fext=.jsp&c_id=mlb.

12 Quoted in "Interview with Rachel Robinson."

Wendell Smith (1914-1972)
Sportswriter Who Promoted Baseball Integration

Wendell John Smith was born on June 27, 1914, in Detroit, Michigan. He was a good athlete who played varsity baseball and basketball at Southeastern High School. As a sixteen-year-old pitcher in an American Legion baseball league, he led his team to a 1-0 victory in the championship game. A minor-league scout who attended the game told Smith that he would like to sign him to a contract, but that he was unable to do so because African-American players were not allowed in organized baseball. The scout ended up signing the losing pitcher instead. "That's when I decided that if I ever got into a position to do anything, I'd dedicate my life to getting Negro players into the big leagues,"[1] Smith remembered.

Smith attended West Virginia State University, where he was captain of the baseball team and editor of the student newspaper. After graduating with a bachelor's degree in physical education in 1937, he took a job as a sportswriter for the *Pittsburgh Courier,* a popular black-owned weekly newspaper. Smith's main beat was baseball. He covered Major League Baseball's Pittsburgh Pirates as well as the city's two Negro League teams, the Homestead Grays and Pittsburgh Crawfords. These all-black squads featured a number of future Hall of Famers, including catcher Josh Gibson, outfielder James "Cool Papa" Bell, infielders Buck Leonard and Judy Johnson, and pitcher Satchel Paige.

Advocates Baseball Integration

Watching these outstanding black players made Smith more determined than ever to end racial segregation in professional baseball. He wrote about the topic regularly in his newspaper column and argued his case from a number of different perspectives. Smith interviewed longtime commissioner of baseball Kenesaw Mountain Landis, for example, who claimed that there was no official policy in place prohibiting black players from joining the majors. Landis insisted that he left it up to team owners to decide when or whether to hire black players. Smith then conducted surveys of team owners, players, and fans and determined that a large majority of them supported integration. He also pointed out that black athletes and white athletes played with and against each other in other professional sports—and even in college baseball.

Once the United States entered World War II in 1941, and African-American soldiers made important contributions to the war effort, Smith called attention to the similarities between segregation in baseball and Nazi Germany's hateful treatment of minorities. "Big league baseball is perpetuating the very things thousands of Americans are overseas fighting to end, namely, racial discrimination and segregation,"[2] he wrote in a column published on July 25, 1942. Smith also chastised black baseball fans who attended major-league games in spite of the league's exclusionary policies. He declared that racial unity was essential to winning the fight against segregation.

Smith also used his columns to praise baseball insiders who voiced support for integration. One frequent recipient of his praise was Branch Rickey, the anti-segregationist president and part-owner of the Brooklyn Dodgers. "It appears to me that Branch Rickey, one of the wisest and shrewdest men in baseball, looms as a valuable friend," he wrote on April 28, 1945, "both for organized Negro baseball and the cause of the Negro player in the majors."[3]

When Rickey expressed interest in hiring a black player, Smith and fellow journalist Sam Lacy suggested Jackie Robinson, an outstanding collegiate athlete and military veteran who was then playing in the Negro Leagues. "Wendell and I had a friendly exchange," Lacy remembered. "He thought Jackie Robinson would be the best choice. We agreed Jackie wasn't the best player at the time, but was the most suitable player. He had played against white competition, was a college guy. So we went with Jackie. Wendell approached Branch Rickey first and got a promise from Branch to think about it."[4]

Covers Robinson's Rookie Season

Rickey ended up taking their advice. After scouting Robinson on the field and meeting with him in person, Rickey signed the Negro League star to a historic contract with the Dodgers' top minor-league team in late 1945. Following a successful season in the minors, Robinson made his major-league debut with the Dodgers on April 15, 1947, finally breaking Major League Baseball's long-standing color barrier.

Delighted with this turn of events, Smith was determined to do everything in his power to ensure that Rickey's "noble experiment" succeeded. He accompanied Robinson throughout his rookie season with the Dodgers and carefully controlled the media coverage of his experiences. When the Dodgers traveled to ballparks in the segregated South, where blacks were not allowed to stay in the same hotels or eat in the same restaurants as whites, Smith arranged for alternative accommodations for himself and Robinson. "When I think back [on] all we went through," Smith recalled, "it's hard to conceive. Going into a town and finding a decent place to stay was not easy in those days. Eating in the places we ate, second and third rate. Always having this stigma hanging over your head. But I knew Jackie would make it. And I knew if he made it things had to open up [for other black ballplayers]."[5]

Smith also emphasized the positive aspects of Robinson's experience in his reporting. He often wrote about opposing players and fans who were friendly and supportive toward Robinson, for instance, and he downplayed the verbal and physical abuse that Robinson received. Smith portrayed Robinson as a regular player who was just trying to earn a living and help his team win, with the goal of helping fans identify with and accept him. Since Smith was close to Robinson and often roomed with him on road trips, he became a resource for other reporters looking for stories about the first black player in the major leagues. Smith provided quotations and anecdotes that helped defuse potential controversies and shape the positive public perception of Robinson. "I always tried to keep it from becoming a flamboyant, highly militant thing," he explained. "And I think that's why it succeeded."[6] His friendship with Robinson led to Smith co-authoring the player's autobiography, *Jackie Robinson, My Own Story*, released in 1948.

Breaks Barriers of His Own

Later that year, Smith accepted a position with the *Chicago Herald-American*, becoming the first black reporter for a national white-owned newspaper. "When he came to Chicago to write, he told the Hearst people [owners of the newspaper], 'I will not be your black writer,'" remembered Smith's wife, Wyonella. "'I'm not going to just write about blacks in sports. If you want me to be a sportswriter here I'm going to write about all sports, and I'm going to do it fairly.'"[7] Smith covered boxing as well as baseball during his fifteen years with the paper.

Smith also continued his fight to end segregation in sports and in society. On January 23, 1961, he published a front-page story entitled "Spring Training Woes" that exposed the unfair treatment of black major-leaguers in Florida during the annual pre-season preparations. While white players stayed in some of the finest hotels in the state and ate in gourmet restaurants, black players were forced to sleep and eat in separate, inferior facilities. Smith revealed the "growing feeling of resentment" among black stars like Hank Aaron, Willie Mays, and Ernie Banks as they suffered "embarrassment, humiliation, and even indignities"[8] during spring training. His article led directly to the desegregation of Florida hotels and restaurants patronized by big-league ball clubs.

Smith left the *Chicago Herald-American* in 1964 to become a sports anchor for the WGN television network. He also wrote a weekly column for the *Chicago Sun-Times*. Smith died of cancer at the age of fifty-eight on November 26, 1972—only a month after his friend Jackie Robinson's passing. Smith received a number of posthumous honors for his role in baseball integration. The Baseball Writers Association of America presented him with its prestigious J. G. Taylor Spink Award in 1993, for example, and the following year he was enshrined in the writers wing of the National Baseball Hall of Fame.

Smith is remembered as a forceful early advocate of civil rights. "What Smith did as effectively as anyone was to point out that discrimination in organized baseball symbolized the dubious status of blacks in American society," wrote historian David K. Wiggins. "Smith expressed the feeling that until blacks could participate fully in the national game, they could not lay claim to the rights of a full-fledged citizen. He made it clear that the campaign was not merely a fight to wear a baseball uniform. It was a struggle for status, a struggle to take democracy off of parchment and give it life.... Smith believed that the desegregation of baseball would give blacks a new sense of dignity and self-esteem, ingredients that were not only inspiring in and of themselves, but necessary components to the ultimate destruction of discrimination in this country."[9]

Sources

Robinson, Jackie, as told to Wendell Smith. *Jackie Robinson, My Own Story.* Whitefish, MT: Kessinger, 2007.

Schall, Andrew. "Wendell Smith: The Pittsburgh Journalist Who Made Jackie Robinson Mainstream." *Pittsburgh Post-Gazette,* March 29, 2012. Retrieved from http://www.post-gazette.com/stories/opinion/perspectives/the-next-page-wendell-smith-the-pittsburgh-journalist-who-made-jackie-robinson-mainstream-300714/#ixzz20EuBK2v8.

Wiggins, David K. "Wendell Smith, the Pittsburgh Courier-Journal, and the Campaign to Include Blacks in Organized Baseball, 1933-1945." *Journal of Sport History,* Summer 1983. Retrieved from http://www.la84foundation.org/SportsLibrary/JSH/JSH1983/JSH1002/jsh1002b.pdf.

Notes

[1] Quoted in Schall, Andrew. "Wendell Smith: The Pittsburgh Journalist Who Made Jackie Robinson Mainstream." *Pittsburgh Post-Gazette,* March 29, 2012. Retrieved from http://www.post-gazette.com/stories/opinion/perspectives/the-next-page-wendell-smith-the-pittsburgh-journalist-who-made-jackie-robinson-mainstream-300714/#ixzz20EuBK2v8.

[2] Quoted in Wiggins, David K. "Wendell Smith, the *Pittsburgh Courier-Journal*, and the Campaign to Include Blacks in Organized Baseball, 1933-1945." *Journal of Sport History,* Summer 1983, p. 16. Retrieved from http://www.la84foundation.org/SportsLibrary/JSH/JSH1983/JSH1002/jsh1002b.pdf.

[3] Quoted in Wiggins, p. 27.

[4] Quoted in Mayo, Jonathan. "Ink-tegration: Writers Lacy, Smith Played Big Role in Baseball Integration." MLB.com, February 2002. Retrieved from http://mlb.mlb.com/mlb/history/mlb_negro_leagues_story.jsp?story=lacysmith.

[5] Quoted in Holtzman, Jerome. "How Wendell Smith Helped Robinson's Cause." *Chicago Tribune,* March 31, 1997. Retrieved from http://articles.chicagotribune.com/1997-03-31/sports/9703310169_1_clyde-sukeforth-jackie-robinson-kansas-city-monarchs.

[6] Quoted in Schall.

[7] Quoted in Schall.

[8] Quoted in Carroll, Brian. "Wendell Smith's Last Crusade: The Desegregation of Spring Training, 1961." In Simons, William, ed. *The 13th Annual Cooperstown Symposium on Baseball and American Culture.* Jefferson City, NC: McFarland, 2001. Retrieved from http://www.cubanxgiants.com/J242.htm.

[9] Wiggins, p. 28.

Tom Yawkey (1903-1976)
Owner of the Boston Red Sox, the Last Major League Team to Integrate

Tom Yawkey was born as Thomas Austin on February 21, 1903, in Detroit, Michigan. Orphaned in his early teens, Tom was adopted by his maternal uncle, William Hoover Yawkey, and took the name Thomas Austin Yawkey. The elder Yawkey was a wealthy industrialist with extensive business interests in lumber, mining, and oil. He also owned the Detroit Tigers baseball franchise for several years in the early 1900s. Tom enjoyed a privileged upbringing in Michigan, New York, and Connecticut. As a boy, he loved baseball and got the chance to meet some of his favorite players, including future Hall of Famer Ty Cobb.

Yawkey attended the Irving School in Tarrytown, New York, where he was a star athlete. He went on to earn a bachelor's degree in mining engineering and chemistry from Yale University in 1925. Upon graduation, Yawkey went to work in the family business empire. Over the next few years, he earned a reputation as an innovative executive. In 1933, when he reached the age of thirty, Yawkey inherited his uncle's fortune, which was estimated at $40 million. The avid outdoorsman also received title to a 50,000-acre property along the coast of South Carolina, which he turned into a hunting, fishing, and bird-watching retreat.

Purchases the Boston Red Sox

Shortly after gaining access to his trust fund, Yawkey fulfilled his lifelong dream of owning a big-league baseball team by purchasing the Boston Red Sox for $1.5 million. The franchise had entered a long downhill slide in 1919, when it had traded legendary slugger Babe Ruth to the rival New York Yankees. In 1932—the year before Yawkey took over the reins—the struggling team had lost 111 games. Yawkey immediately demonstrated his willingness to spend money in order to return the Red Sox to greatness. He hired former player Eddie Collins to manage the team, brought in a number of talented veteran players, spent another $1.5 million to renovate Fenway Park (the home stadium of the Red

Sox), and established a minor-league farm system that eventually turned out such greats as Ted Williams.

Yawkey's rebuilding program led to significant improvements in the team's record. Boston became a contender within a few years, finishing second in the American League (AL) to the Yankees in 1938, 1939, 1941, and 1942. In 1944 Yawkey married Jean R. Hollander. Two years later, under new manager Joe Cronin, the Red Sox finally captured the AL pennant. Yawkey's dream of winning an MLB championship remained unfulfilled, however, as his team lost the World Series to the St. Louis Cardinals in seven games.

Yawkey remained the sole owner of the Red Sox for forty-four years—the longest stretch of any team owner in baseball history. Throughout that period, he gained a reputation as a kind and generous man who was well-liked by his players and staff. Unlike most of his fellow team owners, Yawkey paid his coaches and players above-average salaries and rarely haggled over the details of contracts. He also became a father figure to many of his players and often helped those in need. Most of all, Yawkey was the number-one fan of his team, and his enthusiasm helped revive fan interest in the Red Sox and turn Boston into a loyal baseball city.

Resists Baseball Integration

The main blot on Yawkey's long tenure as owner of the Red Sox was his resistance to integration. Boston was the last team in Major League Baseball (MLB) to add an African-American player to its roster. The first black player to take the field for the Red Sox, Pumpsie Green, did not do so until 1959—twelve years after Jackie Robinson broke baseball's color barrier, and three years after Robinson retired from the game. During the 1950s, as other franchises signed former Negro League stars, Yawkey's refusal to sign black players made the Red Sox less competitive. After challenging for the pennant in 1948 and 1949, the Red Sox languished in the standings through most of the next decade.

The Red Sox had ample opportunities to hire talented black players during this time. In fact, Yawkey could have signed Jackie Robinson in 1945, several months before he joined the Brooklyn Dodgers. Toward the end of World War II, many civil rights advocates were fighting to end the segregation of organized baseball, including sportswriter Wendell Smith of the *Pittsburgh Courier* and Boston city councilman Isadore Muchnick. They pressured Red Sox management to allow Negro League players to try out for the team, and Yawkey reluctantly agreed.

Three black baseball stars—Robinson of the Kansas City Monarchs, Marvin Williams of the Philadelphia Stars, and Sam Jethroe of the Cleveland Buckeyes— arrived in Boston in April 1945 with high hopes. These hopes were soon dashed, however, as the Red Sox repeatedly postponed the promised tryout, day after day, for a week. When the three players were finally allowed inside Fenway Park, the tryout lasted less than an hour, with only one Red Sox coach and no other staff or players present. Although all three players showed impressive skills, none ever heard from the Red Sox again. "Robinson himself was satisfied with his performance," wrote baseball historian Glenn Stout, "although by the time he left Fenway he was smoldering about what he felt to be a humiliating charade."[1]

As Boston maintained its all-white roster deep into the 1950s, many observers branded Yawkey a racist. The Red Sox owner rarely discussed baseball integration or his attitudes with regard to race. His coaches and front-office staff, however, denied that prejudice was involved. They claimed that Boston's scouts could not find any African-American prospects who met their standards, for example, or insisted that the best black players preferred to remain in the Negro Leagues. They also expressed concern that the Red Sox's minor-league affiliates played in the South, where the racial atmosphere might be uncomfortable or unsafe for black players.

Robinson, for one, did not buy these arguments. He blamed Yawkey directly, arguing that the team owner had the power to integrate the Red Sox at any time if he wanted to do so. In a January 1959 interview with the *Chicago Defender*, Robinson argued that if Yawkey had hired a few African-American players during the 1950s, "maybe he would have won another pennant or two."[2] Years later, Yawkey finally addressed the controversy. "I have no feeling against colored people," he told *Sports Illustrated*. "I employ a lot of them [at my winter estate] in the South. But they are clannish, and when that story got around that we didn't want Negroes they all decided to sign with some other club. Actually, we scouted them right along, but we didn't want one because he was a Negro. We wanted a ballplayer."[3]

Leaves a Legacy

Yawkey served as vice president of the American League from 1956 to 1973. His Red Sox won the AL pennant in 1967 and 1975, but lost the World Series in seven games both seasons. Yawkey died of leukemia on July 9, 1976, in Boston, Massachusetts. On his passing, many of his current and former players expressed deep affection for him. "I feel so badly I don't know what to say," said Hall of Famer Ted Williams. "He had a heart as big as a watermelon. I loved the man from the bottom of my heart. He was unselfish, fair, sincere, and honest."[4] Yawkey's place in baseball history was secured in 1980, when he was inducted into the National Baseball Hall of Fame. Yawkey's widow, Jean, retained ownership of the Red Sox until her death in 1992.

During his lifetime, Yawkey contributed generously to a number of causes, including the Boys and Girls Clubs, the Dana-Farber Cancer Institute, and the Georgetown Memorial Hospital in South Carolina. His will granted thirty square miles of land to the state of South Carolina to establish the Tom Yawkey Wildlife Center. This pristine natural area consists of marshes, wetlands, forests, and beaches that are preserved for waterfowl, turtles, alligators, and other wildlife.

Sources

Bryant, Howard. *Shut Out: A Story of Race and Baseball in Boston.* Boston: Houghton Mifflin, 2002.

Stout, Glenn. "Tryout and Fallout: Race, Jackie Robinson and the Red Sox." *Massachusetts Historical Review,* Volume 6, 2004. Retrieved from http://indiepro.com/glenn/tryout-and-fallout-race-jackie-robinson-and-the-red-sox/.

Stout, Glenn, and Richard A. Johnson. *Red Sox Century.* Boston: Houghton Mifflin, 2000.

"Thomas A. Yawkey." Yawkey Foundations, 2012. Retrieved from http://yawkeyfoundation.org/thomas_yawkey.html.

Notes

[1] Stout, Glenn. "Tryout and Fallout: Race, Jackie Robinson and the Red Sox." *Massachusetts Historical Review,* Volume 6, 2004. Retrieved from http://indiepro.com/glenn/tryout-and-fallout-race-jackie-robinson-and-the-red-sox/.

[2] Quoted in Stout.

[3] Quoted in Mann, Jack. "The Great Wall of Boston." *Sports Illustrated,* June 28, 1965. Retrieved from http://sportsillustrated.cnn.com/vault/article/magazine/MAG1077374/1/index.htm.

[4] Quoted in "Nice Guys Don't Always Finish Last." The Deadball Era, n.d. Retrieved from http://thedeadballera.com/NiceGuys_Yawkey_Tom.htm.

PRIMARY SOURCES

Sportswriter Wendell Smith Promotes Baseball Integration

Wendell Smith, a sportswriter and columnist for the Pittsburgh Courier, *worked for many years to generate public support for the integration of Major League Baseball. As part of this effort, he conducted extensive interviews and surveys of players, coaches, team owners, and fans to determine their attitudes about allowing black players in the majors. In 1939 Smith interviewed Ford Frick, the president of the National League, and published excerpts of their conversation in the newspaper article reprinted below. Frick insists that there is no formal color line in baseball, and he claims that the big leagues will welcome black players whenever American society seems ready to accept their presence.*

Ford Frick, President of the National League, told us in an exclusive interview Sunday morning that major league baseball is willing to accept Negro ball players today!

Aroused early Sunday morning in his luxurious suite at Pittsburgh's William Penn Hotel, the former school teacher, ex-New York and Colorado sports writer and radio broadcaster, gave us the major league's angle on the most widely-discussed question in the sports world today.

The National League chief is a tall, lanky individual. Easy to approach. A willing conversationalist. Along with Kenesaw Landis, baseball's high commissioner, and William Harridge, president of the American League, Frick is one of the "Big Three" of the national pastime.

Says General Public Not Educated to the Idea

"Many baseball fans are of the opinion that major league baseball does not want Negro players," commented Frick, "but that is not true. We have always been interested in Negro players, but have not used them because we feel the general public has not been educated to the point where they will accept them on the same standard as they do the white player."

The National League president went on to say that he believes the time is near when Negro players will be starring on big league teams.

"The big leagues," he said, "are in the same position as newspapers. We cannot do anything we want to until public opinion is ready for it."

Frick said there are many problems that must be ironed out before Negroes would be accepted in the big leagues.

"A ball club spends six weeks in the deep South and have the season on the road," he pointed out, "and there are many places where we could not take a Negro player because of social problems. Such situations bring about embarrassment and dissatisfaction for all concerned."

Frick doubted that in places where the color line is drawn it would be advisable to separate the players.

"A ball club must be a unit. The only way a manager can develop team spirit is to keep his men together as much as possible, especially on the road. It would also mean that ball players who were not broadminded would take advantage of the situation and use it to further their own cause. It might go so far as to demoralize a winning team."

Majors Interested in Colored Leagues

Asked just what attitude the major leagues had toward Negro leagues, Frick assured us that it was very interested in the various sepia diamond organizations.

We pointed out that Negro baseball was having a difficult time making ends meet because of major league competition and financial problems. We asked if the majors would possibly give Negro baseball a helping hand if approached.

"As far as I know," Frick replied, "we have never been approached from that angle, but I think we could give them some valuable advice if they wanted it. We certainly would like to see the Negro Leagues prosper."

The National League prexy went on to name numerous cities where sepia baseball could flourish if handled in the right manner.

"Cities like New York, Chicago, Philadelphia, Detroit, and a number of Southern towns have Negro populations capable of supporting ball clubs easily," he said.

Returning to the question of the Negro player in big league baseball, Frick said that there is no written law against the sepia player. He said that baseball is biding its time and waiting for the social change, which is inevitable.

"I think that in the near future people will be willing to accept the Negro ball player just as they have the Negro boxer and college athlete. Times are changing."

Recalls Noble Sissle and Indiana Incident

Frick pointed out a particular incident which happened when he was a basketball player at DePauw University as an example of the gradual social change.

"We had a very well-mannered player on the basketball team by the name of Noble Sissle, who is now a great orchestra leader. We were playing a game in Richmond, Indiana one night and before game time decided to get a bite to eat. We went to a restaurant and ordered our meals. When the owner saw Noble Sissle he refused to serve him. Angry, we all got up and walked out."

Frick said that he does not believe they would refuse a Negro today under similar circumstances.

"It is a distasteful problem, but one we must face. I am sure that any of the major league managers would use a colored player if he thought the fans in his particular city would stand for it. There was a time when Jewish players were not wanted. Johnny Kling, famous old catcher, was one of the first Jewish boys in baseball and he was treated very poorly at first. Now, the Jewish players are just as popular as any of the others."

Many Sepias Capable of Playing in Majors

Commenting on Negro baseball, Frick stated that he had seen a number of sepia players capable of making major league teams.

"One I remember rather well is Satchel Paige," he said, "and there are others whose names I do not know off hand."

Frick said that no plans had been formulated by the majors to include the Negro leagues in their one hundredth celebration of baseball this year.

"This celebration is not a major league affair, but one of the fans, players and everyone concerned with baseball," he told us. "We are anxious to see all groups and individuals celebrate. Organized baseball is celebrating in its own particular way. We have not agreed to foster any programs for colleges or other institutions. However, we would be willing to give the Negro leagues suggestions as to how to develop a similar celebration program. After all, this is not our game, baseball is everybody's game."

Before departing, we jumped back on the question of Negroes in the majors, asking the National head if he would venture to say how long it will be before sepia players are admitted into the big leagues.

"I can not name any particular day or year, but assure you that when the people ask for the inclusion of your players we will use them. I do not think the time is far off and with constant crusading by the press of both races it is bound to come. However, you must keep fighting. Never let the issue die, because there is no way to measure public opinion. It may change tomorrow."

Frick, whose speech is typical of the mid-westerner, refused to make any predictions as to the outcome of the 1939 National League race, but said that New York, Pittsburgh, Chicago, Cincinnati and Brooklyn look like the teams to beat, and that it is bound to be a close race.

Source

Smith, Wendell. "Says Organized Baseball Willing to Accept Colored Players." *Pittsburgh Courier,* February 25, 1939, p. 1.

The Sporting News Supports Segregation in Baseball

As civil rights activists and progressive sportswriters like Wendell Smith promoted the integration of Major League Baseball in the years surrounding World War II, they faced opposition from baseball commissioner Kenesaw Mountain Landis, team owners, and the mainstream media. In the following editorial, published on August 6, 1942, The Sporting News expresses its support for maintaining separate professional baseball leagues for black and white players. The editors argue that baseball fans would never accept integration, and that integration would cause irreparable harm to the Negro Leagues.

There is no law against Negroes playing with white teams, nor whites with colored clubs, but neither has invited the other for the obvious reason they prefer to draw their talent from their own ranks and because the leaders of both groups know their crowd psychology and do not care to run the risk of damaging their own game. Other sports had their Joe Louis, Jesse Owens, Fritz Pollard, and like notables, respected and honored by all races, but they competed under different circumstances from those dominating in baseball.

The baseball fan is a peculiar creature. We believe no one will question that fact. He deems it his inalienable right and privilege to criticize and jeer in words that not always are the choicest or the most gentlemanly. Not even a Ted Williams or a Joe DiMaggio or a Babe Ruth is immune. It is not difficult to imagine what would happen if a player on a mixed team, performing before a crowd of the opposite color, should throw a bean ball, strike out with the bases full or spike a rival. Clear-minded men of tolerance of both races realize the tragic possibilities and have steered clear of such complications, because they realize it is to the benefit of each and also of the game.

However, there are agitators, ever ready to see an issue that will redound to their profit or self aggrandizement, who have sought to force Negro players on the big leagues, not because it would help the game, but because it gives them a chance to thrust themselves into the limelight as great crusaders in the guise of democracy. There would be as much point in the reverse being tried and an attempt made by Negro teams to bolster their lineups with white stars. It is not difficult to visualize what would happen in the latter case.

As it is, players of both races have been permitted to develop in their own environments and rise to the heights of stardom within their own circles. Proper tribute has been paid to Satchel Paige, for instance, as being a great pitcher. Whether he would be held in such esteem had he attempted to win his laurels elsewhere is problematical. The same is true of other Negro stars. They have blossomed forth with the inspiration of the encouragement and sympathy of their own followers. It is doubtful if the road would have been so easy, otherwise.

As a result, the country has a great Negro major league, which draws heavy support from the colored folk. If its ranks were raided by the American and National leagues, with their tremendous resources, it would have fewer stars and the caliber of ball which has made it an attraction would be so lowered that the Negro loop, of necessity, would sink to the status of an inferior minor circuit, with consequent decline in enthusiasm by fans and prestige of performers.

Organized Negro baseball has become a million-dollar business annually and is beginning to emerge from the red-ink stage into the profit column. It would be a staggering blow should its leading players be drawn into the majors and, with them, its fan support. It is doubtful if the colored game could survive. Instead of gaining anything, Negro baseball would lose everything and without a medium for developing talent there would be no players, in a short time, who could make the grade, even if given the opportunity, in the American or National, not to mention the minors.

Joe Bostic, sports columnist of the *People's Voice,* a Negro newspaper published in Harlem, commenting on the agitation, wrote: "While we are not against Negroes playing in the American or National leagues, at the very best, we are only lukewarm to the idea. Our reasons for this position are: (1) Our approach to the question is strictly mercenary; (2) We're deadly practical about the entire situation; (3) We're not convinced that the baseball played in the organized leagues necessarily represents the best caliber of ball played per se. We feel that the net results would be written in red ink on the ledgers of Negro baseball. On the second count of practicality, why subject any player to the humiliation and indignities associated with the problems of eating, sleeping and traveling in a layout dominated by prejudice-ridden southern whites?" And he might have added: "The criticism of sometimes-cruel and hot-headed fans."

Or take Candy Jim Taylor of the American Giants, who has been playing with and managing Negro teams for almost a half century. Taylor was quoted by Irv Kupcinet of the *Chicago Daily Times:* "We know there's no law against hiring colored boys in the majors. Just as there's no law against us hiring white boys for the American Giants. But we are going to stick to our colored boys and I know the majors are going to stick to the whites."

Of course, there are some colored people who take a different view, and they are entitled to their opinions, but in doing so they are not looking at the question from the broader point of view, or for the ultimate good of either the race or the individuals in it. They ought to concede their own people are now protected and that nothing is served by allowing agitators to make an issue of a question on which both sides would prefer to be let alone.

John P. Carmichael of the *Chicago Daily News* relates a story that is especially pertinent and probably expresses the sentiment of clear thinkers on both sides: "There's still the story of Joe Louis, one of our favorite guys of all time, being interviewed in his Chicago home the morning after he whipped Jim Braddock for the heavyweight championship of the world," wrote Carmichael. "As the talk progressed, the fumes of pork chops on the fire assailed the nostrils of both men. Each allowed as how he could do with some. Quick as a flash Louis set up a card table, arranged for one luncheon to be spread thereon. "'If you'll excuse me,' he told the reporter, 'I'm gonna have lunch with some friends in the kitchen. When we get through we'll talk some more.'"

Source

"No Good from Raising Race Issue" (editorial). *The Sporting News,* August 6, 1942, p. 4. Retrieved from http://www.baseball-fever.com/archive/index.php/t-90105.html.

A Ballplayer Shares Memories of the Negro Leagues

Retired bricklayer Jim Armstead played professional baseball during the era of segregation. He traveled around the country as a member of all-black barnstorming teams, and he also played in the Negro Leagues from 1939 to 1949. In the following memoir published in a special issue of Footsteps *magazine, Armstead shares some of his experiences as a young ballplayer.*

I grew up in Louisville, Kentucky. When I was young, we played softball. We had Negro softball teams then, too, that would travel and play games around the country. Later I played for some black semi-pro teams and then in the Negro Leagues. I played and managed for a number of different teams—the Baltimore Elites, the Philadelphia Stars, the New Orleans Creoles, the Cleveland Buckeyes, and the Indianapolis ABCs.

There was a sports promoter, named Abe Saperstein, who would come through the towns of the South looking for young black ball players to play on semi-pro teams he put together. He heard about me and asked if I would come play. I said, "Yes, okay." I'd play outfield mostly, but sometimes I would pitch. There would be ten or twelve of us on a team, and Saperstein would take us all up to Chicago, where he would rent two old Cadillac limousines and we would travel six apiece in these old limos. Of course you couldn't carry too much luggage, and it was kind of a rough life—one night you'd be here, then get in the car and drive on to the next town. We'd play at least one game every day, sometimes more.

Sometimes we'd play in big towns with minor-league parks. Other times we'd just play in town parks. After the game, we'd pass the hat among the spectators, and we'd probably make $8 or $9 of an evening. The owner of the team would take 40 percent, and the other 60 percent would be split among the players. You'd always drive as soon as the game was over, to make the next town in time for the next game. There was no time to practice—practice was the game.

Sundays you were either at a major- or a minor-league park in a large town. Sunday was the day you made your money. The rest of the time you were just playing for eating money—enough to exist on. You would always hope the weather was good on Sundays.

I quit playing the game in 1949. By then, I was too old, really, to be considered for the new integrated major leagues. I was tired of life on the road by then and I had a family to support. So I just gave it up and concentrated on my bricklaying.

At times, I miss baseball, but, you know, it was a tough way of life. And I never did understand why it took so long for the game to be integrated. I mean, we played against the white teams. After the World Series every fall, we'd play the white teams and, in the winter, white and black players went to Cuba and South America and played on the same teams. I just couldn't see it. It seemed to me that it was always that it's got to be some big white person that gives the okay and that's the only way things happen.

I don't go to baseball games. I never cared to go watch the game somehow, though I look at it on television. When I watch, I think about some of the players who are still around who spent their whole careers in the Negro Leagues, and what do they have to show for it? A small pension, but no insurance. And they don't have anything to fall back on, no occupation other than playing ball. That's another reason I left it. I wanted to build a career that would take care of me and my family. I don't know, it was a time of my life that was a long time ago now. Not much I can do with it now. But I kept the glove I played with.

Source

Hambleton, Vicki. "Jim Armstead: Memories of Playing in the Negro Leagues." *Footsteps*, March 2000, p. 36.

Branch Rickey Explains His Integration Plan

The innovative baseball executive who hired Jackie Robinson to become the first black player in the major leagues was Branch Rickey, president and part-owner of the Brooklyn Dodgers. Knowing that he must proceed carefully in order to successfully break the sport's longstanding color barrier, Rickey came up with a step-by-step plan designed to gradually win the support of team owners, fans, players, and the media. He explains his plan—as well as his views on race relations in the United States—in the following speech, which he presented to a group of African-American leaders in Atlanta, Georgia, in 1956.

D r. May, gentlemen—ladies and gentlemen. My plane doesn't leave until tomorrow at 10:35 A.M. and I haven't a thing to do between now and then but to talk if I get the chance—and I feel like talking.

I asked Mr. Lawson and several others today about my time limit, and I think I was rather insistent upon it—and I never did get a time limit and I just concluded that I would talk as long as I pleased. I don't know what time you gentlemen have engagements for tomorrow morning's work but I want to talk about a thing or two.

I feel a little remote—the speaking spot is not as close as I would like it. I should like to feel that each one of you were my guests tonight at my own home, and that I could talk to you just as I would if you were there. And I am going to try to maintain that attitude of mine from my remarks that I am very close to you and whether you may agree with what I have to say or not, you will know that I am trying to be intimately confidential and frank about my remarks.

Now I could talk at some length, of course, about the problem of hiring a negro ball player after an experience of 25 years in St. Louis—where at the end I had no stock at all in the club and no negro was permitted to buy his way into the grandstand during that entire period of my residence in St. Louis. The only place a negro could witness a ball game in St. Louis was to buy his way into the bleachers—the pavilion. With an experience of that kind in back of me, and having had sort of a "bringins up" that was a bit contrary to that regime— milieu—in St. Louis, I went to Brooklyn.

Within the first month in Brooklyn, I approached what I considered the number one problem in the hiring of a negro in professional baseball in this country. Now that is a story and that could be a fairly long speech. Namely, ownership. Ownership must be in line with you, and I was at that time an employee, not at that time a part owner of the club. And when ownership was passed, then five other things presented themselves. This is not my speech. I am just giving you this as a preliminary. But I want to get out of the road of this thing, and have you say that—well, I wish he had talked about that thing.

The second thing was to find the right man as a player. I spent $25,000 in all the Caribbean countries—in Puerto Rico, Cuba—employed two scouts, one for an entire year in Mexico, to find that the greatest negro players were in our own country.

Then I had to get the right man off the field. I couldn't come with a man to break down a tradition that had in it centered and concentrated all the prejudices of a great many people north and south unless he was good. He must justify himself upon the positive principle of merit. He must be a great player. I must not risk an excuse of trying to do something in the sociological field, or in the race field, just because of sort of a "holier than thou." I must be sure that the man was good on the field, but more dangerous to me, at that time, and even now, is the wrong man off the field. It didn't matter to me so much in choosing a man off the field that he was temperamental—righteously subject to resentments. I wanted a man of exceptional intelligence, a man who was able to grasp and control the responsibilities of himself to his race and could carry that load. That was the greatest danger point of all. Really greater than the number five in the whole six.

Number one was ownership, number two is the man on the field, number three the man off the field. And number four was my public relations, transportation, housing, accommodations here, embarrassments—feasibility. That required investigation and therein lies the speech. And the Cradle of Liberty in America was the last place to make and to give us generous considerations.

And the fifth one was the negro race itself—over-adulation, mass attendance, dinners, of one kind or another of such a public nature that it would have a tendency to create a solidification of the antagonisms and misunderstandings—over-doing it. And I want to tell you that the committee of 32—it was called, in Greater New York—eminent negro citizens, and Judge Kazansky, and my secretary and myself—those 32 men organized all eight cities in the National League and did a beautiful job of it. And for two years not one of those things was attempted or done and I never had any embarrassments in Brooklyn. They did have a great trainload of people go to see you play in Montreal and Buffalo and other places—and I tried to stop that but I was too late.

But the greatest danger, the greatest hazard, I felt was the negro race itself. Not people of this crowd any more than you would find antagonisms organized in a white crowd of this caliber either. Those of less understanding—those of a lower grade of education frankly. And that job was done beautifully under the leadership of a fine judge in New York who became a Chairman of an Executive Committee. That story has never been told. The meetings we had, two years of investigations—the Presidents of two of the negro colleges, the publisher of the *Pittsburgh Courier,* a very helpful gentleman he was to me, a professor of sociology in New York University, and a number of others, the LaGuardia Committee on Anti-Discrimination, Tom Dewey's Committee in support of the Quinn-Ives Law in New York state.

And sixth was the acceptance by his colleagues—by his fellow players. And that one I could not handle in advance. The other five over a period of two and one-half years, I worked very hard on it. I felt that the time was ripe, that there wouldn't be any reaction on the part of a great public if a man had superior skill, if he had intelligence and character and had patience and forbearance, and "could take it" as it was said here. I didn't make a mistake there. I have made mistakes, lots of mistakes.

A man of exceptional courage, and exceptional intelligence, a man of basically fine character, and he can thank his forbearers for a lot of it. He comes from the right sort of home, and I knew all this, and when somebody, somewhere, thinks in terms of a local athletic club not playing some other club because of the presence on the squad of a man of color. I am thinking that if an exhibition game were to be played in these parts against a team on whose squad was Jackie Robinson—even leaving out all of the principles of fair play, all the elements of equality and citizenship, all the economic necessities connected with it, all the violations of the whole form and conceptions of our Government from its beginning up to now—leave it all out of the picture, he would be depriving some of the citizens of his own community, some wonderful boys, from seeing an exhibition of skill and technique, and the great, beautiful, graciousness of a slide, the like of which they could not see from any other man in this country. And that's not fair to a local constituency.

I am wondering, I am compelled to wonder, how it can be. And at the breakfast, recently, when a morning paper's story was being discussed and my flaxen hair daughter said to me, "He surely didn't say it." I thought, yes it is understandable. It is understandable. And when a great United States Senator said to me some few days after that, "Do you know that the headlines in Egypt are terribly embarrassing to our State Department?" And then he told me, in part, a story whose utter truthfulness I have no reason to doubt, about the tremendous humiliation—"The Land of the Free and the Home of the Brave"—"where we are talking about extending to all civilizations, tremendous and beautiful freedoms, and the unavoidable, hypocritical position it puts us in internationally." "How could anybody do it," said my daughter.

That night we had a family discussion. It lasted a long time. My five daughters were there, mother was there, auntie was there, four sons-in-law were there—it was Christmas time. And I said to them what I want to say to you tonight. It is understandable that an American with a certain background, certain exposures in the field of education, would represent a more or less plausible inheritance in regard to the assimilation, the relationship, the acceptance in our current life of the negro.

The whole thing as a difference between the acceptance in Brazil, for instance, Spanish and Portuguese countries, and the British West Indies and America, a very remarkable thing, but understood by all historians and all writers on the subject. Portugal was the first one to import slaves from Africa—took them into Portugal. It was the last one to give up the slave trade. 19,000,000 go into one country alone in South America—imported slaves over a period of over four hundred years. Now, slavery antedated negro slavery—oh many years, really thousands of years, before any negro was taken out of Africa. It was an accident, a misfortune, a thing that could be remedied. All slavery throughout the centuries preceded African importation of slaves. It was the result of war, it was a result of debt. There were several things that led to it, but always there was manumission [granting freedom to slaves] in front of the man. Freedom obtainable. And the laws going back clear beyond Seneca, and Cicero refers to it—all the way through all those centuries, manumission was a comparatively easy thing. The law of that time, all of it—Plato, the Roman jurisprudence is based upon it, that you can become free. You may be a slave today—you can be a Moor, you can be a Greek, you can be a man of high intelligence. Slavery was a matter of accident or misfortune. And the Spanish Law, the Latin nations inherited that law both in its enactment and in its interpretation were favorable to manumission—making men free. It was not a matter of color at all and the law supported that and the importation of slaves into South America, and all of South America, into Mexico earlier, a few were there subsequently, and in all the Caribbean countries which are now predominant—all of it came in the line of probable manumission, so that when, say, 90% of all the slaves who had been

slaves came to be free in Brazil, for example. Then would come in the other importations and the other men who were slaves. There was a group of qualified free men to take care of the small number, 10%, who were slaves. That was Latin America.

They had no problems such as we had here in the south following the Civil War, where there was nobody to take care of a great number of free men and no previous free men in the colored race to adapt themselves to those conditions. And, of course, there was disgraceful governmental conduct. Now the difference, miracle that it is, mystery that it is, and yet greed at the bottom of it the slave trade was immensely profitable—Liverpool was, I was going to say, was built out of it, and America followed suit on it. And whereas the law that men are equal long before, I say, the negro came into the picture.

The church has always, and it has been a tendency of the Christian church too to undertake to establish the equality of all men in the sight of God. And to the extent which that prevailed to that extent it became inevitable that all men should ultimately become free. That was the greatest force in the world—to give every man moral stature. Of course the Emancipation Proclamation by Lincoln made the southern negro slave free, but it never did make the white man morally free. He remained a slave to his inheritances. And some are even today.

I believe that a man can play baseball as coming to him from a call from God.

I was in Cleveland at a dinner when I was a youngster, just out of college, and a man in Cleveland who was called, editorially in the *Cleveland Plain Dealer,* on the occasion of his death, the foremost citizen of Cleveland—George Shurtliffe was his name. I never had met him except at that luncheon that day up there in the cupola of that building, 12 or 13 gentlemen around the table, and I was asked to take a job—a certain job that I had never thought about taking. And I didn't feel that I was qualified for the job, and I didn't know whether I wanted it—I was quite ill at ease about it, but the strengthened force of the men who were asking me to take it was influential with me. And we had this dinner and Mr. Shurtliffe was asked to come.

He was identified with the organization in some capacity, and when we had just about finished the meal—I was sitting the second one on the left side of the table and he was down yonder at the end, he said to me, "Branch," he said, "do you believe in the call of God?" No, his first question was, "If you thought God wanted you to do something would you do it?"

168

I said, "If I knew what God wanted me to do, I think any boy would."

He said, "Do you believe in the call of God?" I didn't answer.

He said, "Do you know what the call of God is?"

I said, "I don't know that I do," but I said, "I don't think it is a little bird that comes and sits on your ear and whispers and says to you go do this."

He said, "I think you are right."

"Well," I said, "Bishop Basford said that to me and it's not original," but I said, "I don't. . . ."

He said, "Would you like to know what I think it is?"

And I said, "I would," because he was a distinguished man.

He said that the first thing in the call of God is aptitude. God doesn't want any man to do something that he can't do. He made me define the word in front of those gentlemen.

He said, the second thing in the call of God is the advice of his friends, and he made me tell him all my friends and we got down from the 8,000 people that had seen that professional football game that fall where I had made a touchdown—I was a great big fellow, and I couldn't name all those 8,000. I thought they were all my friends. They gave nine rahs with my name on the end of it and it got down to the place where I named my father and mother and then the girl that I had announced I was going to marry. He accepted her. And that made two and then he took a professor in school after questioning me about it. And then he took a boyhood friend that I had grown up with way down in the hills of southern Ohio—a country boy. He said, no man has more than a handful of real friends under adversity. He said, they are God's angels—go talk to them. God speaks to men through his friends. Be careful who your friends are. The second thing he said.

And the third thing, he said, was opportunity. He said, when you are prepared to do something and your friends all tell you that you should do it and then the chance comes to do it, he said, that's where God shows His face. Now, he said to me, and I didn't quite know what the word meant when he said it. And he said there may be some sophistry [deceptive reasoning] about that. But whether there was or not, I have used it often. And I have thought about it in connection with ball players. What should they be doing in this thing that emphasizes the physical over the mental or spiritual or whatnot. And what are the weaknesses of opportunity in the field? What are the great chances for moral deterioration on the part of great men who go into this thing where they have been under hours of labor previously and now have leisure time—the most damnable thing in the world.

Leisure in the hands of the man who has no creativeness—lots of young men don't have it. That thing that can write great symphonies, that can write great tragedies in this use of time. I have often wondered where God may come into the picture. There are some boys who shouldn't be playing ball. This chap, and others—it's a wonderful thing to have a family background and to have something you can hold on to that is basic and firm and strong.

Character is a great thing to have in an athlete, a team. It's a great thing. And when I wonder if there is any condonation [acceptance], any explanation, anything that can be done to make an extenuating circumstance out of something that violates the right of a part of our citizenship throughout the country when I know that the Man of 1900 years ago spent His life and died for the sake of freedom—the right to come, to go, to see, to think, to believe, to act. It is to be understood, but it is too profoundly regretted.

Education is a slow process. It may solve it. It is inevitable that this thing comes to fruition. Too many forces are working fast. This so called little Robinson—we call it the "Robinson Experiment"—tremendous as it will be for Jackie to have so placed himself in relation not only to his own people in this country, but to his whole generation and to all America that he will leave the mark of fine sportsmanship and fine character. That is something that he must guard carefully. He has a responsibility there.

Frank Tannenbaum, in his book on *Slave and Citizen*—he is a professor of Latin American history in Columbia University—points out—I think it is the bible on the subject—it really is. I'm not sure, I'm not sure that legislators ought to drive against a prominent and very antagonistic minority. I'm not sure that they should drive F.E.C. too fast too far. I'm not sure that the 18th Amendment might repeat itself. That you would have an organization of glued antagonisms that would be able to delay the solution of a problem that is now in my judgment fast being solved, and when you once gain an eminence you do not have to recede from it. The educational process is something.

Four things, says Tannenbaum, are solving this question, with an unrealized rapidity. First, proximity. Clay Hopper, Jackie's first manager. I've never told it in public. I've never allowed it to be printed if I could help it, took me by the lapels of my coat as he sat there sweating in his underclothes watching a game over on the inside park at Daytona Beach. And this boy [Robinson] had made a great play in the fourth inning and I had remarked about it and the two of us sitting there together, and this boy coming from—I shouldn't have given his name—forget the name and I will tell you the story. I'll deny that he ever said it. He took me by the front of my coat when in the seventh inning Jackie made one of those tremendous remarkable plays that very few people can make— went toward first base, made a slide, stabbed the ball, came with it in his left hand glove and as he turned with the body control that's almost inconceivable and cut off the runner at second base on a force play. I took Clay and I put my hand on his shoulder and I said, "Did you ever see a play to beat it?"

Now this fellow comes from Greenwood, Mississippi. And he would forgive me, I am sure, because of the magnificent way that he came through on it. He took me and shook me and his face that far from me and he said, "Do you really think that a 'nigger' is a human being, Mr. Rickey?" That's what he said. That's what that fellow said. I have never answered him until this minute.

And six months later he came into my office after the year at Montreal when he was this boy's manager. He didn't want him to be sent to him. And he said to me, "I want to take back what I said to you last spring." He said, "I'm ashamed of it." "Now," he said, "you may have plans for him to be on your club," and he was, "but," he said, "if you don't have plans to have him on the Brooklyn club," he said, "I would like to have him back in Montreal." And then he told me that he was not only a great ball player good enough for Brooklyn, but he said that he was a fine gentleman. Proximity. Proximity, says Tannenbaum, will solve this thing if you can have enough of it. But that is a limited thing, you see.

And the second thing, says Tannenbaum, is the cultural inter-twining through the arts, through literature, through painting, through singing, through the professions, where you stabbed through the horizontal strata of social makeup, and you make vertical thrusts in that cultural inter-twining. That inevitably will help solve this problem—and be believes with rapidity.

And third, the existence in our democracy here of a middle class, the middle class in Great Britain—the middle class in probably every country, I think, that makes secure, if anything does, a democracy such as we know. This group here like this—these groups throughout America of all colors. That existence in this country will bring it about surely and faster than people know.

And fourth, the recognition of the moral stature of all men, that all humans are equal. This thing of freedom has been bought at a great price. That all men are equal in the sight of God. That all law must recognize that men are equal—all humans are equal by nature. The same pains, and the same joys, and in our country the same food, the same dress, the same religion, the same language, the same everything. And perhaps quite as questionable an ancestry civically in this country on the part of the black men as we can trace many of the forbearers in the white race of the other settlers of this country.

Gentlemen, it is inconceivable to me that in view of domestic tranquility and home understanding that anywhere, anytime, anybody, can question the right of citizens of this country for equal economic opportunity under the law. How can it be? And how can anyone in official authority, where more attention is given to remarks than would come from an ordinary civilian, be so unremindful of his country's relationship that he could bring us into ... disgrace internationally.

These four things I mention will work, I think, in due time with a sureness that will make possibly the very next generation wonder and look back, as I said that you quoted me in Cincinnati, I had forgotten that I had ever said it look back with incredulity upon everything that was a problem to us today in this country, and will wonder what the issue was all about. I am completely color-blind. I know that America is—it's been proven [by] Jackie—is more interested in the grace of a man's swing, in the dexterity of his cutting a base, and his speed afoot, in his scientific body control, in his excellence as a competitor on the field—America, wide and broad, and in Atlanta, and in Georgia, will become instantly more interested in those marvelous, beautiful qualities than they are in the pigmentation of a man's skin, or indeed in the last syllable of his name. Men are coming to be regarded of value based upon their merits, and God hasten the day when Governors of our States will become sufficiently educated that they will respond to those views.

Source

Rickey, Branch. Excerpt from speech delivered at the "One Hundred Percent Wrong Club" banquet, Atlanta, Georgia, January 20, 1956. Broadcast on WERD 860 AM radio. Retrieved from Library of Congress, Manuscript Division, Branch Rickey Papers, http://memory.loc.gov/ammem/collections/robinson/branch.html.

A Dodgers Scout Remembers the Famous Rickey-Robinson Meeting

Brooklyn Dodgers talent scout Clyde Sukeforth was the only other person in the room when team owner Branch Rickey met with Negro League star Jackie Robinson for the first time in August 1945. In the following excerpt from Peter Golenbock's compilation Bums: An Oral History of the Brooklyn Dodgers, *Sukeforth remembers details about the historic meeting, as well as his role in Rickey's secretive search for "the right man on and off the field" to break baseball's long-standing color barrier.*

They had a colored club in Brooklyn, the Brown Bombers, and Rickey had us believing that we were scouting for them. He didn't give anybody an idea that he was looking for a fella that could break the color line. He just wanted a list of all the colored ballplayers in the Negro National League. We found some pretty outstanding players down there: Robinson and Johnny Wright and Roy Campanella and Don Newcombe.

Josh Gibson was in the league, but he was quite old, and his habits were not especially good. He had the reputation of being a drinker. Satchel Paige, everyone figured, was too old. We might have missed something there.

One day in August 1945, Mr. Rickey called me in and he said, "The Kansas City Monarchs are playing the Lincoln Giants at Comiskey Park in Chicago Friday night. I want you to see that game, go up to that fellow Robinson, and introduce yourself," which is something we never did. Usually when we wanted information we got it through Oscar Charleston, the old Negro League first baseman. He knew all those people. Oscar had worked for the Pennsylvania Railroad in the North Philadelphia station. He had a pretty good job there, and he could get off most anytime he wanted. He knew all the people in the colored league, and if we got interested in somebody, why, we'd call Oscar, and we could find out all about a boy, about his habits, how much he'd been to school, what sort of boy he was. For Jackie we didn't need Oscar, though. His record was pretty well-known. He was a UCLA [University of California, Los Angeles] college boy, and he was better known than most of the colored boys.

So I went to Chicago, and I identified myself when Robinson came on the field, talked to him, and he couldn't understand why I was there. I told him who

---

had sent me and that Mr. Rickey told me to talk to him and to pay particular attention to his arm. Mr. Rickey said, "I want to know if that fellow has a shortstop's arm." I went through all that with Robinson, and he said, "I'll be glad to show you my arm, but I'm not playing. I fell on my shoulder last night, and I won't be able to play for several days." Well, he took batting practice.

Mr. Rickey had told me, "If you like his arm, bring him in, and if his schedule won't permit it, make an appointment for me, and I'll go out and see him." Well, that's when I really became suspicious. That's when I knew it wasn't the Brown Bombers, that this was the real thing. I knew the reports on him were good, and in any event, there are other positions besides shortstop if the fella's good enough. And knowing well how Mr. Rickey liked to talk to people and study them and look right through them, I thought to myself, "This fella's going to be out of the game for several days, why not take him to Brooklyn and let Mr. Rickey talk to the guy?"

I had two berths on the train, he had one and I had one opposite, and before we retired we talked a little bit about race relations. Also, he kept asking me, "Why does Mr. Rickey want to see me?" and I'd tell him, "I wish I could answer that, but I can't." In my own mind I knew why, but I couldn't say.

In the morning I got up and said, "Let's go back to the dining car and get some coffee," and he said, "I don't eat much breakfast. I'll wait and eat with the boys." I said, "Why I think it would be perfectly all right if you went back." He said, "I'll wait," and so he waited and ate breakfast with the [black] porters.

So I brought Jackie in for a conference, and I introduced him to Mr. Rickey, and I said, "Mr. Rickey, I haven't seen this fellow throw," but he evidently didn't hear me because when he wrote his book a few years later, he called me in and asked where it was that I saw Robinson play. I never saw Robinson play! All I did was bring him in for a conference.

I was in the room when Mr. Rickey talked to the fella. His first question was: "You got a girl?" Jackie told him about Rachel, his fiancée. Mr. Rickey said, "When we get through today you may want to call her up, because there are times when a man needs a woman by his side." Then Mr. Rickey said, "Jack, I've been looking for a great colored ballplayer, but I need more than a great player. I need a man who will accept insults, take abuse, in a word, carry the flag for his race." He told him, "I want a man who has the courage not to fight, not to fight back. If a guy slides into you at second base and calls you a black son of a bitch, I wouldn't blame you if you came up swinging. You'd be right.

You'd be justified. But," he said, "you'd set the cause back twenty years. I want a man with courage enough not to fight back. Can you do that?"

Well, Jackie sold himself right quick. He thought about it for perhaps three minutes before he answered, and finally he said, "If you want to take this gamble, I promise you there'll be no incidents." If he had said it right off quick without giving it thought, then it wouldn't have carried as much weight. But he thought it out, and he was a long time in answering.

Afterward Rickey told me that there may have been other boys that could do it, but Robinson had the college background, and he was pretty active with the NAACP. Mr. Rickey felt that he would work hard not only for himself, but the cause, that he had all the qualifications, on and off the field.

Source

Sukeforth, Clyde. Quoted in Golenbock, Peter. *Bums: An Oral History of the Brooklyn Dodgers*. New York: Putnam, 1984, pp. 125-26.

A Sportswriter Recalls Robinson's Major League Debut

When Jackie Robinson made his major-league debut on April 15, 1947, sportswriter Jim Becker was there covering the game for the Associated Press. Sixty years later he published an article, which is reprinted below, recalling the sights, sounds, and atmosphere he experienced at the ballpark on that historic day.

On a chilly, gray, early spring day, a black man in a sparkling white baseball uniform walked, alone, from the dugout onto the green grass of Brooklyn's Ebbets Field.

It was April 15, 1947, and Jackie Robinson was about to break the shameful color line in major league baseball, a feat that would have a lasting impact on sports and society.

There was a feel of history in the air overlaid, perhaps oddly, by a sense of somewhat calculated nonchalance.

I was standing by the batting cage along with a handful of other sports reporters when Robinson strode onto the field with that slightly pigeon-toed walk of the natural athlete.

About 10,000 of a crowd that would swell to almost 26,000 at the tidy old park, many of them black, had gathered well before game time. They made no special sound when Robinson appeared. No cameras flashed. Television was in its infancy, and there were no TV cameras on hand.

It was as if all of us—writers, fans and players on both teams, the Dodgers and the visiting Boston Braves—had come to an unspoken agreement to behave as though it was just another opening day at the ballpark. And, by the way, a black man played for the Dodgers.

There were good reasons for this. The writers knew that the owners of the other 15 teams in the major leagues had voted unanimously to oppose the introduction of a black player.

We knew that Branch Rickey, the Dodgers' major-domo who had signed Robinson against all opposition to a minor league contract the year before (he was the Most Valuable Player in the International League in 1946), had hoped his Brooklyn players would have been impressed by Robinson's obvious talent to ask that he be added to the roster. Instead Rickey had been greeted with a petition signed by some key players—with the conspicuous exception of captain and shortstop, Pee Wee Reese, a Kentuckian—that they did not want to play with a black man. We had heard rumors that at least one national league team was organizing a strike rather than play against Robinson.

It was a time in our country when in many places blacks couldn't stay at the same hotel as whites, eat in the same restaurants, attend the same movie theaters or even drink from the same water fountains in the South. They rode in the back of the bus there.

Schools were segregated in the South, where the majority of major league players had grown up. So were neighborhoods, north and south, some by law, others by tacit agreement.

It was into this atmosphere that the black man in the dazzling white uniform strode, alone, carrying for all of us the banner of decency and dignity and fair play that is the American promise.

There is no rooting in the press box, but many of us in it that day, like Robinson, had served in the Armed Forces and had just helped to defeat Hitler and thought it would be a good idea to defeat Hitlerism at home.

So those of us assigned to cover the game seemed to be of one mind that to turn this day of uncommon courage into a media circus would be both unseemly and unfair.

In the Dodger clubhouse before the game we talked to Robinson one at a time, and then only after interviewing a couple of veteran players first. Robinson said he was nervous, as he always was before a big game, but he was sure the feeling would wear off when the game started. He said he had been made to feel welcome by his new teammates, which may or may not have been true.

On the field Robinson was carrying, somewhat awkwardly, an unfamiliar first baseman's mitt. A middle infielder by trade, he played first for the Dodgers that season.

Robinson glanced around for a few seconds, then picked up a baseball and began playing catch with a utility outfielder named Al Gionfriddo, who would make one of the most famous catches in World Series history that fall, and then disappear from the major leagues.

The PA [public address] announcer read the lineups in a matter-of-fact tone. This was before the hysterical homers took over the PA mikes, and the PA system at Ebbets Field never worked properly anyway.

Robinson, batting second, was thrown out by a whisker at first on his first time at bat. He went 0-for-3 with a sacrifice on the day. He reached base in the seventh on an error and scored on Pete Reiser's two-run double.

The Dodgers won, 5-3.

After the game a half dozen or so writers combed the Dodger clubhouse, making a point to talk to several players. Robinson said he went hitless not because of the pressure, but "because Johnny Sain was pitching." Sain was the Boston ace.

I gave the dressing room quotes to Joe Reichler, the AP's baseball writer, who led his story with the result of the game. So did many others.

Some years ago I traded letters about Robinson's first game with Jack Lang, longtime secretary of the Baseball Writers Association. He reminded me that there were nine mainstream daily newspapers in New York then, and not one of them led its game story with Robinson. This approach persisted for some time. In late December I wrote the wrap-up of the sports year for AP. I relegated Robinson's achievement to the 11th paragraph of a very long story, although when I got to him I pulled out all the stops. Robinson had been named Rookie of the Year, and the Dodgers had won the National League pennant, one of six they would win with Robinson.

I drew the assignment to assist Reichler on Robinson's first day because I had grown up in Los Angeles and had watched Robinson play all sports for UCLA. Robinson was the greatest all-around athlete I ever saw.

In his senior year, 1940-41, he led the nation in yards per carry and was a ferocious defender on the football field. He also led the conference in scoring in basketball, played baseball, ran the sprints, broke the NCAA long jump record set by his older brother Mack (second to Jesse Owens in the 200 meters in the 1936 Berlin Olympics), was a scratch golfer and won two tennis tournaments.

When he left UCLA, the door to all pro sports were closed to him, so he went to Hawaii and played for the Honolulu Bears, one of four teams in a semi-pro league there. He left by ship for the mainland on Dec. 5, 1941, two days before the attack on Pearl Harbor. Robinson served as an Army lieutenant during the war, and then came Rickey and his banner season with the Montreal Royals.

Robinson had agreed with Rickey to hold his fiery temper and natural competitiveness in check, to endure the racial taunts from fans and opposing players. When the wraps came off and he was free to argue with the umpires and return with interest the foul bench jockeying, Robinson told me: "I can hardly wait for an umpire to throw me out of a game." In other words, to treat him like everybody else.

But there was, there is, no way to treat Jackie Robinson like everybody else. His victory was his victory. Alone. His defeat would have been our defeat. All of us. He did not lose.

Source

Associated Press. "AP Sportswriter Recalls Jackie Robinson's Debut." *Editor & Publisher,* April 13, 2007.

Jackie Robinson Looks Back on His Rookie Season

After breaking Major League Baseball's color barrier on April 15, 1947, Jackie Robinson embarked on a difficult but often rewarding first season with the Brooklyn Dodgers. In the following excerpt from his autobiography I Never Had It Made, *Robinson looks back on some of the changes that occurred over the course of his rookie year. He reveals the doubts he felt during an early batting slump, expresses appreciation for the support he received from Dodgers president Branch Rickey, describes a memorable stolen base that helped him get on track, and recalls a racially charged incident that united the team behind him.*

The Dodgers won the pennant that year, and when our club came home in September from a swing across the west, we were joyfully received by our fans. Their enthusiasm for me was so great that I once went into a phone booth to call Rae [his wife, Rachel] and was trapped in that phone booth by admirers who let up only when policemen arrived on the scene to liberate me.

Getting a hero's welcome in September made me remember how bad the beginning of my first season with the Dodgers had been. At that time I still wasn't looking like any kind of winner, even though the increasing acceptance of my teammates had begun to help me out of a terrible slump. I seriously wondered if I could ever make the Rickey experiment a success. Both Manager Burt Shotton and Mr. Rickey believed I would eventually come through. [Dodgers scout] Clyde Sukeforth with his quiet confidence helped as much as anybody else.

During the season I was under even greater pressure than in my Montreal days. It was there that I had earned a reputation for stealing bases, and the pressure eased when I began stealing them again. Late in June, in a night game at Pittsburgh, with the score tied 2-2 I kept a careful eye on pitcher Fitz Ostermueller. I noticed he had become a little careless and relaxed. I began dancing off third base. Ostermueller paid me the insult of winding up, ignoring my movements as antics. The pitch was a ball. Easing open my lead off third, I made a bold dash for home plate and slid in safe. That put us in the lead 3-2. It was the winning run of the game. As I ran I heard the exhilarating noise that is the best reward a player can get. The roar of the crowd.

After I made that comeback, I think Mr. Rickey was as happy as I was. He said to some friends at the time, "Wait! You haven't seen Robinson in action yet—

not really. You may not have seen him at his best this year at all, or even next year. He's still in his shell. When he comes out for good, he'll be compared to Ty Cobb."

Mr. Rickey's words meant a great deal to me but not as much as something he did. Howie Schultz, the player who had been mentioned as a possible replacement for me during the bad days of my slump, was sold by the club.

That 1947 season was memorable in many ways. Some of the incidents that occurred resulted in far-reaching changes for the club. In late August we played the St. Louis Cardinals. In one of the last games, Enos Slaughter, a Cards outfielder, hit a ground ball. As I took the throw at first from the infielder, Slaughter deliberately went for my leg instead of the base and spiked me rather severely.

It was an act that unified the Dodger team. Teammates such as Hugh Casey of the poker game incident came charging out on the field to protest. The team had always been close to first place in the pennant race, but the spirit shown after the Slaughter incident strengthened our resolve and made us go on to win the pennant. The next time we played the Cards, we won two of the three games.

I had started the season as a lonely man, often feeling like a black Don Quixote tilting at a lot of white windmills. I ended it feeling like a member of a solid team. The Dodgers were a championship team because all of us had learned something. I had learned how to exercise self-control—to answer insults, violence, and injustice with silence—and I had learned how to earn the respect of my teammates. They had learned that it's not the skin color but talent and ability that counts. Maybe even the bigots had learned that, too.

The press had also changed. When I came up to the majors, the influential *Sporting News* had declared that a black man would find it almost impossible to succeed in organized baseball. At the end of the season, when they selected me as Rookie of the Year, that same publication said:

> That Jackie Roosevelt Robinson might have had more obstacles
> than his first year competitors, and that he perhaps had a hard-
> er fight to gain even major league recognition, was no concern
> of this publication. The sociological experiment Robinson rep-
> resented, the trail-blazing that he did, the barriers he broke
> down, did not enter into the decision. He was rated and exam-
> ined solely as a freshman player in the big leagues—on the basis
> of his hitting, his running, his defensive play, his team value.

Dixie Walker summed it up in a few words the other day when he said: "No other ballplayer on this club with the possible exception of Bruce Edwards has done more to put the Dodgers up in the race than Robinson has. He is everything Branch Rickey said he was when he came up from Montreal."

Source

Robinson, Jackie. *I Never Had It Made: An Autobiography.* Hopewell, NJ: Ecco Press, 1995, pp. 67-69.

Pitcher Don Newcombe Protects His Dodgers Teammates

Pitcher Don Newcombe, nicknamed Newk, joined the Brooklyn Dodgers in 1949. Along with fellow former Negro League stars Jackie Robinson and Roy Campanella, the imposing right-hander made the Dodgers the most integrated team in Major League Baseball. Newcombe won 17 games that season, made the All-Star team, earned Rookie of the Year honors, and became the first black pitcher to start a World Series game.

Perhaps Newcombe's most important contribution, however, involved shielding his teammates from the verbal and physical abuse they had often endured from opposing teams. Newcombe never hesitated to retaliate if an opposing pitcher threw a beanball at a Dodgers batter, or if an opposing coach shouted racial epithets from the dugout. Once his willingness to take action on behalf of his teammates became known around the league, most opponents were too intimidated to bother the Dodgers' stars again. In the following excerpt from Peter Golembock's book Bums: An Oral History of the Brooklyn Dodgers, *Newcombe describes his role in leveling the playing field for his team.*

In 1949 things hadn't changed to any large degree where you could recognize it. Because they were still stepping on Jackie's foot, and they were still trying to cut Roy's chest protector off him when they slid into home plate with their spikes high up in the air. Jackie knew what to do when they came into second base. Right in the mouth where you can catch them between first base in the double play. But that didn't stop pitchers from trying to hit Jackie and Roy in the head.

And that's where I came in. See, I had a chance to protect Jackie and Roy and the rest of the team, because we had very few pitchers who would knock guys down. Ralph Branca and I, and much later Don Drysdale, when he came up. The others would say, "I can't throw at them. I don't know how. Somebody else is going to have to do it." All right. So I would do it. I would throw at them, because they were throwing at our guys. I don't deny it, and I never did. The way they knocked our guys down, the way they hit Roy in the head, the way they hit Carl Furillo, the way they knocked down Duke Snider, if you don't protect your men, you're just not gonna get any runs, and they're not gonna have any respect for you. We were going to be sitting ducks. Nobody's gonna protect us? Come on! Somebody's gotta help us. And it wasn't a racial thing. I knew the guys, Bob Rush of the Cubs, guys like that; Bob would throw at guys, and the way Jackie would steal on him and make a fool out of him, well, Bob would throw at guys. Sal Maglie would throw at guys, and he never denied it, just like I don't. You do whatever's necessary to help your players.

One day, for instance, in Chicago, they knocked down one of our guys, and it wasn't a black guy, it was Rocky Nelson, because Duke Snider had hit a home run off one of their pitchers. So what do the guys say in the dugout? "Well, there you are Newk. What are you gonna do about it?" I said, "I know what I'm going to do. Every son of a bitch that comes up to the plate with a bat in his hand with a Chicago Cubs uniform on is going on his ass." And I did it. I didn't hit any of them, but they knew what I was up to. I told Roy to tell them. I said, "Put your glove behind their head," and Roy would stand there pounding his glove behind their ear, and he'd say, "C'mon Roomie, right here." If he didn't get out of the way it was too damn bad. Seven straight hitters in three innings went on their ass. Every one of them. Ernie Banks came up and said, "What's he mad at me for?" Campy [Campanella] said, "You got a bat in your hand. You got a Chicago Cubs uniform on." Campy told them, "You're going on your ass, so you better be ready."

The umpires didn't call time, not until after the seventh batter. He finally called our manager, Walt Alston, out to the mound, and he said, "If this guy doesn't stop throwing at these guys, we're gonna suspend you and him." Walt said, "They can get along without me, but we can't get along without you. So I'm gonna take you out of the ballgame." So I got mad at Walt. I said, "You got as much [expletive] guts as the umpire got there, Walt," and I walked off the [expletive] mound. He fined me $300 for saying that to him. I apologized the next day. I told him I was sorry. But Alston finally had to take me out of the game, 'cause I said, "I'm going to get all of them. I'm going to get everybody until I make sure I get the right one." That protects your players, and it breaks that crap up. Because, man, that ball hurts when it hits ya.

I've never had a teammate tell me I was afraid. There was always that talk about me choking up and being gutless, never won the big ones, but I never had a teammate tell me that I wouldn't protect him with that baseball when it was time for somebody to go on their ass. They were going to go on their ass, and if they didn't go that pitch, they'd go on the next pitch. I'd get him sometime during the sequence of pitches. He had to go on his ass. And I wouldn't pick the eighth-place hitter or the leadoff hitter. I would get the best hitter on the ballclub.

Del Ennis with the Philadelphia Phillies in 1950. They had a coach named McDonald, a batting practice pitcher and a bench jockey. He'd call us all kinds of niggers, everything. That's what he was there for. In a very distinct voice, I could hear him in the dugout. And one day in Ebbets Field, I'm pitching against the Phillies, and he's calling us all these names, and Jackie comes over to the mound and says, "Newk, did you hear that son of a bitch over there?" I said, "Jack, I hear him. I got good ears." Jack was playing third base. He said, "What are you going to do about it?" I said, "Well, when the hitter comes up who's the best hitter on the club, you'll see what happens." Del Ennis came up, and I buzzed him, and he went down on his ass. Hat went flying, bat went one way, and he got up and picked up his bat, and I said to Jackie, "All right now. We're ready for a fight." Jackie said, "I'm with you. Don't worry about it. Let him come out here." Ennis turned around and went over to his dugout and said something to that coach in the dugout, and he came back to the plate and struck out, and so some years later I got to play with Del in Cincinnati, and I asked him what he said to the coach when he went over to the dugout. Del said, "I told that son of a bitch, you leave that big son of a bitch alone out there on the mound, because you don't have to go up there and hit against him. I do, and he's knocking me on my ass for what you're saying to him. Now, if that's your feeling, that's fine, but if you say anything more to him while I'm at bat, I'm going to pull your [expletive] tongue out of your head and lay it in your hand. Leave that man alone."

And the coach was released from the club. He had lost his effectiveness. What did they need him for, to be a batting practice pitcher? They had him there to call us niggers and all kinds of dirty names. That's why he was there. But when Del took his effectiveness away from him and shut him up, they got rid of him. They didn't need him anymore. I never saw him again.

Source

Newcombe, Don. Quoted in Golenbock, Peter. *Bums: An Oral History of the Brooklyn Dodgers.* New York: Putnam, 1984, pp. 240-42.

Robinson Pushes Eisenhower to Take Action on Civil Rights

Following his retirement from baseball in 1956, Jackie Robinson continued to champion the cause of civil rights. He gave speeches and raised money for the National Association for the Advancement of Colored People (NAACP) and other organizations, joined Martin Luther King Jr. and other activists in protest marches, and wrote hundreds of letters to public figures. In fact, all U.S. presidents who held office between 1956 and 1972 received letters from Robinson urging them to take a firm stand on civil rights issues.

Robinson and President Dwight D. Eisenhower exchanged the letters reprinted below in 1958. The previous year, Arkansas governor Orval Faubus had surrounded Central High School in Little Rock with National Guard troops to prevent nine black students from entering, in direct defiance of a court order requiring the desegregation of public schools. Eisenhower had responded by sending the U.S. Army to enforce the ruling. Afterward, however, the president had made a speech suggesting that black leaders be patient and give white Southerners time to overcome their long-held prejudices so as to avoid future confrontations over civil rights. Robinson wrote his letter in response to these remarks.

May 13, 1958

My Dear Mr. President:

I was sitting in the audience at the Summit Meeting of Negro Leaders yesterday when you said we must have patience. On hearing you say this, I felt like standing up and saying, "Oh no! Not again."

I respectfully remind you sir, that we have been the most patient of all people. When you said we must have self-respect, I wondered how we could have self-respect and remain patient considering the treatment accorded us through the years.

17 million Negroes cannot do as you suggest and wait for the hearts of men to change. We want to enjoy now the rights that we feel we are entitled to as Americans. This we cannot do unless we pursue aggressively goals which all other Americans achieved over 150 years ago.

As the chief executive of our nation, I respectfully suggest that you unwittingly crush the spirit of freedom in Negroes by constantly urging forbearance and give hope to those pro-segregation leaders like Governor Faubus who would take from us even those freedoms we now enjoy. Your own experience with Governor Faubus is proof enough that forbearance and not eventual integration is the goal the pro-segregation leaders seek.

In my view, an unequivocal statement backed up by action such as you demonstrated you could take last fall in dealing with Governor Faubus if it became necessary, would let it be known that America is determined to provide, in the near future—for Negroes—the freedoms we are entitled to under the constitution.

Respectfully yours,
Jackie Robinson

June 4, 1958

Dear Mr. Robinson:

Thank you very much for taking the time to write me some of the thoughts you had after the meeting of the Negro leaders here in Washington. While I understand the points you make about the use of patience and forbearance, I have never urged them as substitutes for constructive action or progress.

If you will review my talk made at the meeting, you will see that at no point did I advocate a cessation of effort on the part of individuals, organizations, or government, to bring to fruition for all Americans, the employment of all the privileges of citizenship spelled out in our Constitution.

I am firmly on record as believing that every citizen—of every race and creed—deserves to enjoy equal civil rights and liberties, for there can be no such citizen in a democracy as a half-free citizen.

I should say here that we have much reason to be proud of the progress our people are making in mutual understanding—the chief buttress of human and civil rights. Steadily we are moving closer to the goal of fair and equal treatment of citizens without regard to race or color.

This progress, I am confident, will continue. And it is gifted persons such as yourself, born out of the crucible of struggle for personal dignity and achievement, who will help lead the way towards the goals we seek.

Sincerely,
Dwight D. Eisenhower

Sources

Robinson, Jackie. Letter to President Dwight D. Eisenhower, May 13, 1958. Official File, Box 615, OF 142-A (6). Papers of Dwight D. Eisenhower as President, Dwight D. Eisenhower Presidential Library, Retrieved from http://eisenhower.archives.gov/research/online_documents/civil_rights_little_rock/1958_05_13_Robinson_to_DDE.pdf.

Eisenhower, Dwight D. Letter to Jackie Robinson, June 4, 1958. Official file, Box 615, OF 142-A (6). Papers of Dwight D. Eisenhower as President, Dwight D. Eisenhower Presidential Library. Retrieved from http://www.eisenhowerarchives.gov/research/online_documents/civil_rights_little_rock/1958_6_04_DDE_to_Robinson.pdf.

A Major League Baseball Executive Describes Robinson's Impact

During his lifetime, Jackie Robinson inspired countless people—and especially African-American youth—to demand equal opportunities and pursue their dreams. His widow, Rachel Robinson, honored his legacy by establishing a charitable foundation in his name to help deserving students earn college degrees. Former National League president Leonard S. Coleman Jr. is co-chairman of the Jackie Robinson Foundation. He made the following remarks at a 1997 news conference, and they were published in The Sporting News *on the fiftieth anniversary of Robinson's major-league debut. Coleman describes the impact Robinson made on his own life, the game of baseball, the civil rights movement, and American society.*

I grew up in a two-family house. On the first floor, my father was a Giants fan, and my mother was a Dodgers fan; on the second floor, my uncle was a Yankees fan. The wars we had in the household over baseball were seemingly endless. And generally, those wars were carried on over dinner. The unifying force at 39 Central Ave. in Montclair, N.J., was Jackie Robinson. There was one thing we could all agree upon: We all rooted for Jackie. He provided tranquility and unification at my dinner table.

Jackie was my hero. He was my champion. He carried my every hope, my every aspiration, on his broad shoulders. I guess that wasn't uncommon for Jackie because he was used to carrying people. For example, at UCLA Jack was a tremendous football player. He carried would-be tacklers up and down the field. Jack's football exploits, however, were merely a prelude to the greater weight he would carry later in life.

Before breaking the color barrier in baseball, Jackie attacked another segregationist institution. He tacked the military. Jackie fought battles against bigotry and a racist system, and he did it at great personal sacrifice. This part of Jack's life deserves more attention.

Yes, we know about Jackie's breaking baseball's color line in 1947 and the profound effect that had not only on baseball, but also American society. I think it's useful, as we think back 50 years ago to 1947, to put into context what America was like at that time. President Truman had not yet desegregated the armed forces. It was seven years before *Brown v. Board of Education*, eight years before the Montgomery bus boycott, and 17 years before the Johnson Administration passed the Civil Rights Act.

Jackie's breakthrough foreshadowed the greatest civil rights movements in this country this century. He not only foreshadowed it, he was a leader in it his entire life, particularly in civil rights. More should be mentioned about Jackie's post-baseball career, because Jackie may have retired from baseball, but he did not retire from speaking out and providing leadership in the civil rights area. He was a confidant of, and marched with, Dr. Martin Luther King; he held leadership positions in the NAACP.

Jackie was a great ballplayer. Lifetime batting average .311. Rookie of the year. MVP. Spiritual leader of the Dodgers. Jackie was a true Hall of Famer. There's no question about that. But off the field, he was a Hall of Fame barrier-breaker because he knocked down hurdles and created opportunities for people in all walks of life.

As a kid you often remember images, not sequence. I remember Jackie dancing off first base, and the pitchers being so rattled. I looked at that image and I said to myself, "Boy, he's really changing this ballgame." Just by dancing off first base. Now that I am older, I realize Jackie not only was shaking up the pitcher, he was daring America to have a higher standard. The Robinson challenge was compelling. Jackie's message was and is bigger than baseball.

Fiercely independent, Jack possessed a restless soul. He was restless for justice. He was restless for equality and opportunity. Many of us like the song, "Did you See Jackie Robinson Hit That Ball?" I particularly like the Natalie Cole version. But perhaps that song would have been more appropriately named, "Did You See Jackie Robinson Hit Jim Crow?" because he hit him in the military, he hit him on the baseball diamond and he hit him in our society.

In my opinion, Jackie Robinson provided the soul of the modern game of baseball. The Robinson ideal—leadership, competitiveness, passion, energy, a quest for justice and Jackie's challenge to a stained system—should be the foundation upon which the modern game of baseball should be played. Fifty years later we're not just celebrating a life. Jackie's spirit continues to drive us. Jackie once said, "A life isn't important unless it impacts another life."

I think one of the nicest things that has ever happened to me was when Rachel Robinson came to me a little more than a year ago and asked me if I could chair the Jackie Robinson Foundation. It's not often that people in life are able—are asked—to make a contribution to a foundation that bears your childhood hero's name. So I felt very privileged that Rachel would ask me.

Our foundation's motto is, "A life is only important if it impacts another life." JRF has provided scholarships to hundreds of kids across this country; young men and women who may not have had the opportunity to go to college through other means. Rachel started the foundation in 1973 as a living legacy to Jackie. The foundation boasts a 92 percent graduation rate for its scholars. The primary limit on the foundation has been resources. JRF receives 37 qualified applications for every student we are able to fund. As chairman, I am pleased to announce the foundation, in this year of celebration, will be launching a $12 million endowment campaign as a continuing legacy to Jackie.

The good book of Ecclesiastes tells us that for every person there is a time and a season. We should follow Jackie's lead and commit ourselves to his ideals. And if we have that type of commitment, it will continue to be Jack's time and his season.

Source

Coleman, Leonard S. "The Man Who Gave Baseball Its Soul." *The Sporting News,* April 14, 1997, p. 7.

Teammate Carl Erskine Reflects on Robinson's Legacy

Pitcher Carl Erskine, who joined the Brooklyn Dodgers in 1948, was an eyewitness to most of Jackie Robinson's Hall of Fame career. The two players were teammates for nine seasons and close friends until Robinson's death in 1972. In 2005 Erskine published a memoir entitled What I Learned from Jackie Robinson: A Teammate's Reflections On and Off the Field, *in which he shared his memories of Robinson's fight for racial equality. In the following excerpt from the book's epilogue, "The Legacy of Number 42," Erskine describes Robinson's impact on his life and the lives of others.*

"Our whole country has benefited from Jackie Robinson and his sacrifice," Hall of Famer Joe Morgan said during a 2004 ESPN telecast on "Sunday Night Baseball." I couldn't have said it better myself.

Jackie's greatest legacy was his unbelievable self-control and how that self-control paved the way for others to lead great lives. Civil rights got a fresh start with Robinson and transformed the rest of society. Baseball forced America to reevaluate itself and its practices, and in turn proved itself to be more than a game. It showed us that sometimes our national pastime can teach us a thing or two, rather than we as a society shaping our national pastime.

Jackie Robinson was a high-spirited, self-confident, militant man as well as a high achiever who resented being considered second class. His understanding of the major goal of his experience—and that the goal was bigger than him or his personal feelings—allowed him to control his anger and suppress his instinct to retaliate.

He believed in Branch Rickey and Rickey's idea that only a passive response to the indignities and hatred of the times was the right formula. It was this self-control during his first two years that made everything work, and after Rickey's gag order was lifted, responses gushed out of Jackie like a geyser. He was caustic and defensive when he needed to be, and when he went off sometimes and I'd ask him about whether it made him feel better, he responded, "Carl, I just can't let that stuff pass." I understood.

He believed in America—"America the Beautiful" the way Ray Charles sang it. He believed in an America that was united as one—not one united as a white America. I learned patience from Jackie. If he could be patient at times

---

From What I Learned from Jackie Robinson: A Teammate's Reflections On and Off the Field *by Carl Erskine with Burton Rocks. Copyright © The McGraw-Hill Companies, Inc. Reprinted by permission.*

191

over civil rights, I could be patient about trivial things happening in my own life. I learned how to be a better player and a better man from Jackie. I learned the importance of good friendship. I learned the importance of speaking one's mind even in the face of criticism.

It's incomprehensible to estimate the number of lives Jackie saved through his public speaking engagements at inner-city schools. The countless hours he spent at youth clinics and youth tournaments giving encouragement to other people's children do not appear in a baseball bio or stat sheet. Lives turned out positive because of Jackie. Men became men because of Jackie. And through all of this Jackie felt not only happy to be a part of it but an obligation as a famous athlete to do it. He said it was "a calling."

Jackie Robinson is an American hero, an icon. Textbooks used in classrooms around the globe bear his stories. His name lives on through the ballplayers today, and his retired number 42 is honored throughout baseball.

Jackie Robinson is an important part of American history, and in that regard he has saved the Brooklyn Dodgers from fading into oblivion, for we all will be remembered as teammates of Jackie. Our team will live on because of him, and the players will still play. And the great political and social question has been answered....

Whether it's in the political arena, the sports arena, the business world, the entertainment world, or the educational system, our America now is a true mix of human diversity.

There's a song in the famous Broadway show *South Pacific* that says you've got to be carefully taught—taught prejudice, that is, because we are all by nature accepting and loving. Jackie ... helped us connect with that innate good nature. We're a better society for it.

The lion has lain down by the lamb.

Yes, we are a better world because Jackie Robinson rose to the challenge and literally gave his life for it.

The bitter, just as Jackie told Newk [pitcher Don Newcombe] that day in St. Louis, has been made better!

Source

Erskine, Carl, with Burton Rocks. "Epilogue: The Legacy of Number 42." In *What I Learned from Jackie Robinson: A Teammate's Reflections On and Off the Field.* New York: McGraw-Hill, 2005, pp. 149-51.

IMPORTANT PEOPLE, PLACES, AND TERMS

Aaron, Hank (1934-)
African-American baseball star who set a major-league record with 755 career home runs and became the last active player to have begun his career in the Negro Leagues.

Affiliate
A minor-league baseball team that is owned by or under contract to a major-league team and helps develop its young players.

Barnstorming
A form of loosely organized baseball competition in which teams traveled to various cities and towns and played against whatever opponents they could find.

Brooklyn Dodgers
A Major League Baseball team in the National League; Jackie Robinson played for this team from 1947 through 1956.

Brown v. Board of Education
A 1954 U.S. Supreme Court ruling that overturned *Plessy v. Ferguson* and declared the segregation of public schools to be unconstitutional.

Campanella, Roy (1921-1993)
First black catcher in Major League Baseball; longtime teammate of Jackie Robinson on the Brooklyn Dodgers.

Chandler, A. B. "Happy" (1898-1991)
Politician who became the second commissioner of Major League Baseball in 1945 and expressed support for integration.

Chapman, Ben (1908-1993)

Philadelphia Phillies manager who led his team in a particularly vicious verbal assault on Jackie Robinson during his rookie season.

Chock Full o' Nuts

The restaurant chain that hired Jackie Robinson as its vice president of employee relations and community affairs upon his retirement from baseball.

Civil rights movement

A struggle by African Americans and their supporters in the 1950s and 1960s to end racial segregation and discrimination and achieve equal rights to those afforded white Americans in employment, housing, education, access to public facilities, voting, and other areas.

Color barrier or color line

Formal laws or informal policies that enforce racial segregation and prevent African Americans and other minorities from participating in various activities that are available to whites; organized baseball maintained a color barrier from the late 1800s through 1947.

Doby, Larry (1923-2003)

African-American professional baseball player who broke the American League's color barrier in 1947 with the Cleveland Indians.

Farm system

A baseball innovation that allows major-league teams to develop young players by having them work their way up through a series of increasingly competitive minor-league affiliates.

Foster, Andrew "Rube" (1879-1930)

Black baseball player, team owner, and league organizer who established the Negro National League in 1920.

Freedom Rides

Organized efforts by black and white student activists to challenge segregation on interstate buses and bus terminals in the South.

Hopper, Clay (1902-1976)

Minor-league baseball manager who initially resisted the addition of Jackie Robinson to the Montreal Royals roster in 1946.

194

Integration

The process of incorporating or bringing together people of different racial and ethnic groups as equals into an organization or society.

Jackie Robinson Foundation (JRF)

A nonprofit organization established by Rachel Robinson in 1973 to honor her late husband's legacy by helping underprivileged youth attend college.

Jim Crow laws

Laws implemented following Reconstruction that codified segregation and discrimination against blacks in virtually all aspects of daily life across the South.

Johnson, Lyndon B. (1908-1973)

The 36th president of the United States (1963-1969) who worked with Congress to pass the Civil Rights Act of 1964 and the Fair Housing Act of 1968.

Kansas City Monarchs

A team in the Negro National League; Jackie Robinson played for this team in 1945.

Kennedy, John F. (1917-1963)

The 35th president of the United States (1961-1963) who earned praise from Jackie Robinson by sending federal troops to enforce desegregation orders and proposing federal civil rights legislation.

King, Martin Luther, Jr. (1929-1968)

Civil rights leader and founder of the Southern Christian Leadership Conference (SCLC).

Ku Klux Klan

A white supremacist organization that used terrorist tactics, such as cross burning and lynching, to intimidate African Americans and advocates for civil rights.

Landis, Kenesaw Mountain (1866-1944)

Federal judge who served as the first commissioner of Major League Baseball from 1920 until his death.

Montreal Royals

The Brooklyn Dodgers' Class A minor-league affiliate; Jackie Robinson played for this team in 1946.

National Association for the Advancement of Colored People (NAACP)
A civil rights organization founded in 1909 to lobby for political and social changes that would grant equal rights to all citizens.

Negro Leagues
Professional baseball leagues for black players that existed during the era of segregation, when African Americans were prohibited from playing for Major League Baseball teams or in their minor-league farm systems.

Newcombe, Don (1926-)
African-American baseball pitcher and longtime Brooklyn Dodgers teammate of Jackie Robinson; first player to win the Most Valuable Player and Cy Young Awards in the same season.

Plessy v. Ferguson
An 1896 U.S. Supreme Court decision that sanctioned racial segregation laws, holding that states could require black and white citizens to use different facilities as long as those facilities were "separate but equal."

Reconstruction
A ten-year period (1867-1877) following the U.S. Civil War in which the federal government sent military troops into former Confederate states to help rebuild infrastructure and to protect the civil rights of African Americans.

Reese, Pee Wee (1918-1999)
Brooklyn Dodgers shortstop and longtime captain who became Jackie Robinson's friend and double-play partner.

Rickey, Branch (1881-1965)
President and part-owner of the Brooklyn Dodgers who spearheaded the integration of Major League Baseball.

Robinson, Jackie (1919-1972)
African-American player who broke Major League Baseball's longstanding color barrier when he joined the Brooklyn Dodgers in 1947; following his Hall of Fame baseball career, he became a prominent civil rights activist and business leader.

Robinson, Rachel (1922-)
Wife of Jackie Robinson who supported his efforts to integrate Major League Baseball; once her husband's baseball career ended, she became a psychiatric nurse and founded a charitable foundation.

Segregation

The policy or practice of separating people by race.

Sit-ins

Organized civil rights protests in which black college students defied Southern segregation laws by sitting at white-only lunch counters and other public facilities.

Smith, Wendell (1914-1972)

African-American sportswriter who promoted baseball integration.

Southern Christian Leadership Conference (SCLC)

A nonviolent civil rights organization founded in 1957 by the Reverend Martin Luther King Jr. and other ministers from across the South.

Walker, Dixie (1910-1982)

Brooklyn Dodgers outfielder who in 1947 asked his teammates to sign a petition saying that they would not play on the same team as Jackie Robinson.

CHRONOLOGY

1846

The first known baseball game using modern rules takes place on June 19 in Hoboken, New Jersey, between the New York Baseball Club and the New York Knickerbockers. *See p. 10.*

1861

The U.S. Civil War begins. *See p. 7.*

1865

The U.S. Civil War ends in victory for the North. *See p. 7.*

The Thirteenth Amendment to the U.S. Constitution makes slavery illegal. *See p. 8.*

1867

The postwar Reconstruction period begins. The federal government sends military troops into the former Confederate states to protect the civil rights of African Americans. *See p. 8.*

1868

The Fourteenth Amendment to the Constitution extends U.S. citizenship to African Americans and requires states to provide equal protection under the law to all citizens, regardless of race. *See p. 8.*

1869

Baseball becomes a professional sport when the Cincinnati Red Stockings offers salaries to players. *See p. 11.*

1870

The Fifteenth Amendment to the Constitution grants all male citizens the right to vote. *See p. 8.*

1876

The National Base Ball League (now known as the National League) is formed. *See p. 11.*

1877

When Reconstruction ends in the South, white Southerners pass discriminatory Jim Crow laws that restrict the rights of African Americans and force them into a position of second-class citizenship. *See p. 9.*

1878

John "Bud" Fowler breaks professional baseball's color barrier by joining a white minor-league franchise in Massachusetts. *See p. 11.*

1881

Branch Rickey is born in Ohio. *See p. 23.*

1884

Moses "Fleetwood" Walker becomes the first black major leaguer when his minor-league team, the Toledo Blue Stockings, joins the American Association. *See p. 11.*

1885

The first all-black professional baseball team, the Cuban Giants, is formed in Babylon, New York. *See p. 12.*

1887

The Chicago White Stockings refuse to take the field for a minor-league game against the Newark Giants because the Giants' roster includes a black pitcher, George Stovey. *See p. 12.*

1890

An unofficial "gentleman's agreement" among team owners excludes all African Americans from organized baseball. *See p. 12.*

1901

The American Base Ball Association (now known as the American League) is formed. *See p. 11.*

1919

Jack Roosevelt Robinson is born in Cairo, Georgia. *See p. 27.*

1920

Andrew "Rube" Foster establishes the Negro National League. *See p. 14.*

1922

Rachel Isum Robinson is born on July 19 in Los Angeles, California. *See p. 139.*

1924

The first-ever Negro World Series takes place. *See p. 14.*

1933

Team owner Gus Greenlee launches the East-West All-Star Game, an annual showcase of Negro League talent that became the most popular attraction in black baseball. *See p. 15.*

1936

African-American athlete Jesse Owens wins four track-and-field gold medals at the 1936 Olympic Games in Berlin, Germany, under the watchful eye of Nazi leader Adolf Hitler. *See p. 16.*

1938

African-American boxer Joe Louis knocks out German champion Max Schmeling in the first round of a title fight. *See p. 16.*

1939

Jackie Robinson becomes the first four-sport varsity athlete at the University of California, Los Angeles (UCLA). *See p. 27.*

1941

The United States enters World War II. *See p. 18.*

Black-owned newspapers in the United States launch a "Double V" campaign, encouraging African Americans to strive for two victories: over Germany and its allies in World War II, and over racial discrimination and segregation in American society. See p. 20.

1943

After two decades with the St. Louis Cardinals, Branch Rickey takes over as president and part-owner of the Brooklyn Dodgers. *See p. 24.*

Longtime baseball commissioner Kenesaw Mountain Landis, a staunch opponent of integration, dies. *See p. 25.*

1945

World War II ends in victory for the United States and its allies. *See p. 20.*

A. B. "Happy" Chandler becomes commissioner of baseball and expresses support for integration. *See p. 25.*

Jackie Robinson plays professional baseball for the Kansas City Monarchs of the Negro National League. *See p. 27.*

On August 28, Robinson meets with Rickey for three hours and signs a contract with the Brooklyn Dodgers organization. *See p. 28.*

On October 23, the Dodgers announce the acquisition of Robinson from the Negro Leagues. See p. 31.

1946

On February 10, Robinson marries Rachel Isum. *See p. 31.*

Following a successful season with the Dodgers' top farm club, the Montreal Royals, Robinson is named Most Valuable Player of the International League. *See p. 33.*

Jackie Robinson Jr. is born on November 18. *See p. 37.*

1947

Robinson makes his major-league debut on April 15, breaking baseball's longstanding color barrier. *See p. 40.*

Larry Doby plays his first game for the Cleveland Indians on July 5, becoming the first black player in the American League. *See p. 51.*

1949

With the loss of most of its star players to Major League Baseball, the Negro National League disbands. *See p. 53.*

Jackie Robinson, Roy Campanella, Larry Doby, and Don Newcombe are the first black players to appear in the Major League All-Star Game. *See p. 60.*

In July, Robinson testifies before the House Un-American Activities Committee (HUAC). *See p. 62.*

Robinson wins the National League batting title with a .342 average and is named Most Valuable Player. *See p. 59.*

1950

Robinson's daughter Sharon is born on January 13. *See p. 62.*

Robinson acts in a Hollywood movie about his life, *The Jackie Robinson Story. See p. 62.*

Earl Lloyd becomes the first black player in the National Basketball Association (NBA). *See p. 70.*

1952

Robinson's son David is born on May 14. *See p. 65.*

Five years after Robinson opened the door, 150 black players are on major-league rosters or in minor-league farm systems, but half of the eighteen Major League franchises have yet to hire a black player. *See p. 53.*

1954

The U.S. Supreme Court issues its decision in *Brown v. Board of Education,* which outlaws segregation in the nation's public schools. *See p. 75.*

1955

The Dodgers capture the World Series championship; Robinson sets the tone by stealing home in Game 1. *See p. 67.*

Rosa Parks is arrested for refusing to give up her seat to a white man on a public bus in Montgomery, Alabama; her arrest sparks a year-long boycott of the city's public transit system by African-American residents. *See p. 76.*

1956

The U.S. Supreme Court declares segregation of public transportation unconstitutional in its ruling in *Browder v. Gayle. See p. 77.*

In December, Robinson announces his retirement from baseball. *See p. 68.*

The National Association for the Advancement of Colored People (NAACP) awards Robinson its prestigious Spingarn Medal. *See p. 77.*

Three major-league teams have never had a black player on their rosters: the Philadelphia Phillies, the Detroit Tigers, and the Boston Red Sox. *See p. 69.*

1957

Charlie Sifford becomes the first black golfer to win a PGA Tour event. *See p. 70.*

Althea Gibson becomes the first black tennis player to win the prestigious major tournaments at Wimbledon and the U.S. Open. *See p. 70.*

Martin Luther King Jr. founds the Southern Christian Leadership Conference (SCLC). *See p. 79.*

Arkansas governor Orval Faubus surrounds Little Rock's Central High School with National Guard troops to prevent nine black students from entering, in direct violation of the Supreme Court's school-desegregation ruling. *See p. 79.*

1958

Robinson writes several letters urging President Dwight D. Eisenhower to take a firm stand on civil rights issues. *See p. 79.*

1959

The Boston Red Sox, under longtime owner Tom Yawkey, becomes the final major-league team to integrate. *See p. 105.*

1960

Four black college students stage a sit-in at a segregated lunch counter in Greensboro, North Carolina, that denied them service; their actions spark a series of similar protests across the country. *See p. 80.*

The U.S. Supreme Court issues its ruling in *Boynton v. Virginia,* which finds segregation of interstate transit unconstitutional. *See p. 81.*

After meeting with both candidates, Robinson endorses Republican Richard M. Nixon over Democrat John F. Kennedy in the presidential race. *See p. 80.*

1961

Black and white civil rights activists known as Freedom Riders launch a series of integrated bus trips across the South. *See p. 81.*

1962

Robinson becomes the first African-American player to be inducted into the National Baseball Hall of Fame. *See p. 90.*

The era of Negro League baseball ends when the Negro American League closes its doors. *See p. 53.*

1963

King and other civil rights leaders stage a series of peaceful protests against segregation in Birmingham, Alabama, that are violently crushed by local law enforcement. *See p. 82.*

Robinson organizes an annual benefit jazz concert to raise funds for civil rights groups. *See p. 82.*

On June 11, Kennedy makes a nationally televised address calling for strong new civil rights legislation. *See p. 82.*

In August, Robinson attends the March on Washington, which features King's famous "I Have a Dream" speech. *See p. 83.*

Kennedy is shot and killed by an assassin on November 22. *See p. 83.*

1964

President Lyndon B. Johnson signs the Civil Rights Act into law on July 2. *See p. 84.*

Civil rights groups organize the Freedom Summer voter-registration drive in the South. *See p. 85.*

1965

The Selma-Montgomery Voting Rights March in Alabama ends in violence on March 7, when police in riot gear attack the peaceful protesters. *See p. 86.*

Johnson signs the Voting Rights Act into law on August 6. *See p. 86.*

Robinson oversees the successful launch of the Freedom National Bank to encourage and support black-owned small business ventures in New York City. *See p. 86.*

Branch Rickey dies. *See p. 91.*

1967

Robinson publicly disagrees with King's decision to oppose U.S. military involvement in Vietnam. *See p. 86.*

1968

Martin Luther King Jr. is assassinated on April 4.

Robinson's eldest son, Jackie Jr., is arrested for drug possession and carrying a concealed weapon. *See p. 91.*

1970

Robinson testifies in court on behalf of baseball player Curt Flood, who mounted a legal challenge to Major League Baseball's "reserve clause" in hopes of gaining free agency. *See p. 84.*

1971

Jackie Robinson Jr. is killed in an automobile accident. *See p. 91.*

1972

The Dodgers retire Robinson's uniform number, 42. *See p. 93.*

Jackie Robinson dies of a heart attack on October 24. *See p. 93.*

The U.S. Supreme Court rules in favor of baseball team owners in *Flood v. Kuhn*, saying that major-league players must obtain free agency through collective bargaining. *See p. 84.*

1973

Rachel Robinson establishes the Jackie Robinson Foundation (JRF). *See p. 95.*

1974

On April 8, Hank Aaron of the Atlanta Braves breaks Babe Ruth's record of 714 career home runs. *See p. 101.*

1975

Frank Robinson becomes the first black manager of a Major League Baseball team. *See p. 107.*

The percentage of black players in Major League Baseball reaches an all-time high of 27 percent. *See p. 105.*

1984

Jackie Robinson is posthumously awarded the Presidential Medal of Freedom. *See p. 96.*

1990

The Negro Leagues Baseball Museum (NLBM) is founded in Kansas City, Missouri. *See p. 98.*

1997

On the fiftieth anniversary of Robinson breaking the color barrier, his jersey number 42 is permanently retired by every team in Major League Baseball. *See p. 96.*

2003

The National Football League institutes the Rooney Rule, which requires teams to interview at least one minority candidate before filling head-coaching or front-office vacancies. *See p. 102.*

2005

Major League Baseball establishes April 15 of every year as Jackie Robinson Day, which is marked with special events at stadiums across the nation. *See p. 96.*

2007

Major League Baseball declares that all active players, managers, and coaches will wear number 42 each year on April 15 in honor of Robinson. *See p. 96.*

SOURCES FOR FURTHER STUDY

"Baseball and Jackie Robinson." Library of Congress, American Memory Collection, 2007. Retrieved from http://memory.loc.gov/ammem/collections/robinson/index.html. Created to commemorate the fiftieth anniversary of Robinson's major-league debut, this collection includes a timeline, photographs, and resources for teachers relating to Robinson's achievements and the larger history of America's national pastime.

Golenbock, Peter. *Bums: An Oral History of the Brooklyn Dodgers.* New York: Putnam, 1984. This engaging book provides a personal account of Robinson's accomplishments from the perspective of various players, executives, fans, and journalists connected with the Brooklyn Dodgers.

"Jackie Robinson." Biography.com, n.d. Retrieved from http://www.biography.com/people/jackie-robinson-9460813. This multimedia resource features a biographical profile, photos, videos, and historical analysis of Robinson's life and career.

"Jackie Robinson Day." MLB.com, n.d. Retrieved from http://mlb.mlb.com/mlb/events/jrd/. The official Major League Baseball (MLB) site includes a vast array of resources in honor of the April 15 anniversary of Robinson breaking the color barrier, such as a timeline, career statistics, essay contest, videos, and interviews with Rachel Robinson, former teammates, and current stars.

Rampersad, Arnold. *Jackie Robinson: A Biography.* New York: Random House, 1997. This comprehensive book provides a detailed account of Robinson's life, career, and legacy.

Robinson, Jackie. *I Never Had It Made: An Autobiography.* Hopewell, NJ: Echo Press, 1995. In this memoir, initially published shortly before his death, Robinson looks back on his youth, his baseball career, and his civil rights activism.

Robinson, Rachel. *Jackie Robinson: An Intimate Portrait.* New York: Abrams, 1996. Written by Robinson's widow, this biography provides a heartfelt account of the triumphs and hardships the couple experienced, and it is heavily illustrated with candid family photos.

Tygiel, Jules. *Baseball's Great Experiment: Jackie Robinson and His Legacy.* New York: Vintage Books, 1984. This engaging biography tells the whole story of baseball integration, from the drawing of the color line in the 1890s to the experiences of African-American stars who followed Robinson into the big leagues in the 1960s and 1970s.

BIBLIOGRAPHY

Books

Adelson, Bruce. *Brushing Back Jim Crow: The Integration of Minor-League Baseball in the American South.* Charlottesville: University Press of Virginia, 1999.

Bergman, Irwin B. *Jackie Robinson: Breaking Baseball's Color Barrier.* New York: Chelsea House, 1994.

Eig, Jonathan. *Opening Day: The Story of Jackie Robinson's First Season.* New York: Simon and Schuster, 2007.

Falkner, David. *Great Time Coming: The Life of Jackie Robinson from Baseball to Birmingham.* New York: Simon and Schuster, 1995.

Fussman, Cal. *After Jackie: Pride, Prejudice, and Baseball's Forgotten Heroes: An Oral History.* New York: ESPN Books, 2007.

Golenbock, Peter. *Bums: An Oral History of the Brooklyn Dodgers.* New York: Putnam, 1984.

Holway, John. *Voices from the Great Negro Baseball Leagues.* New York: Dodd, Mead, 1975.

Kahn, Roger. *The Boys of Summer.* New York: Harper and Row, 1972.

Long, Michael G., ed. *First Class Citizenship: The Civil Rights Letters of Jackie Robinson.* New York: Times Books, 2007.

Parrott, Harold. *The Lords of Baseball.* New York: Praeger, 1976.

Peterson, Robert. *Only the Ball Was White.* Englewood Cliffs, NJ: Prentice Hall, 1970.

Rampersad, Arnold. *Jackie Robinson: A Biography.* New York: Random House, 1997.

Robinson, Jackie. *Baseball Has Done It.* Brooklyn, NY: Ig Publishing, 2005.

Robinson, Jackie. *I Never Had It Made: An Autobiography.* Hopewell, NJ: Echo Press, 1995.

Robinson, Rachel. *Jackie Robinson: An Intimate Portrait.* New York: Abrams, 1996.

Robinson, Sharon. *Promises to Keep: How Jackie Robinson Changed America.* New York: Scholastic Press, 2004.

Rowan, Carl T., with Jackie Robinson. *Wait Till Next Year: The Life Story of Jackie Robinson.* New York: Random House, 1960.

Simon, Scott. *Jackie Robinson and the Integration of Baseball.* Hoboken, NJ: John Wiley, 2007.

Tygiel, Jules. *Baseball's Great Experiment: Jackie Robinson and His Legacy.* New York: Vintage Books, 1984.

Tygiel, Jules. *Extra Bases: Reflections on Jackie Robinson, Race, and Baseball History.* Lincoln: University of Nebraska Press, 2002.

Periodicals

Berkow, Ira. "Standing Beside Jackie Robinson, Reese Helped Change Baseball." *New York Times,* March 31, 1997. Retrieved from http://www.nytimes.com/specials/baseball/bbo-reese-robinson.html.

Crawley, A. Bruce. "122 Teams, One Black Major Owner." *Philadelphia Tribune,* October 23, 2011. Retrieved from http://www.phillytrib.com/commentaryarticles/item/1164-122-teams-one-black-major-owner.html.

Effrat, Louis. "Dodgers Purchase Robinson, First Negro in Modern Major League Baseball." *New York Times,* April 10, 1947. Retrieved from http://www.nytimes.com/learning/general/onthisday/big/0410.html#article.

Fitzpatrick, Frank. "Jackie Robinson: The Man and the Event." *Philadelphia Inquirer,* April 7, 2007.

Glasser, Ira. "Branch Rickey and Jackie Robinson: Precursors to the Civil Rights Movement." *World and I,* March 2003.

Gonzalez, Alden. "MLB Family Honors Jackie Robinson." MLB.com, April 15, 2011. Retrieved from http://mlb.mlb.com/news/article.jsp?ymd=20110415&content_id=17836932&vkey=news_mlb&c_id=mlb.

Kindred, Dave. "Jackie Robinson: One Man, Alone." *The Sporting News,* April 14, 1997.

Schall, Andrew. "Wendell Smith: The Pittsburgh Journalist Who Made Jackie Robinson Mainstream." *Pittsburgh Post-Gazette,* March 29, 2012. Retrieved from http://www.post-gazette.com/stories/opinion/perspectives/the-next-page-wendell-smith-the-pittsburgh-journalist-who-made-jackie-robinson-mainstream-300714/#ixzz20EuBK2v8.

Online Resources

Bodley, Hal. "No Measuring Robinson's Impact." MLB.com, April 15, 2010. Retrieved from http://mlb.mlb.com/news/article.jsp?ymd=20100415&content_id=9331356&vkey=news_mlb&fext=.jsp&c_id=mlb.

"Breaking Barriers: In Sport, In Life." MLBCommunity.org, 2012. Retrieved from http://web.mlbcommunity.org/programs/breaking_barriers.jsp?content=inside.

Cannella, Stephen. "Black Baseball." CNN/Sports Illustrated, 1997. Retrieved from http://sportsillustrated.cnn.com/features/1997/blackbaseball/frame.html.

"Integration of Major League Baseball." Center for Negro Leagues Baseball Research, n.d. Retrieved from http://www.cnlbr.org/Portals/0/RL/Integration%20of%20Major%20League%20Baseball.pdf.

"Jackie Robinson: The Official Website." Retrieved from http://www.jackierobinson.com/about/bio.html.

"A Look at Life in the Negro Leagues." College of Education, Kansas State University, 2000. Retrieved from http://coe.ksu.edu/nlbm/index.html.

Mayo, Jonathan. "From the Field to the Stands: Minor Leagues Helped Hasten Integration in South." MLB.com, February 25, 2008. Retrieved from http://www.milb.com/news/article.jsp?ymd=20080223&content_id=350776&vkey=news_milb&fext=.jsp.

"MLB Celebrates Jackie Robinson Day." ESPN.com, April 16, 2012. Retrieved from http://espn.go.com/mlb/story/_/id/7817037/mlb-honors-jackie-robinson-ballpark-tributes.

"Negro Leagues History." Negro Leagues Baseball Museum, n.d. Retrieved from http://www.nlbm.com/s/history.htm.

Newman, Mark. "MLB Celebrates Robinson's Enduring Impact." MLB.com, April 14, 2011. Retrieved from http://mlb.mlb.com/news/article.jsp?ymd=20110414&content_id=17767716&c_id=mlb.

"Race Remains 'Flashpoint of Controversy' in American Sports." Phys.org, May 3, 2007. Retrieved from http://phys.org/news97426086.html#jCp.

PHOTO AND ILLUSTRATION CREDITS

Cover and Title Page: *Jackie Robinson crosses home plate after hitting his first home run as a Brooklyn Dodger. Teammate Tommy Tatum offers him a handshake as catcher Walker Cooper of the New York Giants looks on.* (April, 1947). Photo ©Bettmann/Corbis/AP.

Chapter One: Photo by Marion Post Wolcott, FSA/OWI Photograph Collection, Prints & Photographs Division, Library of Congress, LC-USF33-030639-M1 (p. 8); National Baseball Hall of Fame Library, Cooperstown, N.Y. (photo no. Fowler Bud 1885 Keokuk team 194) (p. 10); National Baseball Hall of Fame Library, Cooperstown, N.Y. (photo no. 274.81_HS_PD) (p. 13); National Baseball Hall of Fame Library, Cooperstown, N.Y. (photo no. 1939-1520-72_PD) (p. 14); National Baseball Hall of Fame Library, Cooperstown, N.Y. (photo no. 4581-92_PD) (p. 17); Collection of Civil Rights Archive/CAD VC-UMBC, Smithsonian Institution (p. 19).

Chapter Two: Harris & Ewing Collection, Prints & Photographs Division, Library of Congress, LC-DIG-hec-22983 (p. 25); National Baseball Hall of Fame Library, Cooperstown, N.Y. (photo no. BL-1529.67_Milt_NBL) (p. 27); National Baseball Hall of Fame Library, Cooperstown, N.Y. (photo no. 1529.68WTa_wRickey_NBL) (p. 29); Photo by Maurice Terrell, Look Magazine Photograph Collection, Prints & Photographs Division, Library of Congress, LC-USZ62-119881 (p. 32); Rogers Photo Archive/Getty Images (p. 34).

Chapter Three: akg-images/Newscom (p. 38); National Baseball Hall of Fame Library, Cooperstown, N.Y. (photo no. 3855-68WTy_FL_NBL) (p. 40); National Baseball Hall of Fame Library, Cooperstown, N.Y. (photo no. 858.79_NBL) (p. 43); AP Photo (p. 45); National Baseball Hall of Fame Library, Cooperstown, N.Y. (photo no. 1529-68WT25_Grp_NBL) (p. 47); AP Photo (p. 48); Sporting News Archive/Icon SMI 800/Newscom (p. 50).

Chapter Four: AP Photo/stf (p. 56); AP Photo (p. 58); AP Photo (p. 60); Publicity still/RKO Radio Pictures, Prints & Photographs Division, Library of Congress, LC-USZ62-119880 (p. 63); AP Photo (p. 66); National Baseball Hall of Fame Library, Cooperstown, N.Y. (photo no. 279-71a_Bat_NBL) (p. 69).

Chapter Five: National Baseball Hall of Fame Library, Cooperstown, N.Y. (photo no. 112.2006.3CSU) (p. 74); AP Photo (p. 76); U.S. News & World Report Magazine Photograph Collection, Prints & Photographs Division, Library of Congress, LC-DIG-ppm-sca-19754 (p. 78); FSA/OWI Photograph Collection, Prints & Photographs Division,

Library of Congress, LC-DIG-ppmsc-00199 (p. 81); National Archives (photo no. 306-SSM-4C(54)26. U.S. Information Agency/Press and Publications Service Collection. Rowland Scherman, Photographer.) (p. 83).

Chapter Six: National Baseball Hall of Fame Library, Cooperstown, N.Y. (photo no. 1478.84_HOFInd_NBL) (p. 90); AP Photo (p. 92); Bill Greenblatt/UPI/Newscom (p. 95); AP Photo/Frank Franklin II (p. 97); AP Photo (p. 100); AP Photo/The Birmingham News, Bernard Troncale (p. 103); AP Photo/Carlos Osorio (p. 106).

Biographies: National Baseball Hall of Fame Library, Cooperstown, N.Y. (photo no. 1462-77_HS_NBL) (p. 111); Harris & Ewing Collection, Prints & Photographs Division, Library of Congress, LC-DIG-hec-28633 (p. 116); National Baseball Hall of Fame Library, Cooperstown, N.Y. (photo no. 4440-68HTI_HS_NBL) (p. 121); National Baseball Hall of Fame Library, Cooperstown, N.Y. (photo no. 3142-68WT_FL_NBL) (p. 126); National Baseball Hall of Fame Library, Cooperstown, N.Y. (p. 130); Photo by Bob Sandberg, Look Magazine Photograph Collection, Prints & Photographs Division, Library of Congress, LC-L9-54-3566-O (p. 134); Nina Leen/Time & Life Pictures/Getty Images (p. 139); National Baseball Hall of Fame Library, Cooperstown, N.Y. (photo no. 1254.94_NBL) (p. 144); National Baseball Hall of Fame Library, Cooperstown, N.Y. (photo no. 16-66_FL_NBL) (p. 149).

INDEX